We Were Adivasis

South Asia Across the Disciplines

A series edited by Muzaffar Alam, Robert Goldman, and Gauri Viswanathan
Dipesh Chakrabarty, Sheldon Pollock, and Sanjay Subrahmanyam, founding editors

Funded by a grant from the Andrew W. Mellon Foundation and jointly published by the
University of California Press, the University of Chicago Press, and Columbia University Press.

South Asia Across the Disciplines is a series devoted to publishing first books across a wide
range of South Asian studies, including art, history, philology or textual studies, philosophy,
religion, and the interpretive social sciences. Series authors all share the goal of opening up
new archives and suggesting new methods and approaches, while demonstrating that South
Asian scholarship can be at once deep in expertise and broad in appeal.

We Were Adivasis

Aspiration in an Indian Scheduled Tribe

MEGAN MOODIE

The University of Chicago Press
Chicago and London

Megan Moodie is assistant professor of anthropology at the University of California, Santa Cruz.

The University of Chicago Press, Chicago 60637
The University of Chicago Press, Ltd., London
© 2015 by The University of Chicago
All rights reserved. Published 2015.
Printed in the United States of America

24 23 22 21 20 19 18 17 16 15   1 2 3 4 5

ISBN-13: 978-0-226-25299-5 (cloth)
ISBN-13: 978-0-226-25304-6 (paper)
ISBN-13: 978-0-226-25318-3 (e-book)

DOI: 10.7208/chicago/9780226253183.001.0001

Library of Congress Cataloging-in-Publication Data

Moodie, Megan, author.
   We were adivasis : aspiration in an Indian scheduled tribe / Megan Moodie.
      pages cm—(South Asia across the disciplines)
   Includes bibliographical references and index.
      ISBN 978-0-226-25299-5 (cloth : alkaline paper)—ISBN 0-226-25299-X
   (cloth : alkaline paper)—ISBN 978-0-226-25304-6 (paperback : alkaline paper)—
   ISBN 0-226-25304-X (paperback : alkaline paper)—ISBN 978-0-226-25318-3
   (e-book)—ISBN 0-226-25318-X (e-book)   1. Oraon (Indic people)—India—Jaipur.
   2. Jaipur (India)—Scheduled tribes. 3. Women, Adivasi—India—Jaipur—Social
   conditions.   I. Title.   II. Series: South Asia across the disciplines.
      DS432.O7M66 2015
      305.48'8914—dc23

                                                              2014037588

♾ This paper meets the requirements of ANSI/NISO Z39.48-1992 (Permanence of Paper).

For my mother, Patricia Luise, with love and gratitude

Contents

Acknowledgments

I never intended to write a book about adivasis, or to study adivasi issues. I landed in Shiv Nagar Basti only because a friend of a friend was running a reproductive health initiative in the neighborhood and thought I might want to tag along to investigate gender programs in an urban Rajasthani setting to complement my rural fieldwork. This book's existence, then, not to mention the now decade-long relationships that made the research possible, owes everything to the curiosity and generous spirits of the two young women I call Mona and Kanika Solanki but who will, of course, recognize themselves immediately in these pages should their children ever translate them. My debt to them, and to Ram Lal Solanki, Rajendra, Lakshmi, Richa, Sapna, and so many, many others is one I can never repay. I thank the Dhanka of Jaipur with all of my heart and hope that my small efforts here are a testament to how deeply they have shaped my thinking as an anthropologist and my ways of being in the world as an aspirationally global citizen. There are more chapters to be written, my friends, and I look forward to many more tales to come.

My research in Jaipur has always been undergirded by a foundation of compassionate care from a number of friends. Shakuntala and the late C. P. Bhansali always nurtured my desire to live in India and have served as translators in so very many ways over what seems now to have been my entire adult life. (Mummyji, your gift for gently holding a mind wide open has been a model to me in ways I could hardly articulate). I thank them, as well as Gayatri, Vikrant, and Shelly, for sharing their extended family with me. Purnima, Chandana, Sapna, and Bubbli Burman also deserve a great measure of gratitude for all the years of laughter and silly dancing. I also thank the family of P. P. and Shobha Singh—my adopted elders—and my adopted sister and brother, Priyanka and Peyush, for taking me in, feeding me, and treating me like kin on many occasions.

Over the years, I have also been by given help, guidance, food, and camaraderie by Sunita Bapna, D. S. and Renu Bhandari, Raj Bhandari, Manindra Kapoor, Shail Mayaram, Anu Misra, Fateh and Indu Singh, and Lalita Singha in Jaipur. The research assistance of Shally Vaish was crucial to the earliest days of this project, and I am in her debt for her commitment to it. I also thank Justice Jas Raj Chopra for meeting with me during my most recent visit. In New Delhi, Amita Baviskar, Sharada Nayak, and Virginius Xaxa, have, at different moments, helped facilitate my research, and for this I am very appreciative.

I am very lucky to be surrounded by brilliant and supportive colleagues in the Department of Anthropology at UC Santa Cruz, some of whom I have now known and admired for many years. Mark Anderson, Chelsea Blackmore, Loki Pandey, Lisa Rofel, Danilyn Rutherford, and Anna Tsing all read the manuscript, or pieces of it, in draft form. Their input has been invaluable in its development over time and I am deeply in their debt. I also thank J. Cameron Monroe for his wise counsel on maps and Nishita Trisal for her outstanding research support at a crucial moment. I have benefitted, as well, from ongoing conversations with many of my other colleagues, including Don Brenneis, Melissa Caldwell, Nancy Chen, Mayanthi Fernando, Susan Harding, Andrew Matthews, Renya Ramirez, and Matt Wolf-Meyer. Loki, Annapurna, Alok, and Akash Pandey deserve an added mention for their love and unflagging support (not to mention delicious meals) as I have tried to make my way through this study. I am grateful.

On the wider UC Santa Cruz campus, a number of people have read drafts of this work and given selflessly of their time and intellectual energy toward its improvement. I thank Anjali Arondekar, Neda Atanasoski, Jim Clifford, Lizbeth Haas, Donna Haraway, Mattie Harper, Amy Lonetree, Phil Longo, and B. Ruby Rich for their respective and considerable contributions to my intellectual life here. I am grateful also for the friendship and creative genius of my *comadres*, Irene Luzstig and Micah Perks.

The seeds of this book were sown while I was a Mellon-Sawyer postdoctoral fellow at Duke University in 2007–2008. Thanks to Ralph Litzinger and Dominic Sachsenmaier for providing me with the opportunity to be on the Duke campus and interact with the wonderful people there, including Sandra Freitag and David Gilmartin, who also influenced early drafts of the manuscript. The friendship of Anne-Maria Makhulu and Elizabeth Davis, from whom I have learned so much, was another wonderful outcome of that period.

Srimati Basu, Caetlin Benson-Allot, Lawrence Cohen, Sneha Desai, Meena

Garg, Ann Gold, Thomas Hansen, Rob Linrothe, Townsend Middleton, Jason Rodriguez, Debarati Sen, Alpa Shah, and Kalindi Vora have all been important interlocutors over the last several years, and I thank them each for their work and for their willingness to think through whatever questions I might unexpectedly (and without invitation) throw their way.

Support from the National Science Foundation's Graduate Fellowship program, the Mellon-Sawyer seminar at Duke (2007–2008), the Committee on Research at UCSC, and the Hellman Fellowship at the University of California has been essential to my work and has allowed me the freedom to pursue ideas and peoples down unexpected lanes. I am also indebted to the editorial board at the South Asia Across the Disciplines series, T. David Brent, Priya Nelson, Ellen Kladky, Carol McGillivray, Ryo Yamaguchi, and the two anonymous reviewers for the University of Chicago Press, who all gave this project a chance to become incarnated in ways I had imagined and others I could not. It is a better book for their attentions.

Of course, none of the research or writing that has made this book possible would have happened without the cheerleading and devotion of my wider extended family. Donka and Peter Farkas, the Vamosi-Anand Clan, the Moses Crew, the Boukalik Brigade, Heather & Hayden, and Bahiyyah & Elishyah have been more-than-supportive chosen kin over the years. I am lucky to also have a kind family-in-law, and have benefitted so much from the presence of Ion and Elena Braşoveanu, as well as Irina, Mihai, and Adelina Ignat, in my life. My father and stepmother, Douglas and Cheryl Moodie, have patiently listened to all my wild ideas for decades without flinching—they will never know how grateful I am for the fact that they have never once in all these years doubted me for choosing this path. My sisters, Shannon and Maureen, as well as their beautiful people—Michael, Oliver, and Rob—well, I cannot really write about what they have given me along the way. Not yet. Girls, this is just the beginning. Thank you for being my sisters and my best friends and the two funniest people on earth.

To my partner, Adrian, and our son, Toma: I am so grateful for your indulgence as I have worked on this project, for your extraordinary mapmaking abilities, and for all your loving gestures, big and small. *Sunteți bucuria vieții mele, dragilor.*

Finally, I have chosen to dedicate *We Were Adivasis* to my mother, Patricia. Momma, thank you. No matter what the adventure, I will always call home. Thank you for being patient and brave and full of compassion. Thank you for teaching me to pay attention to my own imagination, as well as to the creative lives of others. And thank you for showing me by example that we never, ever, stop writing the story.

1

Introduction

If you study the picture closely, take your time, you will see it: the low hut, with its exposed brick and unfinished planks and corrugated iron roof, was once where Ram Lal's three-story cement house now stands. The photo is from the early 1980s, on cheap paper, now with a subaqueous cast between its white borders. It is precious as a relic of an earlier time, a small proof that it is past, built over. *This is what it used to be like here in the neighborhood*, Ram Lal tells me. *You can see that things have changed, Meghna-bai. There are still many of us who are poor and backwards. But things have gotten better for some.* This is what Ram Lal sees, the vision he wants me to share. It is irresistible. If you compare the hardscrabble shack of the photo, all opportunism and impermanence, with the planned security of the *basti* today—the electricity and always-functioning household water taps, the uniformity and pride—you cannot help but see perseverance, resilience, a line of flight.[1] Change.

And it is not just the house in the photo. Ram Lal Solanki's personal biography, tied as it is to a history of building, is also such a tale. He has lived in Shiv Nagar Basti—a "slum" just outside the walls of the city of Jaipur, capital of the Indian state of Rajasthan—for his entire life. Having been born just after Indian independence, he has seen firsthand the rapid expansion of the city from three hundred thousand residents in 1951 to 2.3 million as of the 2001 census.[2] Like many other Dhanka men of his generation, Ram Lal took a job in the Public Health and Engineering Department (PHED) working to maintain water and sewer lines for colony after colony that grew up in ever-denser rings around Jaipur's original walled city. As a member of one of India's recognized tribal communities, the Dhanka, he had no caste proscription against dealing with human waste. A strong affirmative action program guaranteed postings in government jobs for men of his community. Unlike many other men, however, he rose up to a position of some authority in the Jaipur office and at the time of his retirement in the early 2000s was making around Rs. 10,000 per month. His daughter is well settled. His sons will inherit his large house, which he owns outright. He is a respected elder in the neighborhood and in his community at large. Ram Lal often reminds me, with a wide grin, that, as an "ST" (member of a Scheduled Tribe) or "*nich log*" ("low man") who also failed the third grade, he has made quite a good life for himself. *This is progress. Things are getting better.*

Since 2002 I have conducted ethnographic fieldwork in Ram Lal's neighborhood, populated almost entirely by members of one of India's Scheduled Tribes (STs), the Dhanka.[3] He was one of the first people I met in the community and has been a supporter, informant, friend, and concerned uncle ever since. His story, and the story of his extended family, figures largely in what will follow here. Even as this story is personal and specific, Ram Lal's photo also captures something important about the daily life of upward mo-

MAP 1. India, with Rajasthan highlighted. Map created by Adrian Brasoveanu.

bility in contemporary India. Here is a home, a symbol whose change over time stands for something—makes a stand, even; it cements improvement and new possible futures. But it is a dwelling, with an inside, a set of relationships between old and young, between women and men. For better or worse, it is an intimate space where the pleasures and struggles—the joy and violence—of much of life happen.

For Ram Lal, as for many Dhanka men, it is a point of pride that women in his family stay home as housewives and do not have to go out to work. This transition to domestic respectability is part of what it means to rise above a historically low status that required women to work (especially as agricultural laborers). Such a status also meant that Dhanka women were accessible to men outside the family. Indeed, what it means when things get better is a highly gendered question even when men and women seemingly agree that they are, indeed, better. For the most part, Dhanka women I know, especially those who are able to stay home and do not have to labor for wages, agree with Ram Lal's narrative of improvement and success. The ability to be a housewife, to be married and protected, is highly valued among women. For many of Ram Lal's female relatives, the proof of Dhanka uplift is to be found as much in this realm as in the concrete of individual houses.

It is also to be found in the annual *samuhik vivaha* ("collective wedding") held by the Dhanka each year. In this large-scale event, which convenes many of Rajasthan's estimated seventy-seven thousand Dhanka as well as participants from the neighboring state of Gujarat, women and men are matched by community elders and married off as couples in one large ceremony. The ideology of the samuhik vivaha is that it is undertaken for the uplift of the Dhanka as a whole, a social project that is intimately tied to the well-being of girls and women. The oft-repeated rationale for the expenditure of money and energy on the annual *sammelan* ("gathering or conference"), as it is known colloquially, is that samuhik vivaha protects girls from the kinds of exorbitant dowry demands that plague the poor in north (and, perhaps to a lesser extent, south) India. As these group weddings do not entail—indeed, do not permit—the giving and receiving of *dahej* ("dowry") and because they are conducted under the watchful eye of the community at large, Dhanka girls are more protected than other young women in Rajasthan today. In contrast to upper-caste Rajputs who harm and mistreat women, or other lower-caste groups not interested in undertaking efforts toward their own betterment, the Dhanka are able to link the protection of girls, group identity, and collective aspiration. When asking Dhanka women about what it means to be a woman in the *samaj* ("community"), one is very likely to hear reference to samuhik vivaha as proof that life is good for women.

But no story about upward mobility is simple. Like other tribal groups in India often referred to as *adivasis* (*adi*: "original"; *vasi*: "one who dwells"), the Dhanka are considered and consider themselves to be descendants of the subcontinent's earliest inhabitants—its aboriginals or autochthones; however, they cannot point to a homeland. The Dhanka identity narrative is that, as historically *jungli* ("wild" or "from the jungle") people who did not possess a defined occupation and were subjected to oppression and cruelty, they have done what it takes to get by: moving, taking up different kinds of work, persevering. It is this doing what it takes to get by, this willingness, that does the work of "culture" for the Dhanka and makes them both unique and indigenous; that is, original inhabitants and outside the Hindu-Muslim fold. The Dhanka do not embrace the term "adivasi," however. In fact, one is more likely to hear them refer to themselves as "ST" or "*chhote-nich*" ("little" or "low") than "adivasi," except in the past tense, as in the statement "*Hum* adivasi *te*" ("We were adivasis"). I have used their assertion "We were adivasis" as a theoretical jumping-off point and literary refrain in what follows.

Before we turn to the story of a research project, let's imagine for a moment other pictures, about as old as that of the rough slum shack. Ram Lal's sister-in-law, Bharati, mother of five and grandmother of five, draws them from a tin box kept in her locked trunk. In the first, she is a young woman. She wears trousers and a button-front shirt, with a towel wrapped around her hair to disguise her braid. Bharati is dressed as a man, for fun. She shows it with a sly smile. *See it's not that hard to be like them.* The second photo depicts her favorite hero, the actor Dharmendra, with one of his leading ladies. The black-and-white image, torn now from ogling devotion, shows them in a passionate conversation, possibly singing to one another. *Dharmendra is really, really good.* A bigger smile. *He's my children's real father.* We giggle. Things could have been otherwise.

Concrete and Otherwise

This is an ethnography of the gendered effects of upward mobility among an urban Scheduled Tribe and an exploration of the relationship between intimacy—as both a scale of analysis and quality of sociality—and what I think of as constitutionally-based collective projects of aspiration. It takes an in-depth look at how one small tribal group has availed itself of the possibilities opened up by India's twinned commitments to democratic freedom and social uplift, both in a literal, material way, as affirmative action quotas, and in a more imaginative way as the horizons of hope and possibility for making a better life for oneself and one's children. Without romanticizing the "otherwise" captured in Lakshmi's photos, I think that when they are taken together with Ram Lal's pictures they begin to tell an important story about the relationship between gender and social uplift in contemporary India as well as raise a number of questions that I will try to address: What is the relationship between the public, concrete success of Dhanka upward mobility and the quieter, intimate hopes and disappointments of Dhanka girls, women, boys, and men? What does upward mobility look like from inside an aspiring, yet still marginalized, group?

While there have been studies that try to assess the efficacy of affirmative action in India in terms of household income (see, for instance Borooah, Dubey, and Iyer's important 2007 study), or that look at its role in bolstering the political claims of Dalit and other subaltern groups (Ciotti 2006; Corbridge 2000; Michelutti 2008; Prasad 2001), the literature on affirmative action tends to focus on groups that have been either extremely successful or left out completely, with little attention to the complex positioning of those, like the Dhanka, situated in the lowest rungs of government service and urban society. This kind of ethnographic attention highlights collective aspiration as a lived, daily project. It considers uplift as a cultural process, not simply as an economic transition, and therefore asks us to take a new approach to Indian affirmative action, one that neither reduces the social complexities involved in uplift to the isolated quantitative indicators of the success or failure of affirmative action, nor takes a cynical approach to aspiration. I ask, rather, what is it that Dhanka women and men hope for when they hope? How are their aspirations articulated and lived? What happens when they are thwarted or disappointed?

In order to get at these questions, I argue, we must consider the complexity *within* as well as assertions *of* Dhanka identity. Though they are officially recognized as a tribe, a designation that may conjure notions of egalitarianism, the Dhanka are not homogenous but differentiated and stratified by gender, geography, education, employment, piety, and many other social factors. While I certainly write about "the Dhanka" or "Dhanka identity," the ethnographic task is to simultaneously destabilize their taken-for-grantedness by showing when and how these formations appear, and what work they do for different groups of Dhanka. As Gyanendra Pandey argues, "we have to ask how questions of power and privilege, subalterneity and difference, are navigated within subalternized constituencies and assemblages themselves" (2013, 33).

Inequalities of all kinds shape interactions between people; yet, at the same time, aspiration can be a collective project even when its material and imaginative contours vary widely. Thus, what it means to be Dhanka may change according to context. As we will see throughout this ethnography, sometimes Dhanka-ness is equated with a kind of autochthony or historical oppression. At other times, the Dhanka articulate a position that is very similar to that of their non-tribal neighbors and might seem more "Dalit" than indigenous. Tracking this variation is part of the task of grappling with sociality within the tribe, or *janjati* (roughly "tribal caste"; see A Short Glossary), and between the tribe and the broader political sphere.

I focus especially on gender as the site of difference within Dhanka social life because gender is structurally central to the legal-political projects of social uplift and upward mobility in contemporary India. Marriage and family are privileged sites for the articulation of community identity and for the performance of social reform. From the quasi-legal definition of "tribe," which relies on the cultural "difference" of indigenous marriage practices (whether or not these exist), to the continued struggles over separate, religiously based personal laws for the management of marriage, divorce, and inheritance, to the ongoing preference for endogamy among almost all caste and tribe groups, communities often point to marriage and family practices to assert their shared history and beliefs. This is especially the case in Rajasthan, where the "right" of upper castes to cultural practices that harm women, such as Rajput claims about the religious validity of the immolation of a woman on the funeral pyre of her husband, often called *sati*, has been repeatedly asserted and contested since the 1980s.[4]

This book is thus informed by and in conversation with much of the scholarship of gender and social reform in South Asia that has emerged in history, anthropology, and women's studies over the last twenty-five years. Indeed, studies of social reform, whether state, community, or organization based, have been among the most productive for seeing the ways that gender works as an enabling condition and a generative constraint across a variety of domains and social groupings that may not immediately seem to be about gender (Uberoi 1996). Challenging the conventional progress narrative of social reform in India, in which things are seen to improve for women and Dalits in a steady and predictable fashion over the course of the nineteenth and twentieth century (with today being the "most free" moment), feminist scholars have long insisted that we see social reform as a process through which distinctions of class and caste are made (Sangari and Vaid 1989; Chakravarti 1989).[5] Topics given extended consideration include child marriage and age of consent (Sarkar 1993, 2000), widow immolation (Yang 1989; Mani 1998), dress practices and codes (Devika 2005), and marriage practices (Chowdhry 1994; Arunima 1996), among others (see Sarkar and Sarkar 2008 for a sampling).

It is worth pausing for a moment to consider, however, that adivasi women are rarely the subject of such studies and that they have largely focused on colonial and postcolonial reform efforts in areas under direct British rule.[6] As Andrea Major has recently shown, the images and discourses circulating in mid-nineteenth-century Rajasthan, where widow immolation was being practiced with royal sanction, were quite different from those in Bengal; explanatory models with their provenance in one culturally and historically specific location may obscure as much as illuminate (2006; see also Unnithan-Kumar 2000). Perhaps more to the point, however, the literature sometimes treats the ways that Dalit, lower-caste, and adivasi women (and men, to a certain extent) are constructed as the outer limit and discursive foil for upper-caste women's behavior as a conclusion to, rather than incitement for, research.[7] Despite repeated references to the adivasi woman as a limit figure, there are few studies that engage directly with adivasi women's lives today or in earlier historical moments, particularly as agentive political actors.

A promising direction is suggested by those who have investigated the social reforms proposed by socialist, left wing, and Dalit political projects. While we do not want to romanticize the gender politics of such movements—J. Devika shows, for instance, how late-nineteenth-century scriptings of womanhood in Kerala played out in twentieth-century communist rhetoric (2005)—we should note that there have been other visions of what good women and the proper arrangement of marriage might look like. It seems important that non-elite leaders such as B. R. Ambedkar, Periyar E. V. Ramaswamy Naicker, and Jyotirao Phule all sought to remake marriage practices in quite a different way than those proposed by the upper castes or middle and upper classes, to include inter-caste, widow, and consent marriages free from Hindu ritual or priestly sanction (S. 1991; Chakravarti 2006). Studies that deal specifically with communities caught up in Ambedkarite internal reforms are useful here, particularly if we read them as being gendered in the sense that they track the emergence of a kind of marked masculinity, because they describe gender norms and processes that are constructed in direct opposition to the very ones proposed by upper-caste reform movements (for two very different examples, see Lynch 1969 and Ambedkar 2013).

In this ethnography, then, I am concerned with the overlaps between the practices it takes to assert a community identity and the work of cultivating the dispositions of Dhanka masculinity and femininity. Rather than implying that "men and women are already constituted as sexual-political subjects prior to their entry into the arena of social relations" (Mohanty 2003, 26) and that the feminist agenda of this book lies in its focus on gender, one of basic starting points is that what it means to be a man or a woman is not fixed but changes over time—the course of a lifetime, the span of political-economic eras, the cycle of a day. Part of the task of a feminist ethnography is to provide nuanced, descriptive accounts of intersectionality as it is lived in the world (Crenshaw 1991; Collins 1999); I therefore stress difference within social categories seen as stable, including "tribe" and "women," and map the emergence and reshaping of consequential differences as they occur across a variety of sites.

The Time of Adivasis

It is requested that the competent authorities empowered by the State Government to issue Scheduled Caste/Scheduled Tribe certificates may kindly be directed accordingly to strictly abide with constitutional provisions, exercise due care and follow proper verification in issuance of Scheduled Tribe/Caste certificate to an eligible person only, failing which action is to be initiated under the provisions of Indian Penal Code (sic) (Section 420 etc.) as well as appropriate disciplinary proceeding under the rules applicable to them.

—MINISTRY OF TRIBAL AFFAIRS, Government of India,
from a letter dated July 13, 2010, to the Chief Secretary
of the Government of Rajasthan.[8]

The Indian Constitution makes special provisions for tribes and castes that were listed (or "scheduled" in British English) as deserving of what legal scholar Marc Galanter calls "compensatory discrimination," known in the United States and other locations as affirmative action. The justification for compensatory discrimination derives from several Articles under the Directive Principles of State Policy in the Constitution, especially Article 46 (see Chapter 2).

The policies currently derived from this mandate include three main features: (1) reservation of seats (quotas) in legislatures, government postings, and educational institutions; (2) special expenditure and provision of resources for STs and SCs; and (3) special protection under the law. Scheduled Castes and Tribes are those groups designated as deserving and in need of special measures for their social uplift in recognition of their historical oppression by or isolation from the mainstream Hindu caste system.[9]

Tribes' particular claims rest on the assumption of their profound difference from the rest of Indian society, an assumption that has held sway since the colonial era. Land and culture have been the main tropes for the identification of India's tribal communities. Land-based definitions include those groups who claim to have an autochthonous relationship to a piece of land, as well as to the more generalized notion that certain *kinds* of land, notably hilly tracts, are home to "wild" tribes. Culture-based definitions rely on the documentation of particular customs and rituals that are outside so-called mainstream norms, such as the worship of animistic deities outside the Hindu pantheon. Sometimes land and culture come together as in the case of defining tribes based on their use of slash-and-burn agriculture. Other culture-land convergences include general qualities of "backwardness" and, notably, a resistant or rebellious relationship to state formations throughout history, including the British, the Mughals, various Rajput kingdoms, and the contemporary nation-state.

Importantly, culture-based definitions of tribalness have often found the heart of cultural difference to reside in gender arrangements. As Maya Unnithan-Kumar and others have shown, colonial ethnology and contemporary common sense (often reproduced in social-scientific arguments) converge on the idea that tribal women are more free than their Hindu or Muslim sisters (1997).[10] This freedom is largely defined in terms of social rules surrounding sexuality and marriage. That is, because tribal women have more choice in marriage partners, can divorce of their own accord, and may practice bride-price rather than dowry, they are thought to enjoy a higher status than other, non-tribal women.

Tribes were identified by individual states and their lists presented to the president of India for ratification. Those groups listed on the original schedules are to be found in the Constitution itself. Criteria for the definition of tribes, however, are not ensconced in the articles and have more or less been laid down in nationally mandated, but nonbinding, commission reports.[11] There is, therefore, a great deal of room for confusion about a group's particular status.

In 1956, Dhanka living in the Abu Road area of southern Rajasthan were included on the list of tribes eligible for the newly independent state's affirmative action program; in the 1970s, with the abandonment of the place-based policy, all Rajasthani Dhanka became eligible for ST status. Numbering about seventy-seven thousand according to the 2001 census, they are part of the 6.6 percent of Rajasthan's tribal population not made up of Minas and Bhils, the state's two most populous tribes. Of this population, about forty-four thousand Dhanka live in urban areas, with the majority being found in Jaipur City itself. This statistic flies in the face of most received wisdom about tribal groups in India. Despite the fact that tribals have been among the most affected by large development projects, like dams, and many have moved to cities in recent years, the notion of an urban tribal still strikes many as an oxymoron. It may also make the Dhanka vulnerable to challenges to their ST status. In 2010, a complaint filed with the state government about Dhanka recognition resulted in the circulation of a bureaucratic order, quoted above, to revert to the 1956 system and only provide ST certificates to those Dhanka able to prove that they or their parents hailed from the small area of Abu Road first included on the schedules. This memo effectively barred the Dhanka of Jaipur from obtaining the necessary documents to avail themselves of reservation benefits.

Throughout this book, I will argue that the Dhanka work hard to cultivate dispositions that reflect a positive relationship with the state and the promises of constitutional uplift.[12] Their use of the constitutional category "ST" as their chosen label reflects this positive relationship. Yet, their use of "adivasi" in the past tense says a great deal about its complications. The alternation between "ST" and "adivasi" that roughly corresponds to the present and the past points to the extent to which the Dhanka must negotiate a tricky, even impossible, legal-cultural terrain that resembles that of other indigenous groups around the globe. "We were adivasis" allows Dhanka women and men to both index and distance themselves from the low status and primitiveness that are associated with tribalness.[13] The statement is made in the past tense—we *were* adivasis—and yet its very utterance does not put adivasis-ness entirely in the past. Dhanka identity claims circulate in a temporality, past and yet not, that is often necessitated by regimes of recognition such as the Indian system of schedules and reservations. The fractured time of tribal citizenship, the disjuncture between the "now" of enunciation by a modern, intelligible subject and the "past" of authentic autochthony has been described aptly by Elizabeth Povinelli in the context of Australia: "Every time indigenous subjects provide content to their traditional practices, they do so in present time—linguistic time—and this marks their alteration by history . . . all Aboriginal subjects are always being threatened by the categorical accusation: 'You are becoming (just) another ethnic group' or 'You are becoming a type of ethnic group whose defining difference is the failure to have maintained the traditions that define your difference' (2002, 55).[14] The problem of maintaining difference is all the more marked in an urban social context and when a tribal group identifies itself as Hindu, as do the Dhanka in Jaipur.

The Dhanka, as we will see, want to refer to a certain amount of alteration by history, to mark their willingness to be altered, while at the same time fulfill the ubiquitous requirement of being "traditional"—as in, both in some prior temporal moment and unproblematically undifferentiated—for both of these qualities are central to ideologies of tribal economy and society.[15] Which is not to say that Dhanka do not see themselves as tribal, and here is what is perhaps the constitutive contradiction of their urban tribal identity:

many Dhanka who reject their "tribalness" have also benefitted greatly from the system of reservations that marks them as a Scheduled Tribe and in need of special measures for social uplift. We can read "*Hum* adivasi *te*" as a statement that precisely indexes this contradiction; in marking them as no longer adivasis, it also creates adivasi-ness as a possibility. We might read it this way: "We were adivasis (but we are no longer). We were adivasis (could we be again? does our tribalness linger?). We were adivasis who have tried to change, so we deserved, and continue to deserve, special measures for our welfare." Discussing the Gaddis of Himachal Pradesh, Kriti Kapila has summarized the general paradox of being a modern tribal: "It is as modernist, reformist, national citizens that the Gaddi affirm their right to negotiate with and be recognized by the state, in order to acquire the benefits that should rightfully accrue to them. And yet, at the same time, their actions as citizens involve the ambivalent connections to a traditional past and to a way of life that is increasingly portrayed as not-modern" (2008, 128).

In other words, Scheduled Tribes, and particularly those, I would argue, like the Gaddis and the Dhanka who are "insignificant"[16] in the sense of not evoking the specter of separatism and militancy or abject primitivity, and whose numbers do not make them an important electoral constituency, must engage in collective practices that communicate both internally and externally that they are both worthy of the benefits that accrue from tribal identification (really tribal) and in need of them (backward). They must demonstrate that they are, in sum, willing to change (but never quite capable of change).

On Collective Aspiration

Ram Lal's photograph, his narrative of the improvement of life in the basti over the last thirty years, the cultural work of (partially) locating adivasi-ness in the past and willingness in the present—these are all part of a familiar story about upward mobility. There are others. Consider Ram Lal's uncle Deepak, the cousin of his now-deceased father, who lives across the alley in Dhanka basti. He wears thick glasses over rheumy eyes, which betray his age, and a pressed white *kurta* and *dhoti* when he leaves the house. Deepak is often to be found sitting on the cot in his room at the front of his house, thronged by his grandchildren, of whom he is a favorite playmate. He is calm and generous. Like many men in the neighborhood, he is a devotee of the local saint Sri Garibdasji Maharaj, a teetotaler and a vegetarian, and often goes to sing *bhajans* ("devotional hymns") in events that last all night. (*Dil ka hujra saaf kar jana ke aane ke liye* . . .) For all intents and purposes, his household is exemplary of the rise from backward adivasi-ness to the rungs of the urban, working class. Like many families in the neighborhood, Deepak's family saw their income and cement house grow as the result of his position with the Jaipur PHED. They were able to educate their sons. And they saw some of the stigma of tribal-ness lessen as well. Deepak learned bhajans in his youth because tribals were not allowed to enter temples, being considered too far outside the Hindu fold, too unclean, to approach the gods. In those days they were still subject to the bonded-labor system known as *begaari*. Now, not only can the Dhanka enter temples, they are married by Brahmins, and they have built their own temple in the basti.

One of Deepak's daughters-in-law once confided to me that in his youth Deepak left his wife, Payal, for three years to wander like a *sanyasi* ("mendicant") and sing these spiritual hymns. *What did she do?* I asked. *Well, she just waited for him to come home. What could she do?* In their old age, Deepak and Payal seem to have made peace with one another, and Deepak's brief abandonment is a family secret, if only a partially guarded one. For her part, whatever memories she has of her husband's departure, Payal has settled into married life and old age and does not speak of the incident. But while Payal has adjusted to city dwelling—she married into Jaipur from a rural area—she has never really embraced it. She speaks only a few phrases of Hindi and communicates mostly in her native Marwari dialect. She rarely dons a sari, preferring to simply wear her blouse and petticoat. Simply put, Payal is not a vision of an urban, middle-class housewife but has remained what her granddaughters would call a *gaon-walli*, a village women, a bumpkin. While she has been able to stay home as a housewife during her married life, she often contends that things were better *before* the city grew and everyone built new houses. Families were closer, children more respectful, the streets less crowded and frightening. Payal is utterly devoted to, and protective of, her extended family. But she is often cranky about the social world she encounters in the neighborhood and the city beyond. Despite their new "equality" in the city, Payal's favorite son cannot find a permanent job; even with his education he does not bring in enough money.

Payal's complaints about how much better things were in a previous era was something I heard repeatedly from many older—and sometimes even young—residents when talking about the growth of Jaipur.[17] It could be that cities always generate anti-urban nostalgia for an imagined, lost rural past.[18] But it could also be that Payal and many other Rajasthanis are conflicted about progress, even when that progress entails an agenda they support and are engaged in pursuing. To return to Deepak, was his choice to wander as a spiritual seeker also partly a social protest against the strictures of a caste system in which he was beyond the pale of the hierarchy itself? I can imagine it so. Perhaps motives cannot be parsed in this way, but it seems that at some point being a householder—even one employed with a good job—was not enough for Deepak. He sought something else that made him leave his family behind. His period of *sanyas* pushed the bounds of the kind of middle-class civil-service ethos he and other Dhanka men were seemingly cultivating. So it is not surprising that when he did return the incident was scarcely mentioned again, and Deepak's religious practice became a private matter that added to, but did not supplant, earthly concerns.

The story of Deepak's abrupt departure hints that he and his wife did not always share the same goals or vision for their future and that their experiences of the changes in Dhanka religious life that occurred in their lifetimes differed significantly due to gender expectations. He left. She stayed with their children. *What could she do?* Gender is not incidental to people's experiences of collective aspiration but at the heart of how these hopes—and accompanying doubts—are lived. Both Deepak and Payal had to work through contradictory and sometimes ambivalent feelings about the collective, familial, and individual life projects of which they were a part. They both inhabited a number of different dispositions in their adult lives, sometimes all at once. Deepak was both archetypal Hindu householder and renunciate, Payal respectable housewife, *goan-walli*, and critic of contemporary urban life. Now surrounded by grandchildren, and even great-grandchildren, in a cement home that they own outright, are Deepak and Payal Dhanka? Rajasthani? Tribal? Adivasi? Middle class? Working class? Have they "moved up"?

The classical account of upward mobility follows an almost inevitable progression from worse to better, primitive to modern, uneducated and poor to literate and (at least potentially) middle class. The story accords not only with what Pierre Bourdieu identified as the "common-sense picture of the social world, summed up in the metaphor of the 'social ladder'" (1984, 125), but also with the enduring vision of caste hierarchy noted by Louis Dumont.[19] The ladder and its rungs remain fixed, and movement is always from down to up, past to present, backward to forward. We saw in the previous section that the regime of recognition ensconced in the Indian Constitution creates a contradictory temporality in which Scheduled Tribes must be simultaneously past and present. However, the *ideology* of upward mobility and social uplift continues to posit unidirectional ascent—call it progress, development, modernization—as attainable for STs and other groups suffering social and economic discrimination.

Many popular, legal, and scholarly understandings of social mobility in India replicate the view of society as a ladder that one may ascend. A classic example of this formulation is M. N. Srinivas's theory of Sanskritization.

"Sanskritization" is the term Srinivas coined to refer to the process through which low-ranking castes and tribes rise up through the structures of caste hierarchy to attain higher status. While he revised his theory several times, in his classic (1952) formulation Srinivas contends that

> [t]he caste system is far from a rigid system in which the position of each component caste is fixed for all time. Movement has always been possible, and especially so in the middle regions of the hierarchy. A low caste was able, in a generation or two, to rise to a higher position in the hierarchy by adopting vegetarianism and teetotalism, and by Sanskritizing its ritual and pantheon. In short, it took over, as far as possible, the customs, rites, and beliefs of the Brahmins, and the adoption of the Brahminic way of life by a low caste seems to have been frequent, though theoretically forbidden. (quoted in 1962, 42)

In Srinivas's view, the highest positions in the caste hierarchy are the most "Sanskritized," meaning that they follow exclusionary practices deemed appropriate only for Brahmins. These include religious practices—hence the reference to Sanskrit, the language of the Vedas, the knowledge of which was historically confined only to Brahmins—food proscriptions, marriage and kinship patterns, education, and so on. Through the emulation of these practices, or through the abandonment of non-Brahminical practices, a group could move up (interestingly, never down) in the caste hierarchy; the overall structure, however, would always remain the same: the ranked ladder.[20]

It is important to note here that one of the central markers of Brahminical status was the treatment of women, particularly in marriage relations. Srinivas and later commentators argued that marriage arrangements confer more freedom of choice and movement on low-caste, Dalit, and adivasi women. Upper-caste women, such as Brahmin and Rajput women, in contrast, observe strict *purdah* (a set of "veiling practices"), are married young to men not of their own choosing, and are forbidden to divorce or remarry if widowed. Sanskritization, then, can be pursued through, and is registered in, what Srinivas calls "increasing harshness toward women" (1962, 46).

Leaving aside that the top echelons of a local caste hierarchy may not be occupied by Brahmins—in Rajasthan, they are far more likely to be Rajput and the hegemonic ethos one of the martial Kshatriya varna[21]—the structural view proposed by Srinivas has had an enduring effect on discussions of upward mobility and social uplift in scholarly and popular sources—even as these are now more often conducted in the language of class than of caste. This is most clearly seen in a marked focus on *emulation* as the key technique or modality of aspiring groups. Such communities are thought to try to replicate upper-caste norms of behavior with an eye to proving their own higher-caste status through this replication; the implied audience for such cultural performances is almost always external—either the upper castes or colonial and postcolonial officials who will accept the group's new status.

The problem with this view is that it privileges an external orientation over a view of what happens within aspiring communities. Surely public demonstrations of Dhanka willingness-to-be-altered—especially in the form of the annual samuhik vivaha—are directed toward a larger audience. Part of the event's success is its ability to draw a substantial crowd and therefore a certain media presence. But as I show throughout this ethnography, the cultivation of gender-appropriate, upwardly mobile dispositions is undertaken as much with an eye to internal differentiations as to some imagined upper-caste outside. Furthermore, as David Hardiman (1987) has noted of the Devi movement among Bhils in Southern Rajasthan in the 1920s, Dhanka claims go further than simply asserting a higher-caste status.[22] Hardiman critiques Srinivas and others who have assumed that movements for adivasi uplift, such as the reformist Devi movement that asked tribals to abstain from liquor, become vegetarian, and join the nationalist cause, represent a kind of Sanskritization or move from tribe to caste. Hardiman's basic objection is to the assumption that adivasis pursue such programs in order to claim a rank in the caste hierarchy and thus implicitly accept this hierarchy. He argues, instead, that what is claimed is "*equality* of status with high-caste Hindus" (159, emphasis added). For it is not simply the case that adivasis in the first half of the twentieth century pursued purification by emulating upper castes in behavior—Srinivas's focus; such movements also presented "a sharp challenge to the existing social structure" (160).

Recent incarnations of the emulation approach to understanding upward mobility can be seen in narratives about the rise of consumerism and the middle class in "liberalized" or "liberalizing" India.[23] In everyday talk in middle-class households in Jaipur, one is likely to hear references to the growing consumer aspirations of groups formerly unable to purchase consumer goods like televisions, refrigerators, coolers, scooters, and stylish saris. I have repeatedly heard members of households employing domestic servants comment on these servants' recent purchases of such goods and the perceived gap between their desires and real purchasing power; the implications is that now "they" want to be like "us" and naively believe that consumer goods will make it so, rather than education or hygiene (see Liechty 2003). Emulation is once again understood as the central operation of upward mobility in a local common sense.[24] Yet this is an emulation that never quite works because the very same consumption patterns and desires that mark and create what is often called the "new middle class" of India are decried in others, particularly Dalit and tribal women, who often mark the boundary of the middle class' self-proclaimed inclusiveness and openness to anyone who embodies "the right structures of feeling" (Bhatt, Murty, and Ramamurthy 2010, 136).

The pervasiveness of the emulation model in its commonsense variant is why I think a revisitation of theories of Sanskritization is an important, if admittedly revisionist, task. Both the simplicity of its visual image—the ladder to the sky, with its rungs at regular, predictable intervals—and the message that life above is always better than the life you have, make it powerful and persuasive to those in its upper reaches even if it is no longer common currency in the social science of South Asia. It is the hegemonic aspirational formation in relation to which actual striving takes place.

Upward mobility and social uplift comprise a socially complex constellation of aspirations that are rarely, if ever, experienced in a singular or simple manner—this is precisely why studies of Sanskritization seem outmoded. Research on the middle class in South Asia has stressed this point repeatedly, particularly the cultural effort it takes to situate one's social group and one's self as both "traditional" and "modern" (Liechty 2003). Yet low-caste, Dalit, or adivasi aspiration, particularly as it is lived in relation to constitutionally guaranteed reservations, has yet to be the subject of much reflection. We may have a sense of the kinds of "hegemonic aspirations" (Fernandes and Heller 2006) toward which all Indian citizens are supposed to strive and infer that one must aspire to be a citizen at all. But there are important questions to be asked about how groups who define themselves below, or tangentially, to the new middle class—those often seen to embody "tradition," which is most often a euphemism for poverty (see Pyburn 2004)—relate to and play a role in the politics of hegemony.

Throughout this book, I argue that attention to the structures of inequality, such as local caste politics or the legal regime described in the previous section, as well as the presence or absence of signs of upward mobility, such as televisions, needs to be combined with an ethnographic approach that attends to what it means for the daily lives of women and men to engage in collective aspiration as a cultural project. I foreground a set of questions about how differences, such as gender, cut across legal identity categories and the kinds of dispositions that women and men cultivate in relation to such cultural projects, even when these dispositions are ambivalent or imperfectly inhabited.

I have chosen, then, to use collective aspiration as a kind of general term to describe practices and dispositions cultivated as part of striving for upward mobility and social uplift for several reasons. First, as pointed out above, theories of upward mobility imply both a structure and a trajectory that are untenable in the current era of privatization and contract work. It is not just Payal's educated son who is currently having trouble finding work in the city. The Dhanka of Jaipur are increasingly concerned about the possibility of *downward* mobility, an issue rarely raised in any of the literature on mobility in Indian society.[25] The triumphant progress narrative, in which improvements in education and income lead to a better life and the erasure of caste stigma, must necessarily posit that these changes are lasting to the extent that the central question posed about reservations is often "How much longer?" The question ties affirmative action to the time of the nation and asks Indian citizens to declare an end to special protections for oppressed groups. Underwritten by global linkages to places like the United States, which declares itself beyond racism and routinely undermines its own commitment to equal opportunity by reducing the scope of an already limited affirmative action policy, the understanding of adivasi groups as a temporal diagnostic for Indian modernity is remarkably tenacious (Pandey 2013). I hope to use aspiration precisely to move away from temporal diagnostics toward an ethnographic account of how one group is weathering the transition from an era of state-backed protections to an era of contract labor.

The second reason to frame my discussion in terms of aspiration is that the concept of upward mobility tends to focus attention on individuals or families. While I highlight important differences within the urban Dhanka community based on things like education, income, and marriage, it is also important to consider what is shared. Jaipuri Dhanka highly value commitment to one's community or "giving back," as it might be called in the United States.[26] Responsibility to the community, especially its less fortunate members, is a value that is frequently reiterated—in the building of the temple, in collective weddings, and in electoral politics. Such a perspective provides an important counter to the widespread notion that elites within scheduled communities, the so-called "creamy layer," take advantage of affirmative action benefits for their own personal gain. Thus, I want to stress that contrary to many media portrayals, the aspirations of the Dhanka are to a large extent collective and not individualistic opportunism.

Third, I use aspiration to get at the imaginative aspects of Dhanka efforts, the extent to which social status, at least as one perceives it, is ill-captured by simple material measures. It is not just what you have or do not have—a television, a primary school education—but what you are able to imagine for yourself that shapes the lived experience of social identity. Aspiration implies both a larger, public dream and that there may be possibilities that have not yet been conjured, that start as intimate practices of imagining things otherwise. It opens up theories such as Sanskritization and its commonsense equivalent, in which the goal is already assumed: to be accepted as, or at least as similar to, upper castes. Thus, while collective aspiration includes some elements of upward mobility and social uplift, it is meant to open up ethnographic questions rather than invoke a familiar narrative about a group's "arrival"—in modernity, in the middle class, or in consumerist citizenship.

Dhanka strategies for the inhabitation of tribal roles and norms of good citizenship may be read as emerging from what Lauren Berlant calls "cruel optimism": an affective structure in which that which you desire is the very thing that keeps you from finding more viable ways of living in the present (2011, 1). Clearly there are important differences between the contemporary Euro-American context that is Berlant's site and context and the political terrain I am describing here, and we must be cautious about importing theoretical models from one to the other. But Berlant's deep attention to the ordinary as a space of survival practice, and the conventional as a seemingly inhabitable aspirational promise, are instructive to my case. In her analysis of the ways that people manage in conditions of ordinary crisis that have made the activity of social reproduction more difficult and eroded its best fantasies for a good life, including and especially the dream of upward mobility, she opens up a number of possibilities for feminist ethnography.

Instructively, for Berlant optimism is a structure of orientation, not an emotion. It does not have to feel good. While it may be that the dispositions I describe are optimistic in that they rely on, invoke, and sometimes demand the promises of the aspirational structure of Indian citizenship, they are not about happiness. In the ethnography that follows, I register a wide range of ways that the dispositions of the era of service produce rage, frustration, and ennui. These responses and performances are exacerbated in the present era of the contract, but remain optimistic. My choice to highlight how getting by in the day-to-day can relate to dreams of political participation and upward mobility is, then, an effort to also refuse to turn "the objects of cruel optimism into bad and oppressive things" (15). I do not think that democracy, for instance, is such a thing. The Dhanka are not symbols of larger structures and struggles, but speaking subjects who build and manage the city where they live. Their story is consequential, not emblematic.

Berlant's insistence that the ordinary is not a space of conventionality out of time but "a zone of convergence of many histories" (10) parallels anthropological arguments that, in the words of feminist anthropologist Lila Abu-Lughod, "intimate details of one particular life world" are one way to render "socially grounded understandings of choice, and shake up ideological and culture-bound notions of freedom and constraint" (2008, xxii). Focusing on this intimate scale, Berlant sees convention not as false consciousness, but as the best fantasy that may be on offer. Getting by in this world as it is, with its routine shocks and rote deprivations—missed meals and owed interest payments and paltry stories for making sense of a world—is not the antithesis of politics. Taking "the messy dynamics of attachment, self-continuity, and the reproduction of life that are the material scenes of living on in the present" (15) as her object, Berlant indexes a history within feminist anthropology of attention to the spaces and modes of the reproduction of social life and more recent studies in which reiteration, repetition, and inhabitation are viewed as agentive, historical, and sites of, not just subject to, change (Abu-Lughod 2008; Mahmood 2005; Butler 1993; 2006).[27]

With Hesitation, Mona's Story Begins

In the winter of 2003, when her relatives began to make her marriage arrangements, Mona was nervous but sanguine. Optimistic and anxious all at once. In some ways, though we won't really encounter it until Chapter 6, Mona's story comes first. It's the one I know best, both because Mona was the first person in Dhanka basti who trusted me and because it is Mona's struggle that forced me to think about the Dhanka community project of aspiration in relationship to the work on one's feelings it might entail: cultivation, pruning, cutting back what has wilted, cutting back in an effort to produce particular flourishings, augmentations. Mona, I learned in the first year I knew her in Dhanka basti, often dreamed of other lives for herself. She resisted her wedding for as long as she could. Highly intelligent, empathetic, and curious, she saw herself and her own potential reflected in the basti's visiting nurse midwife—and in the visiting anthropologist—and felt that her marriage, while inevitable, was not the only possible path that her life could have taken. Her insistence that things could be/could have been different is the key to this book.

Mona's husband, whom she and I often imagined before he actually appeared, turned out to be fond of insulting her and threatening her with his defection to old sweethearts in the early years of their marriage. His mother, with whom Mona has lived since her wedding, was even more abusive. During my single meeting with her new *sas* ("mother-in-law") a few years later, she commented repeatedly on Mona's uselessness and stupidity, expecting me to agree. At first I fought back; by the end of the afternoon, I just hung my head, exhausted from the effort of struggling against her unreasonable vitriol. All of Mona's friends and female relatives said she was different in those days: quiet, reserved, angry. I wouldn't have believed it until I saw her unhappiness myself.

Things didn't stay that way; Mona put a great deal of effort into changing them and transforming her relationship with her new family so that she felt like she had more control over the things she wanted to control. When we got together in 2012, just before I heard that this manuscript would be considered by an academic press for publication, Mona was happy and hilarious. Her husband had told her she couldn't come back to Shiv Nagar Basti with their children to see me for the weekend. Her mother-in-law herself told him he was crazy—*Her friend is here from America! What is wrong with you? Of course she's going!* Mona would not want me to tell her story as a tragedy, at least not anymore. But since the labor and the risk and the pain that it took to get to where she is now are not something either of us can ignore, I will not write it as simple triumph, either.

One possible feminist rendering of this story would blame Dhanka men for pursuing their political project of recognition at the expense of women and girls—for their traffic in marriage. Why couldn't Mona pursue the path she wanted? Become a nurse or an anthropologist? Wander as a *sanyasi*? If the Dhanka truly want to embrace modernity and uplift all of their members, then girls should be given options other than early marriage and child-bearing. This is a feminist orientation I cannot totally disavow myself. I have often asked, with Mona, *If only . . . then what might have been?* And more often, alone: *At what cost, at whose cost, does recognition come?* And it is true, I think, that men often know when they gain at the expense of women (Derné 1994). Thinking about gender as often-unarticulated norms of both masculinity and femininity does not necessarily mean that men do not recognize when they are operating through, or operationalizing, unequal power. I will argue that marriages, especially samuhik vivaha, allow Dhanka men to pursue many political ends all at once, in a way that is in keeping with their cultivation of good dispositions in relation to the state and that relies on their ability to command the reproductive lives of girls and women. That is to say, Srinivas's contention about harshness toward women may not be wrong. I think this line of questioning is a beginning, not an end, to analysis.

A critique of the Dhanka traffic in marriage always risks recapitulating the problem of the gift (Strathern 1988), in which women are not subjects themselves, but objects of exchange that make relationships between others (men and men or men and the state). This is also a view that treats women as "a unified group" prior to the "fact of their 'exchange'" (Mohanty 2003, 27) rather than attending to the ways that it is precisely through the social relations characterized as "exchange," and in the differences between a girl's status before and after such a social initiation, that gender is fashioned. Such an approach also dismisses Dhanka women's active efforts to create a certain kind of marriage and family life, and their enthusiasm for samuhik vivaha, as simply "culture" at best or false consciousness at worst. Rather, I want to take women's efforts to cultivate their lives and their families in particular ways quite seriously, especially since, in the case of the Dhanka, the respectability that is supposed to accrue from properly arranged marriage and family life has to be earned and is seen as part of an agenda of making life better. The ability to stay at home signals having "arrived" historically. Dhanka women work hard to embody community norms in ways that are agentive, but not necessarily resistant (Mahmood 2005). This is not to say that they are not sometimes of two (or three or four) minds about their role in their families and community. If we are going to treat agency as a mode of embodiment rather than as a political position with positive content, then we need to learn to see agency in modes of inhabitation and embodiment that are sometimes ambivalent. Further, the cultural projects that Dhanka women undertake are rarely as clearly articulated as those of a textually-based piety movement; yet, they are no less real and challenging.[28]

To locate the problem of the limitation of girls' choices simply with Dhanka men is to ignore the long history through which marriage and gender arrangements become one of the possible, and most legitimate, modes of identification (we might even say citizenship) for scheduled groups in India. If, as I have argued above and as many scholars assert, part of what makes scheduled communities—especially tribals—"other" are the perceived differences between their gender arrangements and those of the Hindu or Muslim mainstream, to bring these arrangements in line with the norm is to disavow an important aspect of historical stigma. This is, we might say, an instance of Sanskritization at work. But samuhik vivaha takes this collective effort a step further: it produces the right kinds of unions (endogamous, sanctioned by religious authority, subject to community scrutiny) but through a ceremony that marks the Dhanka as still not quite developed and therefore still in need of special efforts on their behalf. Because of the political-legal structures of recognition for India's Scheduled Tribes and because of the centrality of questions of women's worth and value for articulating community identity in contemporary Rajasthan, marriage is an especially opportune and charged location for political articulation.

We are better off, then, I think, asking about the social history and political-legal structures that necessitate the enactment of gender inequality through marriage in order for the Dhanka to pursue their aspirations of upward mobility and social uplift.[29] I take inspiration here from Chandan Reddy's discussion of commemorations of *Loving v. Virginia*, the Supreme Court decision that invalidated anti-miscegenation law in the United States. He argues it is more useful to see the marginalization of others by minoritized social actors—in the case discussed by Reddy, acts of African-American homophobia—in ways that do not chalk such acts up to culture or "communal values" but rather "enable one to better specify the unique conditions that organized particular forms" of exclusion (2008: 2862). He is specifically referring here to the ways in which the anti-racism of the *Loving* decision, articulated as it was in and through the institution of marriage, shored up the heterosexual family and affirmed African-Americans as part of the heterosexual norm as opposed to the homosexual other. In the mid-twentieth-century United States, admission to the norm (read: white society) required this exclusion.

In the Indian case, marriage is an important way that communities assert themselves as rights-bearing subjects because it is one of the main social relations to fall under separate "personal laws" for each recognized religion. Marriage, divorce, custody, and inheritance issues are supposed to be decided in accordance with religious tenets, and the right of communities to legislate social relations has been upheld repeatedly in the courts. One famous case, the Shah Bano controversy of the mid-1980s, showed clearly that the right to condone, interpret, and sometimes sever reproductive unions is a matter that goes to the heart of groups' ability to retain their cultural uniqueness.[30]

In Rajasthan, powerful Rajputs have taken this argument to its furthest extreme, arguing that their right to administer marital relations extends to the sanction of the immolation of widows. Public debates about the rights of Rajputs to legislate "cultural" practices having to do with marriage were most visible in the mid-1980s (at the same time as the Shah Bano controversy), following the 1987 immolation of a young widow, Roop Kanwar, in Deorala village not far from Jaipur. These arguments certainly continue to shape all local discourse about the relationship between women and community in the region. To be a visible, politically empowered community is to register and secure collective existence through marriage as both endogamy—vastly preferred by all castes and tribes, including the Dhanka—and a deep community investment in how individuals are married. This investment is bolstered by resonances with the earlier Deorala moment and the continued, widespread veneration of *satimatas*, despite a law making their glorification illegal. Political inclusion relies on a particular configuration of intimate gender relations.

★

Pause.

Does this help explain Mona's story? Perhaps. But it also leaves so much out.

✳

To take as my only task of writing the effort to provide a legal-historical context for the Dhanka embrace of housewifery or collective marriages is to make Mona's story a kind of ethnographic parable about the inevitability (the righteous virtue?) of her painful transition from a girl-who-imagines to a woman-who-is-stuck-but-survives. I confess I am often inadequate to the task of writing outside such parables. My best effort is to attend to what I think of as partially told tales of the intimate. The discussion introduced above about the relationship between politico-legal structures of recognition, marriage, and the arrangement of the everyday lives of Dhanka women and men is an important part of telling these tales; it will occupy me throughout what follows. This project helps illuminate the saturation of a sphere thought to be private by public forces and effects as well as the preoccupation of public debate with questions about the arrangement of people's intimate lives. In this sense, the intimate is a scale of analysis.[31]

But I also take intimacy to be a specific quality of relations, one that energizes and troubles. What makes intimate sociality different than other kinds of sociality is a kind of riveted attention to possibilities that are not as yet present. It is often both the focus of an ethnographer's gaze and the condition in which ethnographic research is conducted. I take Gayatri Chakravorty Spivak to be describing something related in her discussion of "ethical singularity," which emerges in intense interaction with one person.[32] Spivak says "in such engagements, we want to reveal and reveal, conceal nothing. Yet on both sides, there is always a sense that something has not got across. This is what we call the secret; not something that one wants to conceal, but something that one wants desperately to reveal in this relationship of singularity and responsibility and accountability (1999, 384). What is important is that there are secrets on both sides, questions and answers in two directions, rather than the rhetoric of persuasion.[33] Both parties come away enervated, altered, but not converted. It is the revealing that is the "(im)possible ethical relation" (384), the intimacy.

Intimate interactions do not claim, or flourish in, conditions of something like full disclosure. They rely on a sense that not everything has been said, that there is still more to relate, that the present can move in unexpected— sometimes marvelous, sometimes dangerous—directions. Intimacy implies an intricate inter-ness that is not easily swept up in the bifurcating logics of what is true and not true. In this sense, there is—a nice bit of luck for the writer—that other meaning of "intimate," which is to hint, suggest, or communicate indirectly.[34] To explain and to intimate. If my account moves between the different registers that each of these imperatives implies, it is because an important part of my interactions with Dhanka girls and women have been to ask this question—*If only . . . then what?*—and to play games of imagination that require that their meaning be intimated; that is, gestured toward and marked as a fiction—one that was perhaps co-produced, but a fiction just the same.

Outline of the Book

In Chapter 2, I introduce readers to this little-known group as well as to the criteria through which they have been judged to be a Scheduled Tribe (ST). In giving the reader some background on the legal history of ST definition, I also point out the difficulties created by the "tribal role" that groups must occupy in order to be able to make claims for state benefits, particularly "reservations," the hotly debated quotas reserved for protected groups in educational institutions, legislative bodies, and government jobs. I show that "Who are the Dhanka?" is a question that the community must answer repeatedly (hence the answer "We were adivasis") and that creates special problems for this group in particular. Almost half of the Dhanka population of Rajasthan lives in urban areas; they cannot point to a well-documented history or a homeland as proof of their indigeneity; they are largely Hindu, and thus their religious practices are not immediately recognizable as "other"; there are recognized castes with very similar names, including the Dhanak and Dhankiya, which calls into question their specifically "tribal" status; and the Dhanka rarely use the popular term "adivasi" except in the past tense, preferring the more constitutional language of "ST." The Dhanka must work in collective ways to solve these problems of identity, a task they achieve largely by writing and telling their own histories. In this chapter, I therefore trace out the accounts of their origins and history presented by contemporary Rajasthani Dhanka in relation to other accounts, largely colonial, that have been authored about them by outsiders and show that one of their most important strategies is to let mutually contradictory histories exist side by side—in essence, to refuse the kind of closure that is sought through state attempts to define tribal groups but without nurturing the kind of resistant stance to the state that is thought to be prevalent among India's tribal groups. Indeed, what emerges is a historical portrait of a community that has worked very hard to avail itself of the opportunities for uplift that have been made available over the last hundred years.

The remainder of the book roughly corresponds to the two historical periods I am labeling the "era of service" and the "era of contract," though it will
become quickly apparent that I do not think that one has been overcome and
supplanted by the other. In Chapter 3 I discuss the gendered dispositions that
emerge as the Dhanka undertake the cultural work of collective aspiration,
particularly masculine "willingness," a term I use to refer to a constellation of
attitudes, inclinations, and performative practices cultivated by Dhanka men
who highlight their willingness to do what it takes to get by despite historical oppression. I argue that willingness is the disposition that gives force and
shape to Dhanka collective aspiration—it is an orientation that has the community at its center, rather than the individual, and as such is not reducible
to the self-interest that anchors many analyses of upward mobility among
subaltern groups. In the first part of the chapter, I return to Dhanka histories
to show how they read willingness back into the past as their history of taking
up any available work and therefore surviving the cruelty of kings who forced
them into bonded labor and menial service. I show how this attitude continued on as the Dhanka began to settle in the Jaipur region and took up various
"low" occupations, from firing lime bricks to laying sewer pipes, which over
several generations brought them into government jobs and allowed them
to convert their impermanent slum into a neighborhood with many cement
houses. In the second half of the chapter, I describe some of the differences
between men that have been created and exacerbated by Dhanka collective
aspiration and upward mobility, such as those drawn on the basis of religious
values (particularly manifest in teetotalism and vegetarianism) and ability to
get permanent government postings versus temporary contract labor.

Chapter 4 centers on the women of the era of contract through an extended consideration of the emotional and social emphasis of Dhanka women
on love between husbands and wives. It focuses on "respectability" as an important disposition for Dhanka women and further considers how life events
that fall outside the realm of the respectable are accepted and re-narrated by
women whose intimate labor must therefore be seen as part of the project
of collective aspiration. By tracing the stories of three women whose lives do
not conform to the ideals of a good woman, but who continue to insist on
their respectability in the face of misfortune, I highlight the ways in which
all gendered enactments are imperfect inhabitations of norms that not only
determine what it is to be a man or a woman but also influence many forms
of identity, including those of tribe and nation.

Chapter 5 describes the emergence of annual collective weddings, known
as *samuhik vivaha sammelan*, as the centerpiece of Dhanka articulations
of tribal identity and a moment in which the values of the era of service

directly impact the marriage and family arrangements of a younger generation. It locates these yearly events both in the historical-legal context of tribal
identification described in earlier chapters and in community gender relations to explain collective weddings' efficacy. I argue that the centrality of
marriage to community definitions in contemporary Indian politics as well
as histories of tribal definition, which often based the difference between caste
and tribe on the position of women with regard to marriage practices, means
that contemporary tribal identity politics must still be worked out within this
terrain. Thus, Dhanka men demonstrate willingness, in part, by engaging in
a "traffic in marriage" in which they undertake collective weddings for the
stated purpose of protecting poor girls and their families in the community
from the rising costs of dowry and possible related violence; however, other
implicit political goals guide the organization and enactment of the yearly
rituals, such as demonstrating the size of the state's Dhanka population and
thus winning political patronage for their potential role in electoral politics,
printing and distributing group histories, and drawing distinctions between
the Dhanka and Rajasthani upper castes that stress the positive orientation of
Dhanka to the state and its goals of uplift.

Chapter 6 shifts us to the era of contract, which is centered on the generation entering adulthood. It begins with a look at marriage and weddings,
including samuhik vivaha, from the perspective of young unmarried women
who are its stated beneficiaries. This chapter demonstrates how marriage has
become the horizon of possibility for young Dhanka women, replacing all
other modern goals such as education and employment, while at the same
time describing the deep ambivalence that young women sometimes articulate about this horizon via their stories about love and education. I present
ambivalence as another disposition that is cultivated as part of the cultural
work of collective aspiration, though in a less explicit and directed way than
masculine willingness. I consider ambivalence as a strategy of girls to keep
themselves open to the possibility that their lives might have been otherwise
and as a methodology that is important to a feminist ethnographer trying
to adequately portray the complex positioning of interlocutors in a time of
anxiety and excitement. The chapter centers on the story of Mona, one of my
earliest and closest friends in Shiv Nagar Basti, whose engagement, wedding,
and marriage I describe.

In Chapter 7, I consider the position of young Dhanka men in relation
to the broader community projects of their fathers and grandfathers. I argue
that an earlier generation of Dhanka men, men of what I call the "era of
service," were able to obtain the government jobs that became the launching
pad for the group's upward mobility. Today, however, in what I call the "era of

contract," the Dhanka are under threat of downward mobility. The privatization of many utilities in the city and the increasing use of temporary workers by government departments means that young men simply do not have access to the institutions and benefits that have shaped collective aspiration. The change is a fraught topic that repeatedly causes friction as older men attempt to convince younger men that the dreams of the past are still worth their attention.

In the final chapter, I expand the scope of my account to reflect on aspiration and affirmative action as instructional themes for all of us thinking about political mobilization in the contemporary world. I discuss recent struggles around reservations in Rajasthan, including the Dhankas' efforts to maintain their ST status in the face of challenges to their legitimacy, in order to reflect upon the creativity of subaltern citizenship. *We Were Adivasis* demonstrates that such creativity emerges *because of*, not in spite of, proximity to those state institutions the theorization of which usually produces subalterneity as an exclusion, or outside. And yet, this citizenship is never singular. The emerging world described here, one in which the era of service is being eclipsed by the era of the contract, demands attention to how projects for social uplift can be both collective *and* differentially experienced based on axes of gender, age, and religious devotion. In the final analysis, then, I argue that the ethnographic material I present here makes a strong case for the ongoing work of feminist ethnography through which we engage critically—in the many senses of that adverb—with the possibilities of the otherwise, which is spoken in many different voices and registers.

Who Are the Dhanka?

Early 2011. I am surfing the web and find an unexpected link: a PDF copy of a letter written by the National Commission for Scheduled Tribes (NCST) and forwarded to the Chief Secretary of Rajasthan.[1] The subject of the letter, dated July 13, 2010, reads: "Clarification of the Synonymous/Phonetic Similarity name of 'Dhanak, Dhanuk'/ . . . (S.No.20), 'Dhankia' . . . (S.No.21)" as Scheduled Castes; and 'Dhanka, Tadvi, Tetaria, Valvi' as Scheduled Tribes in the State of Rajasthan." The letter describes complications that have arisen in the process of certifying members of the Dhanka tribe. In several cases, individuals of the Dhanak caste, a Scheduled Caste (SC, not a Scheduled Tribe (ST), have obtained certificates stating that they are Dhanka (thus members of an ST, not an SC). They have then used these certificates to access state benefits, such as reserved government jobs, meant for STs. The cases bring to light a problem with the Dhankas' ST status.

According to the NCST, when the first list of Scheduled Tribes in Rajasthan was compiled in the constitution in 1950, Dhanka was not listed as an ST in Rajasthan, though they were listed as such in the then-named State of Bombay. In 1956, the states of the newly independent India were reorganized, resulting in a piece of Bombay state, known as the Abu Road *taluka*,[2] being transferred to Rajasthan. The letter argues that only those Dhanka from this small area are eligible for an ST certificate[3] and that "the place of origin at the time of notification . . . is the only basis to ascertain ST status of a person." It cites as evidence a 1977 circular that declared ST status only for those who are of a particular caste/tribe in relation to a specific locality. Its conclusion on the matter is adamant: "Any Scheduled Tribe certificate in the name of Dhanka, Tadvia, Tetaria, or Valvi tribe . . . issued to a person who does not belong to the . . . tribal community of Abu Road taluka of Sirohi district of Rajasthan . . .

is invalid." The letter further threatens prosecution under the Indian Penal Code of anyone who has not taken "proper care" in issuing ST certificates.

My heart sinks. In 2005, Dhanka elders had mentioned that a claim had been lodged that the Dhanka should no longer have ST status in Rajasthan, but until this notice it seemed to have had little effect on policy or practice.[4] I do not know how many of the Dhanka I met in Shiv Nagar Basti trace their roots specifically to the Abu Road area. But I do know that many middle-aged men report that they and their fathers were born in Jaipur City itself, not in the southern reaches of the state. If the terms of the letter are enforced, many of the men and the few women I know who have gotten jobs through the reservation system will be effectively barred from such benefits in the future. It is as if, as many Dhanka have feared over the last ten years, their entire future has been thrown into question.

It is hardly consolation that the facts marshaled in the NCST's report are debatable and open to interpretation. In addition to the odd attribution of the authentic Dhanka origin site as the Abu Road region—odd both because there are Dhanka found throughout western India, a social reality recognized at least since the nineteenth century, and because the Dhanka have, since that time, been considered a "wild" or "wandering" tribe—there are two other obvious problems with the NCST's assertions. First, in 1976, the area-based approach to scheduling communities was abandoned in favor of an identity-based system of scheduling. Producing the SC or ST certificate of one's parent or other documentation that one belongs to one's group has, in bureaucratic practice, been sufficient to receive official recognition of one's tribal status. Second, the report does nothing to clarify the relationship between the groups mentioned—Dhanka, Tadvi, Tetaria, Valvi—and between the Dhanka and other similarly-named groups, which is the source of the original conflict: whether Dhanak and Dhanka are the same group and which is entitled to what reservation benefit.

This unexpected bureaucratic artifact, the NCST letter, speaks to the struggles faced by many scheduled communities in India today and serves as a starting point for my discussion of the difficult "ST role" created by Indian affirmative action policies and the creative ways in which the Dhanka have occupied this position.[5] The Dhanka women and men I know who live in Jaipur, particularly those of the younger generation, are often ambivalent about their status as tribals or adivasis. This is not, I think, because they are any less tribal than many other groups. I believe that the Dhanka, both rural and urban, have a historically and ethnographically justifiable claim to their ST status when taken in relation to the ST category more broadly. As long as the schedules and reservation system remains intact, they are rightful beneficiaries. Their selective inhabitation of the ST role, rather, indicates how difficult it is to fill this role in a way that answers, rather than raises, questions about a group's authenticity.

From an anthropological point of view, the 2010 letter I describe is confusing. Why are there three groups—Dhanka, Dhanak/Dhanuk, and Dhankiya—with such similar names? What is the relationship between the Dhanka and the other three groups with whom they are listed (Tadvi, Tetaria, and Valvi)? Why are the Dhanka a tribe and the others castes? Where is Abu Road taluka, and is that the Dhanka "homeland"? Are they, indeed, indigenous residents of the land now called Rajasthan?

On one hand, this chapter will hopefully shed light on the basic question "Who are the Dhanka?" As they are a relatively small community without a visible political presence—at least most of the time—most readers will not be familiar with this group. Textual references to the culture and history of the Dhanka are scarce from the late colonial period to the present. Those that do exist tend to be brief and stress their "insignificance"[6] and lowness. On the other hand, I also hope to show that this question becomes the context for much of the political and intimate interaction I describe in later chapters. The Dhanka of Rajasthan must answer the question "Who are the Dhanka?" over and over again in order to secure and maintain their reservations, the path to upward mobility that has inspired their collective aspiration.[7]

Before proceeding to talk about Dhanka history and their particular claim to Scheduled Tribe status, it will be helpful to lay out a bit of the legal history surrounding the Indian schedules of affirmative action beneficiaries. In the following section, I discuss the basic problems posed by the Dhankas' particular settlement pattern and history for their definition as a tribe. I also offer some of my own speculations on the history of Dhanka movements since the 1880s based on my reading of colonial ethnography and censuses in light of contemporary narrations of Dhanka history. In the final section of the chapter, I discuss how the Dhanka go about "solving" the problems of tribal definition. In later chapters I talk about this effort in contemporary sociopolitical events; here, I show how the Dhanka make their lack of occupation and vulnerability to historical events—their *lack* of history—precisely the feature that proves their tribalness.

Scheduled Tribe Recognition

Taken together, the anthropological categories "tribe" and "tribal" and the legal structures of SC/ST recognition in India comprise what we might call the "ST role"—an historical, social, legal, and economic positioning that entitles groups to certain benefits but also demands a particular enactment of tribal-ness.[8] Widely disparate groups in India, with dramatically different cultural practices and histories, occupy the ST role; as such, groups must often do a great deal of performative work to occupy it effectively. One of the most important arenas for this work is the history of settlement and migration. As the NCST letter with which I opened this chapter indicated, the question of origins—where a group comes from, how long they have been settled there, what the conditions of an individual's parents were—makes land-based his-torical narratives central to efforts to prove a group's right to ST status. This relationship to land is familiar from the global movement for indigenous rights. However, as many commentators on India have noted, indigeneity may not be the most relevant category to capture the experience of ST groups because it is based so firmly in the experience of white settler colonies (see Karlsson 2003). To some extent, everyone in the subcontinent could be con-sidered equally migrant and indigenous, current efforts to genetically prove the pre-Dravidian ancestry of ST peoples notwithstanding.[9] More impor-tant is the history of the subordination or "internal colonization" of Indian adivasis; the question of land is more often raised in reference to the loss of rights of use and residence rather than in reference to original inhabitation or autochthony (407). As Archana Prasad (2003, 6) points out, groups now identified as tribal rarely live in areas where they could be considered indig-enous. She shows, for instance, that the Gonds of Central India were subject to "periodic displacement," and not just under the British; in fact, she traces earlier flight to hilly tracts during the Rajput era (1–33).

Cultural distinctiveness, or the maintenance of unique social features in the face of domination by an external ruling group, is thus essential to ST identity claims. Expectations for obvious primitive traits and non-Hindu or Muslim behaviors (from spirit possession to bride-price to swidden agri-culture—even though all are practiced by non-tribal groups as well) struc-ture relationships between STs and the Indian state and between STs and anthropologists tasked with determining their status as a "tribe" (Middleton 2011). Gender arrangements, especially around marriage and family, figure heavily in the distinction of Indian tribes from other groups.

But it is not enough to have been tribal in the past—a group must also be in need of ongoing efforts for their uplift. This is, as I indicated in the Introduction, the basic paradox of Scheduled Tribe recognition. The Dhanka approach to inhabiting the ST role can be gleaned from the offhand remark I heard during fieldwork, "We were adivasis." The statement "Hum adivasi te" tells the listener that, on one hand, there is a quality of adivasi-ness that we are still connected to—that we were adivasis, and not some other category of society. However, this identity is also located in the past. *We have moved beyond it sufficiently that it no longer completely defines us.*

One way to see the vexed positioning of India's ST groups is as symptomatic of a more global problem in the recognition of indigenous groups. Much of the recent discussion of communities that are recognized as, or aspire to be, STs has focused on whether such groups can and should be considered "indigenous" and their growing links to an international indigenous rights movement (for example, see Karlsson 2003). Scholars and activists have been concerned with how the international framework—embodied in institutions like the UN Working Group on Indigenous Populations (IP)—demands a particular *kind* of indigenous person with a particular kind of historical experience. The fear most often raised about indigeneity as a framework for political organizing in India is that the necessary elisions and homogenizations required by the IP framework can undermine local and national political will for other kinds of struggles and link the growing desire to access the international movement to the growth of "adivasi" as a salient identity for groups who previously had little in common. Alpa Shah (2010) argues that the global indigenous rights movement has made indigenous groups "eco-incarcerated" and that "global discourses of indigeneity can maintain a class system that further marginalizes the poorest people. This class dimension to the indigenous rights movement is likely to get erased in the culture-based identity politics in produces" (32). Her concerns are shared by Kaushik Ghosh (2006), who similarly finds those working to insert adivasis into the transnational frame are often the elites from within these groups who have only limited experience with adivasis actually struggling to retain land rights. In a similar vein, Sumit Guha (1998) argues that "indigenous" is a category imported by environmental experts that does not capture the experience of India's forest-dwelling communities. Amita Baviskar (2007) demonstrates the unintentional traction given to Hindu Right nativism and anti-Muslim violence through the language of indigeneity (see also Prasad 2003).

These debates echo earlier debates about the appropriateness of the anthropological category "tribe" for the Indian context or the difference—if any—between castes and tribes, a point to which I return below. It is important to remember, I think, that most ST claims are still made to the Indian government via state apparatuses established for such claims (see Tsing 2007). Even if an ST group works to "keep the state away," as it has been described by Shah (2007) in her rich and nuanced account of groups in Jharkhand, the state is the central interlocutor or foil for Scheduled Tribes. Groups identified and identifying themselves as tribal often take an oppositional or avoidant stance to the state. Indeed, historically those groups considered primitive or outside mainstream Hindu and Muslim culture have often been those who took a resistant position against state formations from Rajput kingdoms in the eighteenth century to the British Raj in the nineteenth to the extent that "tribe" can in some ways be considered a definition of a group's (uncomfortable) relationship with a ruling state.[10]

But Scheduled Tribes in contemporary India do not only take oppositional stances to the state and not all seek indigenous identities. It has been useful for me to think about the Dhanka not as an adivasi group—a term that they anyway use sparingly and strategically—fighting for rights as indigenous people but rather as a recognized Scheduled Tribe who sometimes mobilize the connotations of "adivasi" to help press their claims to the state. The Dhanka occupy the ST role through invocations of adivasi-ness but they do not, in the end, seek recognition as adivasis exclusively.[11] It is also helpful to remember that the term "adivasi" was introduced in the Chotanagpur region of Bihar in the 1930s when it was invoked by a newly-formed political body, the Adivasi Mahsabha (Hardiman 1987, 13). Thus, "adivasi" is as much a political term as "ST" in the sense of being linked directly to state-directed claim making.[12]

CONSTITUTIONAL PROVISIONS

It is necessary to pause briefly here to outline the constitutional provisions that pertain to Scheduled Tribes as they are central to the state's relationship to these groups. The Indian Constitution, ratified in 1950, does not define Scheduled Castes and Scheduled Tribes, but it does allow for preferential policies aimed at their uplift. Article 46 of the constitution, which is a "Directive Principle of State Policy" (not, it should be noted, a clear mandate),[13] reads: "The State shall promote with special care the educational and economic interests of the weaker sections of the people, and, in particular, of the Scheduled Castes and the Scheduled Tribes and shall protect them from social injustice and all forms of exploitation." Thus, despite the fact that discrimination is outlawed, Article 16(4) allows for "any provision for the reservation of appointments or posts in favor of any backward class of citizens which, in the opinion of the State, is not adequately represented in the services under the State"; Article 335 further exhorts the state to take the claims of SCs and STs into account when appointing governmental posts.

Upon the recommendation of specific groups for inclusion in the schedules by the Governor of an individual state, the President is responsible for officially designating "castes, races or tribes or parts of or groups within castes, races and tribes which shall for purposes of this Constitution be deemed to be Scheduled Castes in relation to the State" (Article 341[2]). Subsequently, lists can only be altered by an act of Parliament.

For both Scheduled Tribes and Scheduled Castes, the provisions for their special protection and uplift fall into three categories: permission to create legislation for special protection under the law; the allocation of monies earmarked for SC/ST development; and the reservation of a proportional quota of seats in relation to the general population for SC/ST candidates in legal bodies, educational institutions, and government employment (Galanter 1984). This last has come to be synonymous with India's affirmative action program, such that it is usually referred to as "reservations," though Marc Galanter's term "compensatory discrimination" is perhaps more accurate. He describes the logic of compensatory discrimination: "[it] is premised on the understanding that in a regime of formal equality and open competition, members of a previously victimized group, burdened by accumulated disabilities, will fall further behind (or gain too slowly). The solution is to draw a line between the realm of formal equality and a separate zone of compensatory preference. In this protected zone, the former victims can nourish their accomplishments and enlarge their capabilities until the day that the protective barrier can be lowered and the special provision dismantled" (2002, 311). The uniqueness of the SC/ST provisions in the Indian Constitution lies in its twinned commitment to democratic representation and social uplift, or to formal equality and to substantive equality or redistribution, to use the language of political science. Even if the Directive Principles of the Constitution are not "enforceable" or justiciable, they provide a "frame of reference for judging the goodness of public policy around which public opinion could be mobilized democratically" (Vaidyanathan 2002, 286).

In its goals of "freedom, equality, and social justice" (284), the Constitution is a document of aspiration. It does not begin from a performative "self-evident truth" that all people are equal (which ignores all the ways in which they are not, in fact, equal). Rather, it is based on the idea that the social reality of oppression and inequality demands *efforts* to create the equality that all human beings deserve. In this sense it is radically different from, say, the Constitution of the United States, which refuses/ed to acknowledge that the oppression of slavery, the genocide of Native peoples, and the disenfranchisement of women were built into its vision of the natural rights of "men." It is this aspiration that, I argue, has been taken deeply to heart by groups like the Dhanka who embrace the ST role offered to them by this constitutional vision. There has been a tendency in political theory to see such orientations among marginalized groups as suffering from a kind of false consciousness around freedom; freedom and equality, from this perspective, look more like "means of government" than viable aspirations (Rose 1999: 67). Feminist work, too, has stressed the un-freedom of many liberatory claims and asked us to consider their imperial cultural-historical provenance and demand for a particular kind of liberatory subject (Mahmood 2005). I take such cautions to heart, but there is a danger in assuming a one-to-one correspondence between *rhetorics* of freedom and the collective aspiration of marginalized communities. Putting STs in a constitutional framework helps us think about how such groups engage with the ethno-legal terrain that shapes their identities without limiting this engagement to the terrain itself. The Dhankas' relationship to a constitutional imaginary is as creative as it is constrained.

✻

The identification of Scheduled Tribes and the aims of reservations in their favor has been quite different from that of Scheduled Castes.[14] As Galanter (1984) puts it, "In the case of the Scheduled Castes, the Other Backward Classes, and the Denotified Tribes; [*sic*] it is hoped that the disabilities and disadvantages that separate them from their compatriots will eventually be overcome by preferential treatment. That is, the aim of the policy is to eliminate their distinctiveness by dispelling all of the differences that set them apart from other Indians. The aim of Scheduled Tribes' policy is more complex—to balance improvement of their condition and a degree of assimilation with preservation of their distinctiveness and a measure of autonomy" (153). It is worth noting that compensatory discrimination for Scheduled Tribes has on the face of it been less effective than for Scheduled Castes. While SC and ST groups appear to be approaching an equal footing in terms of income, poverty, and ownership of land, STs have fared far worse in the terrain of education and health than SC/Dalits (Maharatna 2005, 54).

The sense that tribalness is defined by a different kind of outsidership than untouchability (though it should be noted that often tribals like the Dhanka suffered the same discriminations as untouchables, for instance not being permitted to enter temples or the practice of *begaari* ["bonded labor"]) demands that ST groups fulfill a particular set of cultural, historical, and geographic criteria. As mentioned above, the constitution does not define what it means by a "tribe." Rather, the working definition of tribe has been laid out in a series of committee reports since the 1960s. The best known of these, the Lokur Committee (1965) set down the five criteria that are still employed today. These are: indications of primitive traits, distinctive culture, geographic isolation, shyness of contact with the community at large and backwardness.[15] No terms of comparison, let alone recommendations or ascertainable benchmarks, are offered to help measure such vague terms as "isolation" and "shyness."

In the original policy, castes and tribes were scheduled in relation to a specific area (even if the area itself was not scheduled). It would, for instance, apply to members of tribe *x* in district *y* of *z* state. The Lokur Committee recommended the abandonment of an area-based strategy, going so far as to argue that SCs and STs in one state should be recognized in another. This has not been supported by subsequent legislation, but in 1976 intrastate restrictions were lessened, a policy decision that added 2.5 million SCs and 3 million STs (Galanter 1984, 139). While it is still the case that the courts have usually upheld residence requirements in disputes over whether a particular SC or ST candidate is entitled to a reserved position or promotion, in practice intrastate restrictions have not been applied. A Dhanka anywhere in Rajasthan has been a Scheduled Tribe member, at least until the circulation of the memo cited above.

The power and stakes of the letter with which I opened should now be apparent: it is attempting to enforce a letter of law that has not been the enactment or spirit of a policy since the 1970s. The vagueness of the five criteria set down by the Lokur Committee has meant that there is some room for maneuver within the ST role. As several observers of the process involved in obtaining ST status have noted, the success of this endeavor has a great deal to do with the sociality of the encounters themselves (Jenkins 2003; Middleton 2011).

A BRIEF NOTE ON "TRIBE" IN THE INDIAN CONTEXT

Much of the discussion about the category "tribe" in South Asia has focused on the purported differences between tribes and castes and exposing the pointlessness of the distinction. Historical analyses have shown how this distinction was taken for granted by colonial administrators who, under the sway of supposedly scientific anthropological accounts of European history and evolution, saw tribal social organization as a precursor to their own society that was present in Africa and India in much the same way as among the Native peoples of North America (Bates 1995b).

Even if one accepts the term "tribe," there is still no agreement on what criteria have been or should be used to define it. Crispin Bates (1995a) claims that it has been used to apply to people who practice slash-and-burn agriculture or hunting and gathering (5). Andre Béteille (1974) says that the unspoken consensus of early anthropologists was that the tribe was a "more or less homogenous society having a common government, a common dialect and a common culture" (61). But like Bates, he points out that geographic isolation and an attachment to particular kinds of places—hilly and wild tracts—resulted in a kind of "ecological" view of tribe, to use Béteille's term. Both he and Alistair McMillan (2005) note a decided shift from an early focus on the relationship between tribes and places to a focus on tribes as *kinds* of people (121), with tribes being increasingly associated with a particular religious orientation—animist, as opposed to Hindu (63). Thus, while "tribe" cannot be said to have a clear referent, it conjures up a rough sketch of a group of people who are mostly egalitarian, tend to be migratory in order to practice swidden agriculture, do not have a fixed occupation but a common "culture," worship nature, and, implicitly, have been oppressed by groups who either chased them into the hills where they are found today or exploit them because of the naiveté borne of their distance from mainstream society.

Colonial policy created special categories, privileges, protections, and methods of resource appropriation for these groups, however vaguely defined. McMillan (2005) describes British policy toward groups it labeled "tribal" as "founded on a mixture of paternalism, fear, and indifference" (111). Colonial paternalism was based on the view of tribal groups as primitive and unfettered by the social hierarchies of the caste system; tribals were ingenuous and vulnerable and thus had to be protected. Paternalism was most directly manifest in the policy of designating "backward areas." It also involved a romanticized form of masculine identification with groups, such as the Bhils, that colonial officials found preferable to the "effeminate" castes of the plains (Skaria 1997). This identification was, of course, qualified, as it easily gave way to fear evidenced in the labeling of "criminal tribes" and in the suppression of tribal uprisings—sometimes of the very same groups, the Bhils being a case in point (McMillan 2005, 112).

What lay at the base of these policies, however, was an assumption of tribal "difference" and endangerment. Their difference, whether the result of isolation or cultural/religious features, made them susceptible to outsiders who would take their land and loan them money at exorbitant rates. Thus, the British inaugurated a system to list, or "schedule," certain groups or areas to put them under direct administrative control/protection. According to G. S. Ghurye (1980), the first attempt by the British government to create a unique framework for a group they considered aboriginal was in 1782, when the Rajmahal Hill tract was withdrawn from the legal system of British Bengal and a Hill Assembly was formed (70–74).[16] This approach was codified in the Scheduled Districts Act of 1874 which kept listed areas outside the scope of the new legislatures inaugurated by the creation of provincial governments

(McMillan 2005, 112). Indian nationalists later saw this policy as an effort to keep tribal groups away from the politicizing influence of the Congress and as a result many advocated the "development" and assimilation of tribal groups who were merely backward communities in need of uplift.[17]

These two approaches—one, isolationist and the other, assimilationist—are often taken to have been embodied in the debates between Verrier Elwin and G. S. Ghurye (see Guha 1999, 157–161). Verrier Elwin was an Anglican clergyman who became an ardent follower of Gandhi and was encouraged by Gandhi and other Congress leaders to take up the cause of India's tribals—which the Congress largely neglected. In his career, Elwin spent long periods of time living among the Gonds, the Baiga, and eventually in the northeastern states; he became infamous for his marriage to a Gond woman, Kosi, who was nearly twenty-five years his junior. Elwin wrote dozens of books in his lifetime and eventually became the administrator for the North-East Frontier Agency (NEFA) in independent India. His position on the tribals that they needed to be protected from Hindu and Christian missionaries and allowed to develop "according to their own genius" was for the most part adopted by Nehru at Elwin's urging.[18]

Ghurye, on the other hand, saw Elwin's advocacy for positive discrimination for Scheduled Tribes as an affront to the inclusive spirit of the new constitution. The issue of reservation caused the famous rift between Gandhi and Dalit leader B. R. Ambedkar that resulted in Gandhi's fast and the eventual Poona Pact. The details of this struggle are well documented (see Rao 2009, 137–140). Most commentators have contended that the identification and special provisions for tribes has been much less contentious than for Dalits. Galanter (1984) surmises that this may be because so few ST seats have ever really been filled.

THE TRIBAL POPULATIONS OF RAJASTHAN

According to the 2001 census, Rajasthan is home to about seven million Scheduled Tribe individuals. About 93 percent of this population is comprised of members of the Mina, Bhil, and Bhil Mina tribes.[19] The Dhanka are part of the other 7 percent of the population, which includes individuals from thirty different tribes; clearly, these communities have much smaller populations. The census of 2001 reported 77,047 Dhanka, Tadvi, Tetaria, and Valvi living in Rajasthan. In Jaipur, I did not encounter any of these groups except Dhanka, and they did not refer to Tadvi, Tetaria, and Valvi as relatives though they did, as we will see below, claim Dhanuk, Dhankiya, and Dhanak as related groups.

Literacy among the STs of Rajasthan is uniformly low, listed in 2001 as about 44.7 percent; only 26.2 percent of ST women in the state are literate, which is even lower than the national ST average of 34.8 percent. In comparison to these all-state figures, the Dhanka have fairly high rates of literacy: 61.8 percent for men and 45.9 percent for women, though these figures are both still below the national literacy rates. It is interesting to note that while the Dhanka only form about 1.09 percent of the ST population, they comprise 1.57 percent of the *literate* ST population; their representation is greater than other STs relative to overall population size. While there is certainly reason to be circumspect about the criteria used to measure "literacy," such statistics help us render a demographic sketch of the Dhanka of Rajasthan: small, urban, with rising literacy rates that can be directly attributed to the group's upward mobility via reservations.

The Challenge of the ST Role

We might not worry too much about the caste/tribe distinction and consider it an outmoded anthropological debate. But, of course, it is not as though "tribe" does not conjure images and expectations. It is telling that while nineteenth-century accounts of wild and wandering tribes tended to stress difference, wildness, and savagery (references to rumored human sacrifice are plentiful), contemporary discussions of adivasi communities often begin with a note of despair at the death of a romantic dream. In his influential critique of the anthropological distinction between tribe and peasantry, Andre Béteille (1974) describes his first fieldwork among the Oraon in the mid-1950s. He comments: "Although . . . I spent just a month studying material culture, social organization and religion in an Oraon village in Ranchi district, I came away with the strong impression that the inhabitants of these villages corresponded very closely to the ordinary meaning of peasants. I clearly remember my initial disappointment in discovering that, although we had come to investigate proper tribals, the people who confronted us were outwardly no different from the poorer villagers one might find anywhere in rural Bihar or West Bengal" (64). An anthropologist seeking a distinctive "tribal" way of life might be similarly disappointed by the Dhanka of Jaipur.

A relatively large percentage of the Dhanka have lived in urban areas since the 1960s. The 1981 census returns indicated that 43.76 percent of Rajasthani Dhanka lived in cities (Singh 1998, 234).[20] In 2001, this percentage had risen to 56.36 percent of the 77,074 counted as part of the "Dhanka, Tadvi, Tetaria, Valvi" category. Some of my Dhanka interlocutors in Shiv Nagar Basti claimed to have had family living in their current location for the past eighty years.

While this is difficult to verify, it is worth noting that in 1931, the Rajputana census listed a "Dhanak" population of 80,785; the Jaipur census, which was conducted separately by the Maharaja of Jaipur in the same year, found 14,411 Dhanak living in the state. While we might want to resist the urge to attribute an anachronistic kind of urbanity to residence in Jaipur, it was certainly the densest population center in the area at that period, and the presence of Dhanka gives credence to my interlocutors' assertions that segments of the community have long been city dwellers.[21]

Though not entirely urban dwellers (half of the Dhanka population still lives in rural areas), Dhanka today are not isolated in wild hilly tracts, nor are they likely to have been so in the early twentieth century when census-taking procedures were regularized and codified. Neither do they claim Jaipur as a kind of "homeland"—their migration to the city-state is an accepted historical fact. Nor can the Dhanka be considered entirely "outside" the wider organization of social life—as victims of isolation or perpetuators of separateness who are "shy of contact" with the world around them. Most Dhanka refer to themselves as Hindu, even if they tend to follow more syncretic, local gurus than orthodox traditions (a topic I discuss in the following chapter). Aside from older women wearing heavy metal anklets that are welded at marriage (common among adivasis in western India), they do not have special religious rituals or styles of dress not found among other Rajasthani groups. Men wear pants and shirts; women wear nylon saris. If they speak a Rajasthani dialect, so do most rural in-migrants to Jaipur. It is hardly a unique cultural feature, and daily talk is in Hindi sprinkled with many English and Bollywood-inspired phrases, as well.

The Dhanka also do not often refer to themselves as adivasis except, as I discussed in the Introduction, in the past tense of the statement *We were adivasis*. They are much more likely to use the term ST, or *nich* ("low"), or *janjati* ("tribal caste"; see A Short Glossary). The first time I asked a group of adolescents about the predominant jati in the neighborhood—a young man replied that they were Dhanka and an ST. Then he paused and asked a friend, "*Hum ST han ya SC han*?" ("Are we an ST or an SC?"). Clearly, at least at moments, labels like "tribal" or "adivasi" have little salience, especially for Dhanka youth.

How, then, do the Dhanka claim their ST status? Or, perhaps more to the point, how do they manage to present themselves as both of the past—with the correct origin, relationship to land, and cultural uniqueness described in the previous section as the "ST role"—and at the same time committed to their own uplift as participatory national citizens? In the remainder of this chapter, I discuss narratives of Dhanka history, including those written by outsiders and those authored by the Dhanka themselves, in order to discuss how the Dhanka strategically occupy and reinterpret the ST role. In the next section, I take up accounts written by non-Dhanka, including those of nineteenth-century colonial administrators that locate Dhanka origins in what is today Gujarat and stress their relationship to another Scheduled Tribe, the Bhils. In the last section, I highlight the ways in which the Dhanka "solve" the problems presented by the socio-legal category "Scheduled Tribe" via stories of their origins and movements over time. I identify four main strategies used by the Dhanka to fulfill the historical requirements of the ST role: (1) letting multiple, sometimes contradictory, accounts of their origins hang together without attempting to "resolve" them into a coherent story; (2) claiming all groups with similar names or historical links as part of their community, at least in the past; (3) stressing their lack of a fixed occupation, their longstanding commitment to social betterment, and the "clean" nature of their work as proof of their difference from (low-) caste groups; and (4) highlighting their oppression by various regimes, ancient and modern, and their need to do what it takes to survive through time.

I use the term "strategy" here in a Foucauldian sense, not to refer to premeditated gambits but, rather, to the ways in which Dhanka claims must work with and around terms of definition that they did not set and at the mercy of which they now see their future rise or fall.[22] The Dhanka do not "claim" to be a tribe when in fact they are not one. Rather, the history that produced the Dhanka as objects of knowledge and later, intervention, is one shot through with the misunderstandings of a colonial authority that was deeply invested in the idea of the existence of tribes. The Dhanka are a tribe to the extent that we retain this as a meaningful category. The will to knowledge of the ethnographic state (Dirks 2001) was always necessarily geared toward administration; thus, complicated regional histories and social connections such as those linking mobile communities in western India were simplified in ways that continue to have ramifications for groups like the Dhanka.

Dhankas in Northern Bhil Country

There are few written accounts of the origin of the Dhanka authored by outsiders; the ones I have located all pertain to the "Dhanka of Gujarat." For now, we will leave aside the question of whether they are originally from "Rajasthan" or "Gujarat" because, of course, these boundaries did not exist in their current form until quite recently. I will address the efforts of Rajasthani Dhanka to prove their Rajasthani history in the next section. We will instead imagine a wide swath of territory in the northern part of what colonial

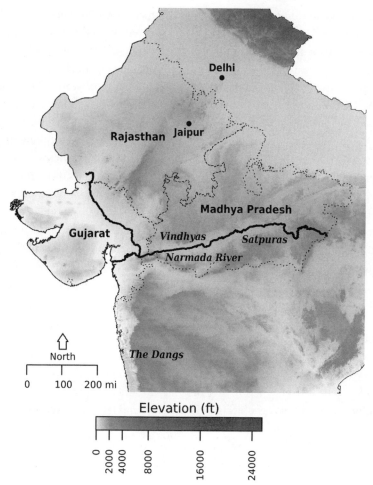

MAP 2. Northern Bhil Country. Map created by Adrian Brasoveanu.

ethnographers and administrators dubbed "Bhil country." This includes the
area from what is now Rajasthan (with the northernmost point being Jaipur
and moving south into Jodhpur, Udaipur, and Banswara) into the Narmada
Valley, south to the Satpura Hills and the Dangs and east to Khandesh.[23] This
area has traditionally been known as Rewa Kantha (*kantha*, in Gujarati, refers
to the bank of a river or an area drained by a river; *Rewa* is another name
for the Narmada). It has also been called the *Pal*, which refers to hilly and
forested land with few yields (Nath 1960, 1–2, n2). Indeed, most of the region
included is hilly and was, at least in the past, considered *jungli*. The Aravallis
in the north, parts of the Vindhyas and Satpuras in the middle, and the Sa-
hyadri Hills in the south are all included.

Here is what the anthropologist P. G. Shah[24]—the only anthropologist to write a full-length monograph on the Dhanka—recorded as the Dhanka origin story during his fieldwork in the 1950s (note that he uses Tadvi and Dhanka interchangeably at times):

> According to the popular belief, the Tadvis were original inhabitants of Pavagadh[25] and they were Chohan Rajputs.[26] In the time of Patei Raja of Pava-Gadh they were living in Pavagadh area. The story of the fall of Patai Raja is well known. It is said that he was a devotee of the goddess Amba[27] and when the goddess was pleased by his deep devotion, she expressed a wish to give him what he wanted. The king asked her to become his wife. The Goddess became so enraged with this demand that she gave a curse that he would perish with all his kingdom and relatives. After some time, when Muhammad Begda, the Emperor of Ahmedabad, invaded Pavagadh, the Patai Raja fought bravely, but he was killed on the battle field.[28] The soldiers fled and took shelter in the jungle. The city of Champaner and the neighbouring areas lost their prosperity and the population fled to the neighbouring fields and forests. Those who took shelter in the fields and fed themselves on Dhan (uncooked grain), were called Dhanka. Some of them came and settled on the bank of the river Narmada. The Gujarati and Sanskrit word for river bank is tat and those living on river banks or in villages near the river were called Tatvis, a word which came to be softened in to Tadvis.
>
> The word Dhanka is also derived from Sanskrit Dhanushyakas, meaning holders of bows; the group of Dhanushyakas as a fighting clan has been mentioned in the Mahabharata war as going to Kurukshetra from western India. They were evidently clever at the use of the bow and arrow, which seems to be the common weapon of the tribal people. The word Bhil is derived from the Dravidian word Bili meaning bow; the corresponding Sanskrit word "Dhanushyakas" for the Dhanka tribe is indicative of the Hinduised development of the tribe in the area. (1964, 22)

Shah does not qualify this story, explain or contextualize it, or refer to its source(s). It is left to speak for itself in a way that is both telling and confusing. I imagine that there are many ways to read Shah's history. I am most interested in the way that it foreshadows more recent Dhanka descriptions of their own origins. Perhaps the most striking aspect of this account is that it presents two entirely different theories of Dhanka origins as if they could both be true at the same time. The second paragraph, which begins "The word Dhanka is *also* . . . ," implies that one unified group may have two separate origins, or there may be divided origins for the same term, one from

the medieval period and the other from the mythological time of the Mahabharata. By the end of the account the reader may even decide that they
have, in fact, been reading about the history of the Bhils, not a separate group
called Dhanka or Tadvi, all along.[29]

Based on contemporary Dhanka narratives, we might guess that this is
not because Shah got it wrong or did not recognize the contradiction between different versions of the origin story but because the Dhanka have,
since at least the 1950s, developed an important strategy for dealing with the
question of their status as tribal: they let mutually contradictory histories
stand together. Shah is quite likely reporting exactly what his informants said
about their early history. As we will see in Dhanka accounts of their own history in the next section, no effort is made to streamline or authenticate one
version of historical or mythological events; rather, evidence for the Dhankas'
Rajput origins (in the first story) or their indigeneity (in the second story) is
piled on, layer after layer, so that even if one version proves to be true, it is
enough to prove Dhanka tribal claims. It is important to note that both versions claim for the Dhanka a place in well-known events. The story of Patai
Raval was retold in what is thought by some to be the first novel in Gujarati in
the nineteenth century; it was based on a well-known *garbo* (lyrical narrative
that accompanies a dance) on the leader's destruction (Yashaschandra 1995).
The story of Patai Rawal's defeat by Mahmud Begada is also recorded as the
origin of the Bhil-Patlias (Nath 1960, 63).

The second story makes the Dhanka actors in the epic Mahabharata, who
are both ancient and slightly separate, "a fighting clan" and thus outside the
mainstream Hindu caste society. References to users and bearers of the bow
and arrow also continue to figure in Dhanka accounts of their origin, as we
will see below. In this reference, intimations of another Bhil link help place
the Dhanka in an important historical context. Colonial ethnographers accepted and repeated the notion that the term "Bhil" was derived from the
Sanskrit "*billi*," meaning "bow." They were more divided, however, on whether
the Bhils were in fact the Nishadas referred to in the Mahabharata, a group
that included the famous archer Eklavya, who cut off his thumb (rendering
him unable to wield a bow and arrow) when it was demanded by a jealous
teacher as tribute.[30] The tale of Eklavya continues to be immensely popular in
India and was the name given to the central character in a 2007 film starring
Amitabh Bachchan. Because Eklavya is perhaps the most well-known tale of
adivasi culture, the Dhankas' link would establish them as important actors
on the historical stage in addition to giving them a martial aura that is highly
valued in western India. As the tale also describes a deep historical injustice
(one is expected to be on the side of the unfairly put-upon archer who must

give up his thumb), it places the Dhanka on the moral high ground of this legacy.

In Shah's record we see the first iteration of an important question in Dhanka history: What is their relationship to the populous and less-contested tribal category "Bhil"? Shah's account, presumably the reported speech of a Dhanka informant, implies that the Dhanka are a more Hindu-ized (we might read "Sanskritized") offshoot of the Bhils. There is the intimation that they are, therefore, of higher status. Colonial accounts that stressed the link between the Dhanka and the Bhils, however, almost unanimously recorded that the Dhanka were of a lower status than the Bhils. As late as the 1950s, Y.V.. S. Nath found that the Dhanka "are so poor and primitive, that even the Bhils mock at them" (1960, 60).[31]

THE GUJARATI STATE

A second, similar version of this history can be found in a report by the Centre for Social Studies completed in the 1980s. The study was commissioned by the Government of Gujarat to provide working knowledge of villages to be submerged by the planned damming of the Narmada River (it has since been undertaken; see Baviskar 2008) in order to aid later rehabilitation. It reads:

> There are two explanations about the migration of the Tadavis [to their current home in the Narmada valley]. The first, which is purely mythological, suggests that the forefathers of the present Tadavi inhabitants were living in the region around Pawagadh. Pawagadh at that time was ruled by a Rajput king named Patai. Once, during the Garba dance, Goddess Durga herself joined the dancing women in disguise. The king, attracted by her beauty and not knowing that she was the Goddess herself, suggested that she should become his queen. Enraged at this impertinence the Goddess cursed him and disappeared. This curse brought ruin to the kingdom. . . .
>
> The second explanation is based on peoples' attempts to escape from the famine at the turn of the century. . . . We [the researchers] were given to understand that the term 'Tadavi' is a corruption of 'Tatvi' where 'tat' means the river bank. Hence, it is logical to assume that the usage of this term began when migrants settled on the banks of the Narmada. Though the Tadavis emphasize that they are actually descendants of an earlier Kshatriya clan and hence are originally Rajputs, the claims seem to contradict the migration theory. On the one hand there is the agreement that the forefathers of the Tadavis came from the jungles in the interior and on the other, they emphasize that they were Rajput migrants. The region they were supposed to have migrated from was a tribal region inhabited mainly by the Bhils. Hence it is more probable that one section of the Bhils migrated during the famines, and another

section even earlier than that, and both had settled in the coastal belt. This means that originally the present Tadavis might have been Bhils, who, later, in an attempt at dissociating themselves from their original counter-parts, started calling themselves Tadavis and subsequently emerged as a distinct socio-cultural group. . . .

The inference that the Tadavis were Bhils once upon a time is also supported by some old writings on the Bhils. Enthovan mentions Dhanka and Tadavi as two different groups of the Bhil tribe. He opines that the Tadavis are half 'Musalman' (Mohmedan) and half Bhil. . . .[32]

At the turn of the century, there were three consecutive famines. This resulted in mass migration from the jungles in the interior to the roadside villages which were formerly only small hamlets. Some families settled in these villages after the famines. The Bhils who came to these villages were not originally known as Tadavis. Those who settled on the bank (Tat) of the river came to be known as Tadavi. They were further divided into 'Dhanka' and 'Tetaria'. The mythology tells us that some time during the famine four boys went out hunting. One shot a 'Tetar' (partridge or pee-wit) and hid it under his armpit for his own consumption. He ate the partridge, while the others ate grain. Those who ate grain (Dhan) came to be known as the Dhankas and one who ate the Tetar was known as Tetaria. (Joshi 1987, 47–49)

Much like Shah's account, the report does not contextualize the origin stories presented above by indicating who told which story, under what circumstances, and where. But unlike Shah, who allowed multiple interpretations to stand together in his account without trying to resolve their contradictions, the political agenda of the authors of the Centre for Social Studies means that they must decide which of the stories from the above account to consider "true." They conclude that since the groups' (Tadvi, Dhanka, Tetaria) emergence can be traced to within one hundred years and since they may just represent different responses to a shared issue (i.e., famine), that it will be best not to treat displaced social groups as groups but as individuals. Different individuals will have different reactions to rehabilitation after flooding from the Narmada dam, and the issue of the dam, like that of the turn-of-the-century famine, will be "to some extent, responsible for cross-cutting the traditional group identities and restructuring of groups" (67). They do not, therefore, recommend treating these groups as communities with rights or stakes in the dam project and speculate that they will be relatively unaffected by dam displacement. This, we know now, has certainly not been the case (Baviskar 2008; Devy 2006).

It is likely that the famine that ravaged western India in 1899 and 1900 did have an important impact on the history of the Dhanka, an issue I discuss below. But the report's claim that the Dhanka emerged as a response to conditions of famine is perhaps the only entirely spurious theory about their history I have encountered. The report and its conclusions, however, are not entirely unlike the case laid out against Dhanka ST claims in the letter with which I opened. In both instances there are strong state motives for questioning whether the Dhanka constitute a legitimate adivasi group (unless they are from a very small part of southern Rajasthan). And though there are Dhanka who can read and write in English and who cite colonial sources about their origin and history, most Dhanka are effectively barred from access to existing documentation via language, class, and education. I have been asked by Dhanka elders on several occasions what I have "discovered" about their history through my research, as well as to access certain documents they are unable to obtain through their own channels. Though I will not attempt here to solve the problem of Dhanka origins—something that I leave to the Dhanka and perhaps allied historians—it seems worthwhile to pause for a moment to consider the—albeit interested and refracted—evidence about their origin, their relationship to the Bhils and other "tribes," and their movements in the more recent past.

A Speculative History

The earliest written traces I have been able to find of the Dhanka as such are unsurprisingly found in gazetteers of Rajputana and the Bombay presidencies in 1879 and 1880.[33] Many studies over the past thirty years have pointed to the ways in which censuses and gazetteers imposed an order and hierarchy on Indian social life that did not necessarily correspond to its lived categories or practices. A preoccupation with textual sources and religion meant that Brahminical accounts of caste and tradition were favored over others and given a solidity that they did not previously possess. Nicholas Dirks has gone so far as to suggest that the British "invented" caste, at least in the form that we now recognize it (2001). There were, of course, always limits to the order imposed by these endeavors, and they were sometimes actively resisted. Dhanka history is interesting in this regard because, in colonial documents, the Dhanka are almost universally associated with the Bhil tribe. The Bhil were averse to all census-taking activities throughout the late nineteenth century. In 1881, the Maharana of Udaipur had to promise not to count them, and in 1901 they were counted via proxy: colonial officials would locate village headmen and ask them how many Bhils were under their leadership.[34]

The tendency to see Dhanka as related to the Bhils may, as is implied by the origin stories discussed above, indicate that Dhanka were at one time part of a larger tribe called the Bhils and by exile or by choice became a separate, endogamous group. When I began looking into Dhanka origins, this was indeed my own assumption. I presumed that the Dhanka were a group who, as reflected in Shah's account, renounced some of their primitive practices during the spate of tribal reform movements that swept through western India in the late nineteenth and early twentieth centuries. But this assumption misunderstood several things: First is the simple fact that Dhanka are recorded as having resided in at least two states in the 1870s, prior to such movements. They could not have been, as the Centre for Social Studies report implies, "invented" due to the famine at the turn of the nineteenth century.

Second, and perhaps more importantly, is that "Bhil" is a term that seems to have been coined by outsiders to refer to a collection of semi-endogamous groups scattered across the region stretching from south of the Narmada river in the Satpura mountains to Jodhpur and Udaipur in southern Rajputana—what I have called Northern Bhil Country. Thus, at the same time that colonial officials and ethnographers treated "Bhil" unproblematically as the name of a discernable "tribe," repeatedly referring to "the Bhils" and amassing descriptions of their customs and habits, they also questioned the status of this classification. In 1824, John Malcolm reportedly wrote of his experience with Indian aborigines that "the names of tribes, or rather of families increase in the ratio the inquiry was pursued. The slightest circumstance, the name of an ancestor, a dispute in the tribe, a favorite spot of residence, gives rise to a name, and forms a tie of brotherhood" (cited in *Gazetteer of the Bombay Presidency* 1901, 9:295n2). He thus implied that "Bhil," like perhaps many other "tribal" designations, was readily differentiated. Another volume of the *Gazetteer* (1880, 12:82) more baldly claimed that the term "Bhil" "was afterwards applied to all the lawless forest and hill tribes."

Modern commentators are even more skeptical of a historically unitary Bhil identity. Writing of the Bhils of the Ratanmal Hills in the 1950s, V. V. S. Nath suggests: "In retrospect, there is plenty of evidence to believe that not all the people known today as Bhils constitute a single tribe. On the contrary, one is inclined to believe that congeries of tribes living in adjacent areas and bearing only a superficial resemblance in their general way of life in the eyes of plainsmen, were probably lumped together under a blanket term. The why and wherefore of such blanket terms being employed is at the present beyond one's comprehension and at best a matter of conjecture" (1960, 21). In his work on the Dangs, Ajay Skaria tells us that "many communities were called Bhils and referred to themselves as such" despite their also using other tribal names such as Gamit and Dhanka (1997, 203).

We might, then, imagine that many of the names given to colonial ethnographers were actually variations or categories within categories and only
sometimes distinct endogamous groups of the kind that would have been
seen to constitute a tribe. The Dhanka tendency to claim every possible affiliation (except, notably, with the Bhil) that we will see in the following
section and the confusion manifest in the NCST's letter—the relationship
between similar-sounding groups like the Dhanka, Dhankiya, and Dhanuk
and between these groups and the Tadvi, Tetaria, and Valvi—can also be seen
as a historically "accurate" practice. The assertion that I have heard repeatedly
from Jaipuri Dhanka that Dhanka, Dhankiya, and Dhanuk were all simply
variations of the same name, rather like nicknames of each other, might also
be considered true.

Here, then, is my speculative history of the Dhanka.

The first thing is to un-imagine state borders. Rajasthan, Gujarat, and
Maharashtra don't exist. Domains are defined by military might and natural
boundaries—by hills, rivers, and forests. Groups fight one another for control
of important tracts. For what is the territory we now call western India in the
centuries following the disintegration of Mughal power? City states. Defen-
sive positions. The quest for territory. The concerted effort it takes to stay out
of the way. If we are to take anything from the Dhanka stories about their
origins, it may be that they give us a new perspective on historical accounts
of this region. Theirs is not a tale of grand exploits—even if it has a vaguely
martial flair, or of subaltern resistance, and even if they are often identified
with the Bhils and their disdain for administration of all kinds—but of doing
what it takes to survive the whims of others.

Written traces of the Dhanka begin with the British colonial effort to
create ethnographic catalogues of their subjects following the rebellion of
1857. They tell us little about their lives, except for their marginal status in
British renderings of caste hierarchy. *The Rajputana Gazetteer* (1879) lists
"Dhanka—a low caste" last in its inventory of Hindu castes in Jodhpur. In
the *Gazetteer of the Bombay Presidency* (1880), the Dhanka are recorded as a
subdivision of Bhils, but there are conflicting accounts of their territory. In
Khandesh, they are listed as "one of the forest and fill tribes in the Satpudas
[*sic*],"[35] while in neighboring Rewa Kantha they are said to be found only
in the Narmada basin.[36] Whatever their status, a group called the "Dhanka"
catches the colonial gaze, if only for a moment.

In 1899, western India is decimated by drought and famine. Commentators at the time note that Bhils suffered more greatly and lost more members
than any other community, though their interpretations of why this is the

case differ significantly. Reverend J. E. Scott, for instance, who worked in the Famine Relief Committee of Rajputana and published his account *In Famine Land* in 1904, reports that "The Hindus of the neighboring country were supremely indifferent to the sufferings of the Bhils; in fact, they thought it would be quite the best thing to allow such a nation of thieves to be depopulated to the furthest degree possible" (89); others blame the greater mortality among the Bhils to "their reluctance to work on wages on relief operations" (Maloo 1987, 191). Kamala Maloo estimates the percentage of mortality among the Bhils in Rajputana to have ranged from 7 percent in Sirohi to 30 percent in the "Hilly Tracts," precisely where most Dhanka were probably living at the time. I imagine Dhanka, like so many others, moving in search of assistance of many kinds. A clue about Dhanka movements, perhaps: Udaipur is said to have very high mortality rates from epidemics "owing to the insanitary conditions of the city and suburbs, which were crowded with Bhils from nearby areas in search of relief" (Maloo 1987, 190). If they are reluctant to work on relief operations, perhaps it is because they fear contagion. Perhaps it is because others assume they are savage, or criminal. At the same time, their participation in relief works is seen to make them more amenable to British authority and administrative practices. According to the 1901 census of India, the Dhankas' need for assistance during the famine rubs off their "shyness, savagery and distrust" (Bannerman 1902, ii).

1901 was a year of great ethnographic production (Dirks 2001). In Rajputana, A. D. Bannerman was tasked with conducting a more complete census than had been possible in 1891, when the Bhil population had simply been estimated by counting the number of huts in Bhil villages (though many in remote areas were not approached). The main obstacle in that year had been the refusal of the Bhils to participate, which, reportedly, was based on their dislike of being counted and of strangers approaching their homes. In his introduction to the census report, Bannerman comments that in 1881 "wild stories" had circulated among the Bhils about the objects of the census to such an extent that the Maharana of Udaipur was forced to promise not to count them. The famine supposedly changed all that. Bannerman describes the new strategy for counting the Bhils, apparently suggested by Risley, as explaining to them that "one object of the counting was to ascertain how many people might require food in the next famine" (Bannerman 1902, ii).

There is an odd alternation between the conflation and separation of "Dhanka" and "Dhanak" as census categories. The Dhanka, who are all considered Hindu, are listed in the Rajputana census of 1901 as part of Group VI, which consisted of "castes from whom twice-born will not take water" and numbered 10,417. The Dhanak were classed in Group VII, which were defined as "Untouchable Castes," with a note that they were less powerful or "strong" than Bhangis; they numbered 21,536. In the census tables of population variation, however, the category Dhanak includes Dhanka and reports that while there were 65,723 Dhanak in Rajputana in 1891, there were only 32,003 in 1901. It is hard to guess what causes the simple arithmetic discrepancy in the 1901 population, but the statistic does imply that there was a large loss of population. Perhaps this is simply because people weren't counted. Or perhaps they emigrated during the famine. But it is also possible that the lack of food, experienced so profoundly by the Bhils in 1899 and 1900, cut the Dhanka population in half. This proportion of mortality would be in keeping with historical estimates of Bhil fatalities.

By 1931, groups of Dhanka have moved as far north as Jaipur state, where they live outside the city walls and tend the king's animals, transport grain, and take other kinds of jobs. They find work; they remember stigma. These are the ancestors of my friends in Shiv Nagar Basti.

A Special Position, a Glorious History

The following account appears in the booklet, known as the *Smarika* ("Souvenir") published on the occasion of the 2003 *samuhik vivaha sammelan*. It is, as far as I know, the most complete version of Dhanka history that has been published by the community itself. I discuss the role of the *Smarika* in Dhanka constructions of identity and collective aspiration in Chapter 5. Below, I will treat the historical narrative itself, as presented in "Our Society [*Samaj*]: An Introduction" (Solanki 2003, 12).

> The Dhanka caste [*jati*] has a special position among other *jatis* in India. This community [*samaj*] has a glorious history. It is called by different names in different regions. Dhanak, Dhanka, Dhankiya, and Dhanuk are variations on the root word "dhanak." We get special mention of this Dhanak tribe in the Rig Ved, Puranas, and other historical texts. In the past, they wore bow and arrows and were considered fighters. In the medieval period, this tribe has helped the Rajput kings to fight against the Mughals. This caste scattered during the Mughal period because they were suppressed. As a result of the cruelty [*atyachar*] of the Hindu states, kings, and the tribal clans, these Dhanka scattered to different states and adopted different occupations.
>
> According to our ancestors, the Dhanka have their roots in Rajasthan. Our rituals, customs, folksongs, and marriage ceremonies all have a connection with Rajasthan in one way or another. At the time of marriage, the custom of taking rings and jewelry to the bride, and the groom striking the ornamental archway [*torun*] is a clear indication of Rajputi influence.

Also in Rajasthan, our ancestors used to live in jungles like adivasis [*adi-vasiyon ke rup men nivas karte te*] and they were dependent on forest yields [*vansampada*] for their livelihood. They used to cut bamboo and from that they used to make bows and arrows and baskets. With time, there was too much deforestation, so that our ancestors had to migrate for their livelihood and they started moving around the greater region of Rajasthan: Punjab, Dilli, Haryana, Himachal Pradesh, Uttar Pradesh, Madhya Pradesh, Gujarat, Maharashtra, and Bihar. In north India, some of our people are working in grain markets, and do different jobs like cleaning grain, weighing them, and work as laborers to transport grain. The name Dhanka is probably a result of this relationship with the grain market [*dhan*]. They have adopted different occupations, like guard, water carrier, band master, musicians, weaver, shepherd, and agricultural laborer, and mason, and musician.

We can come to the conclusion, looking at this information, Dhanak communities and other related people who were called by this name have never done low status jobs [*chota vyavasaya*]. They have served the society. They have earned their living by working in a clean [*saf-suthra*] way to serve the society.

The Hindu caste system was based on the occupation which they do. The Dhanka community was never able to do just one occupation because of the unfavorable conditions [*dur jakar vivashta*], and they have adopted all types of occupations for their livelihood. In the middle ages and the Puranas, though we were concerned with the bow [*dhanush*]; but in different circumstances we were forced to adopt different occupations. Even though our ancestors worked as laborers, they did puja in temple and they have never done the work that has been done by the Dalits.

In spite of the fact that we were doing different jobs and living in different places, our social and cultural customs, social relations, social behavior, caste system, and public behavior remains the same. Having different occupations has not affected our social unity and organization. We never felt alienated from our group. The strength of our gotra system, mutual behavior, similar eating habits, tribal council [*jati panchayat*] system have constantly maintained our sense of unity. The special feature of Indian culture that is unity in diversity can be seen in our culture as well.

Some foreign historians have described different occupations of Dhanka community in their books as below:

Crookes [sic], in his book, the Tribes and Castes of Northwest India, has described Dhanuk caste as a tribe who used to work as water carriers, guards, musicians in marriages, etc. This tribe is called by different names in different states, as Dhankara, Dusadh, Kadhya, Katoriya, Kedi, Ravar. Giving a different opinion, the famous writer Bushman has written that this is a martial race [*vir qaum*]. Ipsen, in 1916, elaborating on Elliott, has described the Dhanak jati as a race [*qaum*] who initially had the dhanush and over time changed into guards, weavers, and hunters. Russel and Hiralal considered the Dhanak community to be petty farmers. The origin of Dhanak is from the Sanskrit word "dhanuksha," which means the one who wears dhanush. Some people think there was a saint [*muni*] named Dhanak, and these were his followers.

The social workers of Rajasthan have a special inclination toward education. According to a survey conducted in 1981, the rate of literacy was 15.43 percent, which is steadily increasing. The end of the feudal system has brought about a positive change in the people of Rajasthan. The inclusion of Dhanka into the Scheduled Castes and Tribes reservation means that people have a greater chance to obtain government jobs. Rajasthan is a living example of caste rivalry, jealousy, discrimination, and prejudice. The Dhanka group who were dependent on the forest yields were included into the SC/ST category according to constitutional amendments in 1950 and 1977. There are some caste prejudiced officers who raise difficulties for us in obtaining certificates. Different associations and political parties connected with this tribe should draw the attention of the government to this problem.

To reiterate several points made above, there are problems that plague Dhanka attempts to assert their Scheduled Tribe identity. Among these are (1) the fact that almost half the Dhanka of Rajasthan live in urban Jaipur, (2) the presence of other groups with similar names in the state who are recognized as castes (not as tribes), (3) the lack of a specific homeland and identifiably "tribal" cultural practices, and (4) a spotty and minor presence in colonial ethnographic records. In addition to the five criteria officially fixed for defining tribes by the Lokur Committee (primitive traits, distinct culture, geographic isolation, shyness of contact with outsiders, and backwardness), a main requirement for tribal recognition is to appear to be, or have historically been, outside the Hindu caste system. This has meant, to varying degrees, being less hierarchical, lacking a fixed occupation, migrating within a fixed domain, being oppressed by non-tribals and being able to assert an ancient, if not entirely autochthonous, presence in an area.

The above essay effectively "solves" many of these problems—for instance, the problem of variations on the name "Dhanka." The account offers several possible explanations for the relationship between the Dhanka, the Dhanak, the Dhanuk, and the Dhankiya. One is that each name corresponds to a unique region. Another is that there was a holy man named Dhanak and they are descended from his followers. Yet another explanation, frequently reiterated to me in conversations with the Dhanka, is that they are all simply variations on the root "dhan" or "dhanush." Ram Lal used to remark that the difference between them was a bit like the difference between a name and a nickname. "Don't people sometimes call out 'Meghna!' or 'Meghi!'" he asked. "Well, this is the same thing." As mentioned below, the Dhanka do not work to solve the problem of resolving these seemingly contradictory derivations. Are the Dhanka defined by their relationship to the dhanush ("bow") or to dhan ("grain")? Both are left open as possibilities, though the former is clearly given precedence in this account, probably to stress historical links with the Rajputs and thus the Dhankas' Rajasthani origins.

Rather than working to address each of the five criteria per se, the effort in this account is to show that the Dhanka have never been a part of caste society. In this regard, three main features stand out. First, that the Dhanka were forced to migrate and scatter over the centuries due to forces beyond their control. One of these is the cruelty of not just one exploitative group, but several: Hindu states, kings, and tribal clans (see Prasad 2003). Another is their dependence on forest produce that over time became scarce, one suspects, not because of the Dhankas' own practices but because the forests were used and controlled by others. In both of these cases, the Dhanka were forced to move in order to secure a livelihood. It was the kind of livelihood that meant the Dhanka "lived like adivasis," a statement made in the past tense, as we might now expect. *We were adivasis.*

The second feature that keeps the Dhanka outside the caste system and, I would argue, the most important in Dhanka everyday talk, is that they did not have a fixed occupation. This point was reiterated to me over the years on many different occasions in forms very similar to that recorded above. On this point, the essay is explicit: "The Hindu caste system was based on the occupation which they do. The Dhanka community was never able to do just one occupation because of the unfavorable conditions." Their lack of power and, importantly, *lack of a cultural imperative to have a set occupation* sets them firmly apart from caste society. And it is not just upper castes from which the Dhanka wish to separate themselves. They also assert their separation from Dalits, especially Dalits who have historically been associated with one kind of work—for instance, Chamars who are leather workers—both by highlighting a lack of fixed occupation and that the occupations they did adopt were always "clean" (*saf-suthra*) and never "small" (*chota*). This assertion is important because it simultaneously places them outside the caste system and yet puts them in a slightly superior position in relation to Dalits, who they consider rivals for state support to some extent. I have often been told that Chamars, for instance, do not need the kind of help that is needed by the Dhanka because they have seen significant upward mobility as a result of their employment in the leather industry. Whatever the veracity of this assessment, it is a powerful ideology for the Dhanka.

The third difference is seen to lie in the unity of the Dhanka community, which the author distinguishes from that of other caste groups in Rajasthan. This is an interesting reflection and one that opens up, rather than shuts down, questions about the internal stratification of the Dhanka. Is the author here trying to counter charges that there is a strong internal class system? Perhaps. Or perhaps it is simply a comment on a salient difference between the Dhanka and the Rajputs. A frequent charge against the latter community is that they are so internally fragmented and prone to rivalries that they have been unable to forge a successful political coalition since independence. Again, whatever truth there is or is not to this statement, we would do well to remember that in Rajasthan the caste system is symbolized less by a Brahmin elite (though such an elite does exist) and more through a coalition of Rajputs-Banias-Jains (Sangari and Vaid 1996). Asserting their place outside the system thus requires a bit of finesse, as the Dhanka of Rajasthan simultaneously want to assert an ancient historical connection to the Rajputs and Rajasthan and a history of oppression at their hands. Specific rulers and lineages of either kind—allies or oppressors—are not mentioned, which again leaves open several possibilities that may or may not agree with each other.

As we saw in outsider histories above, the Dhanka trace their origin to unspecified and ancient moments of the Vedas and the Puranas, which makes them part of a recognizable pan-Hindu tradition, but a part that is difficult to pin down. They are bow-bearers, and thus involved in war and combat, but not specifically identified as soldiers.

Again, rather than posing a problem, this vagueness provides a productive space to make a set of non-historically specific but socially relevant claims about a group. And not just for the Dhanka. Dalit politics has often involved elaborating historical narratives in which an earlier glorious past is unfairly stolen as a counter to Brahminical notions of the karmic basis for caste—its rightness and inevitability. References to the Vedas and the Puranas also, however, give the Dhanka a certain religious sanction and aura. Their mention in these texts puts them on the low side of the caste system, perhaps, but not beyond the pale. Indeed, the claim that "we were so abject as to not even warrant a mention" is not a claim that can carry any historical traction. Subjects are thus rendered needy due to historical oppressions at worst or accidents at best, but also worthy because they are not utterly "other," that is, absent. It is as if the Dhanka are saying, "*There were many important groups in those texts. We were there too.*"

Such a reading is not cynical. Surely contemporary Dhanka writers have an interest in portraying a certain version of events that strengthens and furthers their claim to ST status. Many groups have undertaken strikingly similar strategies to achieve related ends. In the case of the Yadavs described by Lucia Michelutti, the goal is to show that the group has "exceptional qualities" at the same time that "in some places and times [it] has become poor and backward and hence needs 'reservation policies' for improving its well-being" (2008, 91): worthy and needy at the same time. In a similar way, I will discuss the special qualities of the Dhanka in the next chapter. Here, my goal was to highlight the immensely creative and difficult work that must be done in such texts. Rather than treating them as suspect and holding them up to the scrutiny of certain kinds of positivist academic history, we would do better to think about what kinds of narrative and emotional performances are required of those groups seeking uplift through reservations, through the ST role. Formally, across communities in contemporary India, many of these historical narratives are similar; the Dhanka are not at all unique in that they produce such documents or tell such stories. They frequently refer to mythological time, to an inherent specialness, and invoke colonial ethnography as proof of origins.

The stakes for such stories are high when their persuasiveness is the ground from which groups wish to stage their political, moral, and economic claims. The system of scheduling undoubtedly reinforces a particular kind of intensive focus on identity—it is as a *kind* of person, rather than as an individual, that many aspirational groups in India, including the Dhanka, imagine access to the benefits to which they feel they are constitutionally entitled. Because identities require origins, collective aspiration requires that one have a story to tell about one's history that is not simply factual—event following event. Narrating how *bad* history was for one's community is an important part of this articulation and must make an emotional and ethical claim on the reader or listener. But drawing attention to that spark of hope, a glimmer of something in the past that foretells a different future to come, is equally a part of the work of Dhanka history. I discuss how this glimmer of an otherwise is cultivated in the following chapter.

3

What It Takes

On a warm winter afternoon, I met Ravi Lal Dhanka, who goes by Ravi. As was often the case in Shiv Nagar Basti, I was introduced to this community elder by some of his younger female relatives, in this case Ravi's granddaughters, who befriended me via Mona and her sister. The girls thought he could help me with my official research and, indeed, we discussed his career in government service, his work for Dhanka uplift, and the history of the tribe in Rajasthan at length. Ravi was an eager informant and teacher. That afternoon, he carefully drew a chart to explain to me the relationship between the Dhanka and other tribal groups. He also wrote out his full title: "Ravi Lal Dhanka, Gen Secretary Dhanka Samaj Shekhawati Panchayat, Social Worker for whole cast [sic]," so that I would understand his deep commitment to the betterment of the Dhanka people.[1]

At the end of the interview, Ravi told me that he is also a poet. A happy surprise! He explained that he had recently published a volume of his work as a tribute to his son. I asked to buy a copy, but when his granddaughters delivered it to me a few days later they refused payment, saying it was a gift. I promised to translate some of its verses into English, a promise I am in part fulfilling here.

Ravi's self-published chapbook is entitled *Mati Meri Desh Ki (The Soil of My Country)*. It begins with a poem of the same name:

> "The Soil of My Country"[2]
> [Mati Meri Desh Ki]
> The soil of my country
> red, yellow, a bit of black
> With the fragrant, sweet scent of rice

The soil of my country
The soil of my country
Whenever the green scarf ripples,
Swelled with pride, not held in
The bosom of my country
The soil of my country
. . .
A brave new mother is this earth,
To whom the country has remained dear
Man and man's herds have devoted
their lives for the life of this country
. . .
Hindu, Mussalman, Sikh, Christian
Hold the highest love [for each other] here
The governance is of neutral dharm
The merit of universal peace from the fruit of action
The fame of my country
The soil of my country
. . .
Paramount to life here
are the rings of pure relationships—
The slate of my country
The soil of my country

The cover of *The Soil of My Country* features faded, soft-focus photographs of what appear to be arid Rajasthani hills, blending into the waving
crops to which Ravi refers in the poem. Red, golden, and earthy brown grains
line the bottom border in neatly squared photographs of plenty. But for some
of the telling references to secularism (paradoxically called "neutral *dharm*")
and Hindu/Muslim brotherhood, "The Soil of My Country" could be a patri-
otic song of praise for the nation from many countrysides around the world.
Despite the fact that Ravi himself lives in a large urban area and made his
living as a civil servant, the poem is sincere, anthem-like. We could see it as
an example of a genre that the writer knows is bigger than himself. A genre in
which the reality of city life does not carry the same resonance as these other
bucolic images. In its imagined nostalgia—many of the men in Shiv Nagar
Basti are third-generation city dwellers—it is a poem of modern aspiration.

There are sixty-two poems in Ravi's book as well as a great deal of front and
back matter. They are not all as celebratory or nationalistic as these opening
verses. Some are quite critical of contemporary greed and refer extensively to
the plight of laborers: "By whose labor you've acquired/These bungalows, these
lawns and gardens/These gleaming motor cars/These servants all around?"

he asks in "By Whose Labor? (No. 26)." Others, such as "Our Darling Daughter (No. 7)," are personal, romantic, sentimental.[3] But the fact that Ravi chose
"The Soil of My Country" to represent his collected poetic works—the fact
that he chose to write and publish such poems at all—tells us a great deal
about him and, I want to suggest, about a kind of Dhanka masculinity that
emerged in the era of service and upward mobility, a masculinity that is asserted, contested, and remade as the security of government postings through
ST reservations steadily erodes.

   An important aspect of this masculinity, one of its key dispositions, is what
I am calling "willingness," a constellation of orientations, practices, forms of
expression and feeling that I will unpack below. In his personal efforts to
write something larger than himself—and the literacy of the act is essential,
rather than incidental, to its meaning—Ravi provides us with a poignant example of what I want to describe in this chapter: a way of being an agentive
Dhanka man in the face of discrimination and structural constraints that
insist one be both within and without categories such as nation or tribe and
their implied temporalities. (*We were adivasis.*) Willingness, as deeply felt as
it might be by any one individual, always refers back to community, whether
this is family, neighborhood, or country; it is often all three. It is willingness
to change, adapt, sacrifice, move, and humble oneself for a larger vision.[4]

   Ravi's poem, then, is our first glimpse into a non-elite or subaltern masculinity that embraces some of the best promises that modern India has had
on offer: unity, development, and plenty for all. Willingness is an important
part of collective aspiration; it gives both force and shape to mobility projects.
In that sense, it is one of those sites in which the individual and collective
trajectory are closely related; in which, as Bourdieu writes, there is a dialec-
tic established between "dispositions and [social] positions, aspirations and
achievements" (1984, 10). Willingness is a set of ideas, practices, and imaginative frameworks that provides Dhanka men with a sense of identity, collectivity, and purpose. Rather than cultivating or enacting cultural practices
perceived as "other" and "tribal"—as is the strategy of other ST groups (see
Middleton 2011)—performances of Dhanka masculinity incorporate precisely this quality of Dhanka non-essence.

   I want to be clear that "willingness" is my term, my heuristic tool for making something visible, a polysemous descriptor with its provenance deeply in
my own cultural framework—at least the academic anthropology aspect of
this framework—through which I hope to communicate something about
how the Dhanka position themselves in relation to the larger projects of
which they are both subjects and intended beneficiaries. It is not a term that
Dhanka men themselves use. They would be more likely to stress "survival"

(or, we might say, "survivance" [see Vizenor 2008]) and the effort and will it takes. I use "willingness" to reference the positive effort of the Dhanka, both in the sense of their proactive strategies and in the sense of their adaptation or accommodation to circumstances beyond their control.

In light of my discussion of tribal definition in the previous chapter, Ravi's ingenuous nationalism might seem odd or even misguided. In general, "tribes" have been given an oppositional "indigenous slot" vis-à-vis the state. On one hand, the embrace of modern promises evinced in collective willingness might be a particular survival strategy of the Dhanka. It may have brought specific benefits to the group. My own sense is that the importance of the disposition of willingness for Dhanka men (and references to this willingness that date from at least the 1960s) implies that this is the case. P. G. Shah, for instance, makes a telling remark in his monograph on the Gujarati Dhanka, saying that "one remarkable thing is that the tribals are not conservative, and easily believe in innovations in agriculture [and] education" (1964, 204).[5] On the other hand, willingness is tempered by critique of the conditions that make it a *necessary* disposition. In Ravi's poems, in Dhanka histories, and in everyday talk, there is a deep sense of the injustice of being repeatedly subject to forces beyond their control.

To focus on the forms and expressions of willingness and the differences between men these produce is to provide an important counter to the tendency to talk about "adivasis" or "SC/STs" as if these were categories with pan-Indian meaning or even consistency within a particular tribe or caste. We can begin to think about the multiplicity of forms of relationship that non-elite groups might have to larger forces and processes without assuming a (romanticized) oppositional stance and without, as celebratory politicians might, assuming that the promises of the changing Indian nation-state are inspiring to all its citizens, or inspiring in the same way. As I argued in the Introduction, too often it is assumed that non-elite groups aspire to "be like" groups to whom they are in a hierarchically subordinate position, whether these be higher castes or the unmarked middle class citizen-consumers of globalization fantasy. In this case, the goal is not to emulate upper castes so much as it is to gain respect as a good man in one's own community and to demand the enactment of the constitutional promises of upward mobility and social uplift.

The status questions that emerge arise *within* the community, while historical forces of oppression are located outside; in other words, hierarchy between Dhanka is not seen as the most significant problem, while hierarchy in broader society is cited as the source of Dhanka suffering (Chowdhry 2007; Lynch 1969). In the Dhankas' analysis, such inequalities can only be remedied through efforts that combine upward mobility and greater political attention to the community, especially as a vote bank. This assessment informs the shape of collective aspiration not, for instance, the effort to Sanskritize and somehow escape history (see Schaller 1995 for a contrasting case).

Willingness is decidedly masculine, though it is part of a broader vision that relies on gender as a relation: the breadwinner model, which necessarily excludes women and children, at the same time depends on their existence and perceived needs. It is important to distinguish the kind of masculinity I describe here from that invoked in traditional Sanskritization narratives in which gender is fixed and immutable. Such explanations of upward mobility often assume agentive men who oppress women in order to rise in locally meaningful hierarchies. There is a striking tendency to take gender for granted as a unified "thing" to be mobilized rather than a process that generates distinctions at the same time that it stabilizes identities as "men" and "women."

There is also a marked trend to see non-elite groups only in relation to elite groups whose gender norms become hegemonic. As R. W. Connell (2005, 72) notes, "hegemonic masculinity" is not a finished project of assigning roles, but rather a "*process* of configuring practice" that enables the "gender projects" of masculinity and femininity to which it is not reducible. Other masculinities—which Connell describes as subordinate, complicit, and marginalized, though of course these terms are all relative—are in dynamic relationship with the current hegemonic masculinity and may authorize or disrupt it.

Such "other" masculinities have rarely, if ever, been studied in the South Asian context. The introduction to a recent volume on South Asian masculinities, for instance, contains the following disclaimer: "We note with dismay, but a sense of inevitability, the absence in [the] polarized picture [of Hindu versus Muslim men] of the Dalit (ex-untouchable) man . . . and hope to find future work addressing this lacuna" (Chopra, Osella, and Osella 2004, 4). We might want to take issue with their distillation of social categories into simply "Hindu," "Muslim," and "Dalit," but the comment is apt. Such invocations of lack nearly always open discussions of non-hegemonic masculinity in India, pointing up that masculinity is rarely complicated as an intersectional identity in the same way that feminists have insisted we must see femininity (though see Gupta 2010).

Though non-elite South Asian masculinities have yet to be given the attention they deserve, there are some promising recent studies that point to important lines for future research.[6] In her discussion of the gendered meanings of work among domestic servants in Calcutta, Raka Ray (2000, 694) tracks changes in the economic conditions and resultant expectations for service among the *bhadralok* in relationship to the persistent idea that "male servants are better" in order to explore the interaction between these hegemonic ideals and the narratives offered by domestic servants themselves. She finds that while some male servants struggle to retain a sense of masculine independence in the face of their enforced subservience and dependence, others "actively counter the disparagement of their work and life by redefining the notion of a good man" (711). They stress that heroism consists in sacrifice, in this case, sacrifice of one's masculinity to provide for his dependents and secure their safety.

In a similar vein, Annie George (2006) finds that as women in a working-class shanty neighborhood outside Mumbai are presented with new opportunities for work outside the home and begin to exercise greater autonomy over their income, ideas about "honorable masculinity" transform from a deep concern over control of women's sexuality to include evaluative discourses about men's sexual behavior. A good man is one who works to "advance in life," who is not violent toward his family, and who does not engage in coercive marital sex or engage in extramarital affairs (45). Importantly, she finds that women's talk about men's actions is very important in the evaluation of honorable and dishonorable men. George concludes that "masculinities and men's personal honor are co-constituted through men's own actions, public and private, sexual and otherwise, and women's discourses about men's actions. Contemporaneously, emerging masculinities are shaped by, and in turn shape, emerging femininities" (47). Noting that this co-constitution in fact points to the erroneousness of categories of public and private to begin with, George sheds light on the differential performance of masculinity in different local venues.

As we will see, Dhanka men place a similar emphasis on the value of personal self-control and working to better the lot of oneself and one's dependents. Willingness is the drive and commitment to doing what it takes to secure a livelihood in conditions that are not of one's own making. Like the emphasis on sacrifice and sexual propriety described by Ray (2000) and George (2006), willingness also makes distinctions between good and bad (or *bekar* ["useless"]) men. However, there is an important difference between Shiv Nagar Basti and the neighborhood described by George. Namely, that Dhanka women are not being presented with the opportunities that have arisen for women from other groups since the shift to flexible, free market production and so-called woman-centered economic development. The comparison should remind us that particular visions of masculinity and femininity need not necessarily be paired together; men can, for instance, be concerned with both self-control and the control of women in equal measure. Thus, we cannot presume to know what kinds of gender ideals will emerge from any particular large-scale change, even when that change is seen as "national," as India's has been in the last fifteen years.

Ravi is like many Dhanka men of his generation, men who came of age in what I am calling the era of service and upward mobility, which corresponds to a period roughly from the 1960s to the mid-1990s. Their assertions of willingness guided much of Dhanka public life in that time. In what follows, I describe this outlook, the disposition I am calling willingness, in order to show how it both brings together and creates difference within the community. I will be especially concerned with showing how devotion to syncretic saints or *gurus* (spiritual leaders) is invoked as a sign of distinction between individual men.

But in some ways, Ravi speaks to an era that has passed, and many of his poems bemoan this passage. Young Dhanka men today, living and raising families in an era of the contract, inhabit and navigate a world in which they move between the unfulfilled promise of social uplift through guarantees in education and employment (reservations) and new, uncertain hopes that are engendered by local practices of *thekedari*, of giving and receiving a contract (*theka*); I will discuss young men's complex positioning in Chapter 7. The hierarchy between men of service and men of contract is strong: men who have government positions are seen by men and women alike as more reliable than those employed on contracts. While there are a few local fables about individuals becoming rich in private enterprise, government service is the definition of security. It is also where "men like us [*hum ke jaise admi*] deserve to be. After all, *we were adivasis.*" Service, then, is taking on more and more dreamlike qualities as a site of aspiration, and it may be that its best promises are now captured in poetic paeans, rather than in practices of everyday life.

This chapter tells the story of Dhanka willingness as it works to create collective history and distinctions between individual men on the basis of spiritual devotion and discipline. I also try to show that it is Shiv Nagar Basti itself, the neighborhood with its *pukka* houses and cobbled lanes, that embodies the aspiration at the heart of masculine dispositions.

The Cruelty of Kings

An important aspect of Dhanka male willingness is that it is presented as a disposition with a long history. Being able to project willingness back in time helps to deal with the problem of Dhanka identity claims outlined in Chapter 2: the absence of strong land-based or cultural claims to indigeneity.

Because they cannot point to a specific tract of land or hill range to prove autochthony or to a specific cultural practice to assert timeless cultural difference, urban Dhanka locate their tribalness in quite the opposite—in movement and flexibility, or what I am calling willingness. In the absence of land-based or cultural definitions, Dhanka men, particularly those of the era of service, need to find other modes of association that allow them to be a tribe. Dhanka masculinity has incorporated precisely this quality of non-essence into its sense of who the Dhanka are and what makes them adivasis, as opposed to simply "low caste."

To return briefly to the essay "Our Society [*Samaj*]: An Introduction," by Munshi Ram Solanki (2003) and discussed in Chapter 2, let us consider again several sections of the text. Here we will see that tribalness is evoked in the absence of a set profession. Though, as we saw in the previous chapter, the Dhanka clearly construct themselves in relation to Rajput history and a Rajput ethos, this history portrays Hindu men as different from, if equally as valiant as, the high-caste Rajputs. It is the absence of a profession, rather than a relationship with Rajputs, that becomes the ground for historical identity claims:

> As a result of the cruelty [*atyachar*] of Hindu states, kings, and the tribal clans, [the] Dhanka scattered to different states and adopted different occupations....
>
> ... Our ancestors used to live in jungles like adivasis [*adivasiyon ke rup men nivas karte te*] and they were dependent on forest yields for their livelihood.... With time, there was too much deforestation so that our ancestors had to migrate for their livelihood.... In north India, some of our people are working in grain markets and do different jobs like cleaning grain, weighing them, and work as laborers to transport grain. The name Dhanka is probably a result of this relationship with the grain market [*dhan*]. They have adopted different occupations, like guard, water carrier, band master, musician, weaver, shepherd, and agricultural laborer, and mason, and musician....
>
> Dhanak communities and other related people who were called by this name have never done low status jobs [*chota vyavasya*]. They have served the society. They have earned their living by working in a clean [*saf-suthra*] way to serve the society.
>
> The Hindu caste system was based on the occupation which they do. The Dhanka community was never able to do just one occupation because of the unfavorable conditions [*dur jakar vivashta*], and they have adopted all types of occupations for their livelihood. In the middle ages and the Puranas, though we were concerned with the bow [*dhanush*]; but in different circumstances we were forced to adopt different occupations. Even though our ancestors worked as laborers, they did *puja* in temple and they have never done the work that has been done by the Dalits.

. . . Having different occupations has not affected our social unity and organization. We have never felt alienated from our group. . . . The special feature of Indian culture—that is, unity in diversity—can be seen in our culture as well.

References to a lack of occupation are a frequent response to questions about who the Dhanka are. When I asked Dhanka elders to tell me about their *jati* (caste; see also A Short Glossary), nearly all of them invoked their lack of a set profession, indicating that the lack had, indeed, become an important site of identification. For example, echoing the textual account above, an elder who had been tasked by Ram Lal with explaining the Dhanka Samaj to the visiting anthropologist told me at a panchayat meeting: "We have shops. But otherwise, we have no fixed profession. Whatever work we get, we do. And we look after our kids. Since we have no fixed profession, whatever we get, we do. Some graze cattle, some work in the fields, some work for society. Everyone does a different job." One of his friends chimed in: "As the dhobi washes clothes, the carpenter works with wood. In that way, we have no profession. People go to different places for work. Somebody went to Delhi, somebody went to Bombay. We have no fixed profession. In spite of being ST, we have no fixed profession. Like the Minas work in the fields or look after cattle—we have nothing."

As in the account above, movement figures prominently in these men's accounts of Dhanka identity. Movement is not, however, identified as a special feature of culture, as it might be among groups claiming tribal status who highlight nomadism as a unique aspect of adivasi tradition (see Kapila 2008). The tradition, rather, is being forced by conditions beyond one's control to migrate in search of whatever work is available to survive. In other words, the cultural feature that is being illustrated in these accounts is Dhanka willingness: to move, to work for the benefit of society as a whole, and, importantly, to do what it takes to survive in the face of poverty and powerlessness. As another elder at the panchayat meeting put it:

Like in the history of the state of Rajasthan, you see that the kings inherited states and lots of different things. We inherited nothing. Our background was very poor, so we couldn't do much. Our ancestors were also poor and their main aim was to earn enough to eat and survive. And previously there was the question of untouchability [*untouchability ka question*]. So people would look at us with hatred. And the pandits also wouldn't let us be educated. If somebody goes out of India, then he is gone. Or if somebody joins the forces. But there was nobody great enough who could be recorded in history. That's why from the beginning we were trailing behind and could not make history.

The language here is important because it speaks to the ways in which the Dhanka embrace constitutional promises of uplift and maintain their collective aspiration at the same time that they are deeply critical of the historical oppression of their community. This elder refers to "the question of untouchability" in English. This may have been a deliberate choice or a habit of speech, but either way it aligns the speaker with the history of struggles for the legal recognition of the special conditions and needs of Dalits and adivasis. In my hearing, using the term "untouchability" invokes B. R. Ambedkar's legacy rather than, say, Gandhi's on the question of caste and representation in the Indian nation-state because it is a legal-constitutional term rather than a social euphemism (like "*harijan*"). Indeed, this same speaker went on to talk about Ambedkar and the difficulties and prejudices he faced with great enthusiasm; Gandhi was briefly mentioned. The speaker does not, however, use the term "*begaari*" ("forced/bonded labor"), which is occasionally used by the Dhanka in reference to their history; this term would perhaps draw too much attention to the "difference" of Dhanka history from that of the authorized (upper-caste) national version of the story of India coming into its own.

The speaker's final comment is also telling in that it aims to account for why there may not be sufficient written records to prove the timeless indigeneity of the Dhanka in western India. It is perhaps not a coincidence that it was during this meeting that I first heard from the Dhanka about the contention of some researchers and politicians in the state that the Dhanka are an "extinct" tribe in Rajasthan.

Building Shiv Nagar Basti

The conditions which we find today are not what they had been forty or fifty years ago, when the Dhankas were wild, wretched, drunkards and dirty creatures.

P. G. SHAH (1964, 133)

In the absence of land- or culturally based assertions of adivasi identity described in the previous chapter, Dhanka men, particularly those of middle age (which I am defining as the period between becoming a father and the marriage of all of one's children) and the era of service, need to find other modes of association that allow them to be a tribe. I am identifying "willingness" as this mode of association.

How is willingness created and how is its value reaffirmed? What are the ideas, practices, and imaginative frameworks that I am drawing together with this term? Dhanka men locate themselves firmly within the city of Jaipur and their particular neighborhood, which they narrate as inexorably linked to a work history in which they have been willing to seize opportunities as they arise—this interpretation of local history echoes the historical vision discussed in the previous section. The value of being willing to do what it takes is first and foremost manifest in the building of the neighborhood itself. I take building to signal the embrace of a certain nationalized vision of development and a particular, local practice of group articulation that is specific to Jaipur, which often claims to be the world's first planned city.[7]

Consider the following narration of the history of Shiv Nagar Basti as it was told to me by Ram Lal. The conversation from which this translation is taken took place in 2002, but Ram Lal told the same story in 2007, almost word for word. We might think of it then as the authorized narrative of the neighborhood—the story that is locally hegemonic—even though it does not necessarily reflect the collective experience of all residents and quite strikingly leaves out any mention of Dhanka women. Ram Lal began:

> Previously this was agricultural land. . . . There is a Sita-Ram temple nearby; this land was under that temple. Nearby there is also a cremation ground at The Lotus Garden, where holy men used to live; these holy men were given this land by the kings before Independence. Crops were raised in these fields for the domestic animals of the king. Gradually, the kings' rule ended. Then, lime furnaces were set up here and people like us came from the villages in search of work. . . . People like us who migrated here to find jobs settled here. As a result of this, Janata Colony came into existence. Slowly, the government took possession of these lands from the king and developed us.

What is immediately striking about the beginning of Ram Lal's narrative is the way in which there is a historical break at the time of independence after which the Dhanka become part of the building of the city. Whereas the time of kings meant spending life outside the walls, the era of "government" represented a moment when the Dhanka were pulled into the project of making Jaipur in its current form and when the Dhanka became, in their telling, developed. This meant shifting from their previous livelihood—largely agriculture and animal tending—to working in the furnaces that would fire the bricks to build the new Jaipur. There is no mention made of the "pollution" created by proximity to a cremation ground—Ram Lal does not focus on spatial discrimination—but rather, the focus is on the willingness of the Dhanka to move to take advantage of the changing times and learn a new kind of work.

When the lime furnaces were shifted much farther outside the city in the 1960s and 1970s because of rising pollution, the relationship between the

FIGURE 1. A visit to the Lotus Garden. Ram Lal's vision of what Shiv Nagar Basti looked like thirty years ago. *Photo by author.*

Dhanka and the building process shifted but remained intact and fundamentally related to the willingness to learn new kinds of work once again. The willingness to change occupation, which we will hear in Ram Lal's story, is all the more striking for the ways in which it abjures the inextricable relationship between caste and occupation that has served other north Indian communities quite effectively in politics (see Michelutti 2008 on the Yadavs, for example). Ram Lal continued:

> One of the major reasons [that we have been able to develop our neighborhood] is like this: When the furnaces were being shifted, certain of the hard jobs like breaking the stones to prepare lime were being performed only by people [like us]. [But then] a certain kind of awareness developed [among our people]. We were not able to get full wages for our labor. We used to get less than one rupee for breaking fifty baskets of stones. At that time, Jaipur was developing and the Public Health and Engineering Department [PHED] and other departments required employees to work for them. In the waterworks of PHED, the pipes used to be laid near the sewers of the homes. So initially, these pipes were repaired only by low-caste people. Other people would not do this kind of work. In today's context, anyone can repair these lines. Since people were needed at that time, most of the Dhanka were employed in waterworks.

In Ram Lal's story of the basti, the expansion of the city and its government represents an important moment of empowerment for the Dhanka. Government employment with fixed and reasonable wages, it is implied, replaced hard jobs that did not bring adequate pay. Some of the Dhanka loyalty to the state in Jaipur undoubtedly exists because this shift in their employment patterns is seen to have had dramatic consequences and hastened the improvement of urban life for the community. Indeed, the relationship between Dhanka men in Jaipur and the PHED continues to this day. Dhanka men pride themselves not only on their skill in pipe fitting and pump and sewer maintenance, but also on their willingness to seize an opportunity that allowed "people like us" to turn their basti from *kacchi* to *pukki*, at least for those who became attached to such government work. They have built their dreams in concrete.

It is also telling that while Dhanka men will gladly admit that they have benefitted from reservations in government postings and vocally mourn their erosion under the present employment conditions, as we will see, they do not always locate the source of their community's development in the reservations themselves. Often, the key is seen to lie in the flexibility of the Dhanka, which is also implicitly the willingness to come forward and identify themselves with what Achille Mbembe and Sarah Nuttall have called the "underneath" of the city (2004). They had to be willing to embrace their lack, quite

FIGURE 2. Most of life happens on the roofs in winter months. Shiv Nagar Basti. *Photo by author.*

literally the lack of caste standing and a proscription against handling the human waste of a city over whose growth they had little say. The Dhanka are not the only group that have availed themselves of the visibility and invisibility provided by the underneath, but their reiteration of this relationship as an identifying political currency, as the stuff of a collective disposition, points up its importance. "Honorable masculinity" in this case is not in the work itself but, as is the case with the male domestic servants described by Ray (2000), the willingness to do any work to better one's lot.

Men like Ram Lal are upset about the changes they see in recent years in part, I think, because willingness no longer has pride in it but is demanded by the flexible system of labor known as *thekedari*. His 2002 narrative ended on a pessimistic note:

> These people [who come for contract work] are thieves. You see the names of these people in the newspapers. The *local man* who is from here will never steal anything because he is afraid of being caught when all his relatives live here. He will not be engaged in *criminal* activity. These outsiders live together, four to five people in a single room, so it becomes very economical for them. Now I am at the verge of *retirement* but still my three sons are unemployed. We have a home, but we can't eat this. We could rent the house, but then the tenants might acquire the whole home. My father put me in *service*, but I am not able to do the same for my children.

Ram Lal's complaints had intensified when I saw him again in 2005 and 2007. Despite the fact that he had gotten all three of his sons and his daughter married, and despite the fact that he did retire, he continued to bear the majority of the household's expenses from his pension and, perhaps, other sources. (Some residents think that the men who are prominent in the organization of Dhanka collective weddings also embezzle from funds raised for the event, a point to which I will return.)

Contained within his lament, however, is also an implicit critique of the turn from the stability—and morality—afforded by service for "local men" to the monstrous willingness, the distorted flexibility, of "these people" who come to the city for contract work and day labor and are willing to live in a distressingly economical manner that does not evince the proper dedication to the betterment-through-building so valued by the Dhanka. Though he does not identify "these people" explicitly, other similar articulations throughout my fieldwork indicted what I came to think of as the "three Bs": Bangladeshis, Bengalis, and Biharis (see Moodie 2010). Like other middle-class Jaipuris, the "facts" of migration—that, for instance, most migrants to Jaipur come from other parts of Rajasthan (Goyle et al. 2004)—do very little to challenge firmly held and erroneous stereotypes about these groups. That the Dhanka thus choose to align themselves with a bygone era of valued citizenship and to oppose themselves to others with whom they might compete for casual jobs rather than aligning themselves with other workers who must live on the *theka* shows us that recent downturns in employment may have the somewhat paradoxical effect of strengthening, rather than weakening, the connection between subaltern groups and the state.

Making Men Different

Willingness is embodied in houses, in work on Jaipur's underneath, and in histories of survival through seizing an opportunity or evading an oppression; masculinity is about action, about building with an eye to the future. The goal is to create something concrete that can anchor the expectations of the next generation and convey status upon a man so that he is seen as example by his peers and less well-off neighbors. As we might expect, not all Dhanka men have access to the material and rhetorical resources, or even the inclination, to enact masculinity in the same way. There are many axes through which differences between men are created and emphasized, and it is these differences, I would argue, that are more important for understanding Dhanka collective aspiration than any kind of external orientation to upper castes or classes and their norms. Here, I want to focus on spiritual discipline.

Many of the men who are considered to possess good qualities in Shiv Nagar Basti are followers of various devotional movements, from the locally born saint Sri Garib Dasji Maharaj to Kabir to the internationally known Radhasoami. Radhasoami is the name used to refer to a religious tradition that was founded in the 1860s by Swami Shiv Dayal Singh. It combines Sufi mysticism, the *sant guru* tradition, and elements of Sikhism in what is referred to as *shubdh* ("word" or "sound") yoga. The precise manifestation of this sound is a matter of some debate, and this doctrinal issue, along with conflict over succession of the guru, split the Radhasoami movement into two different groups in the early twentieth century, one centered near Agra and the other in Punjab. (The Agra group is further divided into two groups, again due to succession issues [Lane 1992].) Regardless of which school *satsangis* ("members of the community") follow, members of the Radhasoami faith believe that through certain contemplative practices, especially the recitation of sacred sounds, one can rise to a level of consciousness in which one experiences the Supreme Creator. Devotion to a guru, who guides the devotees' spiritual progress and provides a focus for daily devotional practice, is central to this path toward enlightenment (Babb 1986).

Radhasoami has always appealed to men of the managerial classes, to the extent that historian Mark Juergensmeyer (1991) identifies three aspects of the modern personality that are marked among adherents, including individualism, organization-mindedness, and empiricism (135, 193). While these modern values may seem strangely at odds with the practices of esoteric self-realization prescribed by the faith, Radhasoami does not teach asceticism. Its founder was a householder, as were the gurus who succeeded him. A central tenet of Radhasoami is that one can be in the world and be spiritually enlightened.

Service is highly valued among Radhasoami adherents. *Seva*, or service, here does not mean the same thing as it did in other reform movements of the nineteenth century, such as the Arya Samaj and the Singh Sabha—the goal is not social reform.[8] Service is, instead, service to the guru and to the satsang, not society as a whole; the goal of this service remains individual self-fulfillment (Juergensmeyer 1991). Such an orientation works well with the project of collective aspiration because it allows one to embrace the individual qualities necessary to join the ranks of those in government employ while encouraging investment in one's own community. One can hope that one's own betterment will in itself raise the status of the community as a whole; if an individual chooses to undertake social work—frequently referred to as a key positive characteristic by Dhanka men—it is all the better but not necessary for individual spiritual growth and thus takes on even greater merit because the social worker is not supposed to seek any individual gain (see Mayer 1981).[9]

On the other hand, there is a radical message in Radhasoami teachings, as well. Lower-caste groups, including Dalits, have been drawn to Radhasoami, particularly the Beas branch, because it "rejected caste distinctions from the start" (Babb 1986, 56). Indeed, Swami Shiv Dayal Singh, "Swamiji Maharaj," the original Radhasoami preached against caste prejudice and the authority of Hindu priests (Mathur 1974). Radhasoami teachings stress equality and individual merit at the same time—one is not born to be a particular kind of person but can transform one's life through devotion to the sant-guru and proper contemplation. Hierarchy is an impediment to spiritual growth.

Such messages are central to Dhanka understandings of Radhasoami. Adherents stress that anyone can approach the guru and that all devotees are equal before him. The embrace of Radhasoami in Shiv Nagar Basti thus reflects the general trend among tribals, particularly those who settle in urban areas, to both accept and reject Hindu markers. As among the Ravidas

followers described by Joseph Schaller (1995), the egalitarian message of Radhasoami is not best seen as a kind of safety valve to release resentment against
upper-caste hegemony. Rather, the teachings are an exhortation to proper
behavior and a challenge to status quo social hierarchy. There is a striking
correlation between adherence to Radhasoami and employment in government service, and both are interchangeable indications of a man's qualities.
In terms of daily life, adherence means that men generally do not drink and
smoke, that they are employed, and that they provide for their families while
resisting being bogged down entirely by family concerns.

Women in Shiv Nagar Basti are followers of Radhasoami. They are familiar with his teachings and revere his image. However, they rarely take up
devotional practice with the enthusiasm of their male relatives. This may be
because women are responsible for all domestic work and thus have little
time to go and hear local satsangs about the finer points of Radhasoami philosophy; young women, for their part, especially if married, would not be
allowed out on their own for any reason. It may also be because there is what
Lawrence Babb has termed "a discernable element of misogyny in the tradition" (1986, 55). For example, Maharaj Charan Singh, who was the leader of
the Beas branch of Radhasoami from 1951 to 1990, espoused the view that a
woman could be a devoted follower but was unlikely to ever be a spiritual
leader. While devotion was "natural in a woman," "at a later stage a man makes
better progress than a woman because she is tied down to the world by that
same instinct of devotion" and has difficulty separating herself sufficiently
from her family to attain a saintly level of consciousness (Singh 1983). It may
well be that what women find especially compelling about Radhasoami is the
way it demands certain kinds of behaviors and dispositions from their male
relatives.

Followers, both men and women, of Radhasoami in Shiv Nagar Basti
stress the aspects of the tradition relating to service and social equality, rather
than its specific practices of shubdh yoga and devotion to the guru. Still, it
is common to find devotional images of Swami Maharaj or Charan Singh
and others adorning the walls of homes. Everyday accounts of the religion to
outsiders stress the quasi-miraculous powers of the guru, with an interesting
emphasis on his truth-discerning ability and the way his presence evokes a
profound calm, even among crowds.

During the one satsang event I attended in 2003, several thousand followers gathered at an official satsang ground in Bhilwa, a rural site outside
Jaipur. Buses had been arranged for many and waited for returning devotees
in numbered rows. The level of order was indeed impressive. People passed

through metal detectors almost silently. Many of the Dhanka men from the basti had been at the ground since the previous day; their job was setting up and maintaining the public latrines. The friends with whom I was attending the satsang repeatedly stressed the discipline of the scene to me—"Look how orderly"—thus aligning themselves strongly with the modern managerial personality described by Juergensmeyer. They also frequently referred to the idea that anyone, regardless of caste or class, was welcome at the satsang. (The fact that the security guards stationed throughout the tent would not let my young female companions into the VIP section in front of the stage, but motioned for me, the only foreigner present, to proceed, did not elicit much comment. I sat with my friends.)

In the neighborhood itself, at the level of everyday talk, what men and women alike stress about Radhasoami adherents is that they abstain from drinking alcohol and prize service to their family and community above all else. When asking about a particular man "Does he drink?" one is frequently met with the response "Oh, no, he follows Swami Maharaj," abstention from alcohol being seen to flow directly from this religious orientation.

Men and boys who do drink are seen as both spiritually and socially lax. Alcohol is linked to uselessness ("he is *bekar*"), poverty ("he drinks up all the money"), shiftlessness ("he drinks at breakfast, so how can he work?"), domestic violence ("he becomes angry when he's drunk"), and unhealthy sexual appetites ("they drink and also rent pornographic videos") by both women and men. Some distinctions are made between the *pagal* drunks whose speech is frequently senseless and somewhat "normal" men who occasionally get up to mischief; interestingly, the former is sometimes met with less criticism than the latter precisely because normal men should and could know better. From the perspective of those who follow Radhasoami or abstain from alcohol, they properly pursue the betterment of their own lot and the future of the community—essential aspects of masculine willingness—while their drunken peers remain low or backward.

It is also worth briefly mentioning, though the topic deserves greater consideration, that alcoholism has long been seen as a particular affliction of tribals. High-caste Hindus have a religious injunction to avoid alcohol, while there is no such injunction against drinking in tribal communities, particularly in Rajasthan where the dominant caste (at least in terms of the state's imagery), the Rajputs, also approve of alcohol consumption for men and sometimes women. Thus, not drinking and following a vegetarian diet perform a certain kind of annunciation of upward mobility. It is another instantiation of the repeated narrative "we were adivasis," in which backward practices are replaced by developed ones.

Abstention from alcohol has figured largely in Bhil reform movements in Rajasthan and Gujarat since the nineteenth century and has often been interpreted as an indication of Hinduization or Sanskritization. While it is true that many of the leaders of such movements, including Govind Giri and, importantly for the Dhanka in the twentieth century, Vishwanath Maharaj,[10] preached abstention from alcohol as a key component of Bhil spiritual and social redemption, such abstention was most likely not thought to really have an effect on how Bhils or other adivasis were seen by outsiders (see Hardiman 1987; Schaller 1995). To a large extent, the non-adivasi presumption that all adivasis are alcoholics continues to this day. The meaningful distinctions that are drawn on the basis of alcohol (or meat) consumption are therefore largely drawn within the community. For instance, Arjun Patel notes that among adivasis in the Narmada region in Gujarat, Dhanka Tadvis make strong distinctions between Bhagat (followers of Vishwanath Maharaj, vegetarians, and teetotalers) and non-Bhagats, with the former believing that they are more advanced than the latter (1999, 108).

Peace and Knowledge

While spiritual discipline must be undertaken willingly by an individual, followers of Radhasoami also explain that the guru's peaceful comportment is related to his ability to see the truth with his "third eye," which works as a kind of disciplining apparatus that helps to ensure the right kind of behavior in his devotees. For example, I was told that once some women snuck into the gathering with bombs attached to them, presumably disguised as babies wrapped in blankets (their reason for wanting to bomb the satsang was not clear to me). They made it past the security checkpoint and were sitting in the crowd as Swamiji prepared to give *pravachan* ("spiritual discourse"). He sat on the dais meditating and turning his head slightly from side to side. Eventually he announced that all mothers should nurse their children at that moment. A few women noticed that their neighbors were not breastfeeding, so they asked, "Why aren't you feeding your child?" to which the would-be bombers replied that their children were asleep. The concerned women said that it didn't matter if the children were sleeping, that Swamiji had said to feed them, and so they should wake up the babies and feed them. The would-be bombers refused, at which point guards were called over, the bombs were discovered, and the women were taken into custody. The discovery is attributed to Swamiji's omniscience. As to the latter explanation of the "discipline" and "*shanti*" described by Dhanka followers of Radhasoami, one young female devotee recalled that once a gold chain was discovered at a *satsang*. What was impressive to her about this was that, when the announcement was made over the loudspeaker, the true owner was able to come forward and recover the necklace and no one tried to improperly claim it as their own.

It is tempting to see part of the appeal of Radhasoami in the guru's ability to perceive and know all, to illuminate that which is obscure. Recent work on the Right to Information Act and the Mazdoor Kisan Shakti Sangathan ("Workers and Farmers Power Organization") in Rajasthan has stressed the role that transparency is increasingly playing in the political imaginaries of subaltern groups (Baviskar 2010; Jenkins 2004; Webb 2012). After all, despite their proximity as low-level government servants to state institutions such as income tax offices and the PHED, there are obvious limits to Dhanka knowledge about the operations and decision making of the state bodies of which they are a part. They are not privy to high-level interactions or documents or bureaucratic operations. But neither are they so excluded from the state as to feel alienated and unable to seek information. Thus, in the subaltern civil servant, willingness is also curiosity—the feeling that there is more to know and that the truth may set you, if not free, then at least better than you were (see Moodie 2013b).

But as much as Dhanka participation in Radhasoami is an expression of a disposition of willingness to be altered, it is always circumscribed in problematic ways by their ambiguous tribal/ "untouchable"/low status. The Dhankas' ongoing relationship with the PHED and Jaipur's water supply and sewers mirrors their participation in the religious movement: one of the primary voluntary activities of Dhanka men who follow Radhasoami, a form of seva for Swamiji, is setting up the water works (primarily latrines) at the satsang grounds at Bhilwa. Dhanka devotees that I know take great pride in this role and their ability to keep the waterworks running smoothly for a large gathering. What is telling is that the latrine crew is caste-based; one is unlikely to find a Brahmin or a Rajput on the team.

And yet, it is this knowledge of the underneath that deeply links Dhanka men to the city of Jaipur, past and present, as well as to a broader world beyond India. Rajendra, son of Deepak who, as described in the Introduction, left his wife to wander as a sanyasi for several years, loved to tell me that Swamiji's own children had lived in the United States for a time. He also reported that Swamiji sometimes stays in the farmhouse of a "Mr. John" when he comes to Jaipur. Mr. John, whose wife is English, owns Anokhi—an upscale brand of hand-block-printed textiles and, more recently, an organic farm that supplies a small cafe catering to foreigners with raw vegetables— near Jhagatpur. The textile house is very popular with foreigners and elite

Indians alike. Rajendra was able to report a great deal about this family, including the fact that Mr. John's daughter studies in London, because he once
fixed water lines on Mr. John's farm.[11]

Rajendra is referring here to John Singh and his British wife, Faith, who
established Anokhi as an export company in the late 1960s; the textiles went
to the "hippie" market in London. Today Anokhi is run by their son, Pritam,
and his wife (also British), Rachel Bracken-Singh.[12] Stories about Anokhi and
the Singh family are the stuff of everyday conversation among middle- and
upper-caste Jaipuris that I know—they are certainly local celebrities (I myself
have never met them). Rajendra's reference was striking, though, as it spoke
to the circulation of stories about the Singhs among groups who would certainly never be able to shop in Anokhi's upscale, air-conditioned boutiques.
By narrating his relationship to both Swamiji and the Singhs via his work on
pipes at the Anokhi farm in Jhagatpur, Rajendra was casting himself as an *integral part* of Jaipur as both a city itself and as a hub of transnational contact
via tourism and fashion.

In Rajendra's story of the Anokhi farm, three sites that are important for
the enactment of a willing disposition come together: the civil service, the
waterworks of Jaipur and its environs, and the Radhasoami faith. Willingness
is expressed in each realm in ways that speak of a collective history in which
the Dhanka are made visible as a force in city infrastructure and in ways that
make distinctions between men who do and do not comport themselves in
the proper way. Stigma is never far, however, and each site is saturated with
aspiration for a Dhanka future that might be otherwise.

Another Otherwise?

Since 2005, the Dhanka of Shiv Nagar Basti have been in the process of building their own *mandir* ("temple") at the site of an old shrine to the god Shiva in
the basti. This temple is constructed with materials purchased via donations
from the community and serves not only as a religious site where pujas are
held twice daily, but also as a kind of community center and meeting ground.
It is administered collectively, with individual Dhanka choosing to act as
pujaris, or leaders of worship. There is no distinction made between those
whose spiritual lives revolve around the neighborhood temple and those who
are clear Radhasoami devotees. Furthermore, Radhasoami-like messages are
certainly carried over in the everyday talk about the temple, which stresses
that it is a space open to everyone: rich and poor, man and woman, regardless of caste. It is not clear what this local religious movement will become.

Some examples from other sites would perhaps indicate that such local religious activity may make Shiv Nagar Basti a site of increased interest for local Bharatiya Janata Party (BJP) organizers (see Baviskar 2007).[13] Either way, with the entrance of the temple into neighborhood life, it seems likely that spirituality may take on greater importance as a mode of identification and distinction in future.

4

A Good Woman

The Dhanka wife is a quiet, humble person working throughout the year for the welfare of the family. She has few demands and she is fully satisfied with what she gets and she uses a gold-plated armlet on both her arms, besides the silver anklets on her legs. She is the best dressed tribal woman living in the villages of Gujarat. She is frank and talks, with but few inhibitions, inspite [*sic*] of her modest behavior.

P. G. SHAH, *Tribal Life in Gujarat* (1964, 34)

Dhanka masculinity and the cultivation of willingness of course depend on relationships not only between men but also between men and women. For what, after all, is the point of a concrete house without the family arrangement it is seen to anchor and symbolize—a government servant without his devoted wife safely in the home? Marriage and love are both a personal and a community promise. To arrange intimate life in the right way is to allow love to grow *and* to be an agent in the Dhanka effort to improve their lot. This is women's work in the project of Dhanka collective aspiration. The goal of this chapter, then, is to situate conjugal relationships—or, at least, how women talk and think about them—within the broader political framing I have provided in the previous chapters.

I argue that we cannot understand the importance of Dhanka marriage, or why it is at the center of community organizing and assertions of Dhanka identity, without attending to women's ability to occupy and negotiate an emergent femininity, and attendant conjugality, that is at once tribal, Rajasthani, and modern. Even as women remain ambivalent about their individual fortunes in marriage, they are undoubtedly invested in projects of community striving that require them to cultivate dispositions as respectable, good women. In other words, the political project of making claims for uplift and the intimate projects of making a marriage and a family are neither separate nor separable. Taken together, they are the daily life of collective aspiration.

In Shiv Nagar Basti, a woman's life is often narrated in terms of her goodness, or respectability, and how she manages the fate of her marriage. Respectability is not, as many accounts of gender relations in South Asia might imply, adherence to a given structure, Brahmanical Hindu, Kshatriya/Rajput, or otherwise. In this case, respectability is more an improvisation, a mode of interpretation, than a strict definition—respectable women work with what history, the community, and personal kismet have given them.[1] While, as we will see, a generalized Rajput ethos and cultural symbology informs some of the ways in which Dhanka women view their lives, it would be far too easy to see Dhanka cultural practices as somehow echoing Rajput hegemony; like masculine willingness, discourses about being a "good woman" are just as much about making distinctions *within* the community as they are about external perceptions. Respectability is not really about aping upper-caste norms or aspiring to be upper-caste women, even as Dhanka notions of respectable womanhood interact with upper-caste social formations.

Dhanka women's respectability is related to, but not the opposite of, the willingness of Dhanka men I described in the previous chapter. To ask "What does it mean to be a good Dhanka woman?" is to ask about how the intimacies of everyday life are related to efforts to be in the world, to be related to others (not just husbands), and to have a politically salient group identity.[2] It is to ask questions, also, about femininity in Rajasthan from the perspective of those who are excluded from, or seen to be on the low end of, the caste hierarchies that shape social life. We need to ask questions about marginalized groups' relationship to seemingly hegemonic cultural formations—in this case, ideas about femininity and conjugality—rather than assuming both the content of these formations and a unidirectional flow of aspiration.[3] As with willingness, this is a historical question—what respectability means must change over time. Indeed, part of my argument here is that the security of the era of service allowed norms of respectability to become conventionalized in such a way that they came to signal "Dhanka-ness" as opposed to some other social identification. The inhabitation of these conventions, then, has to be taken seriously as women's contribution to the project of collective aspiration I described for men.

A related point is that my intent in this chapter is not to traffic in stories that will somehow expose respectability as a myth or a sham. When presenting this material at conferences, I have been asked several times versions of questions like "Yes, but what do the women *really* think? What about the women who aren't respectable? What about divorce?" On one hand, this chapter will address some of these issues. Most women do not conform to all, or even many, norms of respectability. How they manage in the inevitable gap between life and expectation will be the focus of the second half of the chapter; I show throughout this book that managing is in fact increasingly difficult for Dhanka women as their concrete dreams are eroded by privatization and the rise of contract labor, which does not always bring a dependable wage. On the other hand, it has seemed to me that because respectability is extremely important to the Dhanka women I know, it is on respectability itself that I should focus. I am less interested in how women fail to be respectable or reject the coercions and pleasures of respectability outright, though they certainly do both.

One of the central arguments of Dalit feminists and writers has been that writing can and should powerfully restore dignity by reflecting upon social and individual life as seen by Dalit authors themselves (see Pandey 2013; Rege 2006; Satyanarayana and Tharu 2013). This is especially important for subaltern women who are often subjected to reiterations and reaffirmations of a literary-political caste-ist rape script that "derives its power and meaning from the humiliation and disappearing of Dalit women" (Brueck 2012, 233) in textual accounts of their lives. While this text is obviously not authored by Dhanka women, I have tried to write within the thematics through which they tell their own stories on a daily basis, even as a I draw attention to some of the ways these thematics are implicated in the unequal gender politics of the Dhanka political gambit. I am as interested in what the disposition of respectability has allowed women to say and do as I am in what it has prohibited. What dreams does it entail?

The focus on respectability is, in part at least, a response to the dominant mode of description that has historically been used when discussing women and tribal life—a mode that stresses promiscuity and "freedom." I begin with a discussion of how ideas about the greater freedom of tribal women have played into definitions of tribal-ness since the colonial era as one of the central markers of the difference between tribes and castes. This historical discussion then provides a context for understanding the ethnography that follows, which attends to how Dhanka women, many of them married to men of the era of service, narrate themselves in terms of respectability. The construction of tribal women as "free" can also help us understand certain aspects of upward mobility in India, as well as the history of the social science that has endeavored to explain such mobility.

The final two sections of the chapter provide an ethnographic account of the specific contours of urban Dhanka femininity. In the first, I highlight the interaction between dominant Dhanka notions of female respectability and more general notions of femininity in north India broadly and in Rajasthan specifically. In the second part, I focus on individual stories of women negotiating conjugal life and expectations for respectability in the face of community identity struggles and the vagaries of personal fate. I show how three women—Richa, Gulabi, and Sapna—each managed the trials of the marriages in which they found themselves in such a way as to remain respectable Dhanka women—at least in their own estimation. In each case, we will see how the inevitable gap between the ideal of respectability and the vicissitudes of life as it is lived provide challenges and opportunities for women to assert their individual respectability and that of their family. In other words, we will track the emotional labor and narrative processes through which a Dhanka woman may become a good woman, regardless of the circumstances she faces.

The Freedom of Tribal Women

The idea that tribal women are "more free" than their Hindu or Muslim counterparts has a long history and proves remarkably tenacious even in the contemporary era. Scheduled Tribe women certainly enjoyed rights under precolonial customary law that were eroded first by the codification of legal traditions under colonialism and later through the establishment of separate sets of personal laws for religious communities (Agnes 2004; Arunima, Sudhir, and Basu 1996). These losses included customary rights to property and rights to contract and dissolve marriages, among many others. There are also ways that tribal women's agency in practices surrounding sex and marriage is *different* than that of Hindu or Muslim women (see, for example, Alpa Shah's (2010) discussion of life at the brick kilns in Jharkhand). However, as Maya Unnithan-Kumar (1997) points out, definitions of tribe based on the freedom of women often say as much about the group attributing this quality than the "tribe" itself (see also Gellner 1991). Indeed, Unnithan-Kumar argues that when we examine the similarities between the Girasia tribals of southern Rajasthan and non-Girasia women, rather than taking their essential difference for granted, we see that both groups of women are usually in weaker decision-making positions than men. The "freedom" of tribal women must often be sanctioned by men: bride-price, for instance, means that women's position in the social structures of their communities and their (possibilities for) intimate relationships are still determined by monetary exchanges between men, which does not indicate an especially tribal valuation of women's labor, as has sometimes been argued about bride-price versus dowry marriage. In cases of woman-initiated divorce, to take another example, Unnithan-Kumar reports that such cases are only successful if women have the support of their male kin (1997, 22).

In its most insidious form, the idea of the free tribal woman serves as a way to disavow the pervasive sexual violence against adivasi women in India today.[4] At the very least, it collapses distinctions between adivasi groups (should we, after all, generalize from the experience of, say, Mundas in Jharkhand to Girasias in southern Rajasthan?) and sets up a problematic binary between tribal and non-tribal women.

Since the colonial era, constructions of the sexual freedom of tribal women by outsiders have often worked to construct images of wild, primitive, or childlike peoples who remain outside the pale of civilization, whether Hindu/Muslim or British. Colonial constructions of gender among the tribes of India were complex, however, and it would be a mistake to read current assumption about adivasi women as a simple continuation of earlier discourses. As historian Ajay Skaria (1997) points out, distinctions between the colonizers and the colonized, as well as between castes and tribes, relied on particular constructions of wildness that differed between regions and groups.[5] Tribal women, according to Skaria, came to be thought of as savage and possessing a wild sexuality. Yet, the sexual freedom of the tribal woman was not stressed in the nineteenth century the way that it would be in the twentieth. The reasons for this shift are interesting to consider. Skaria hypothesizes that the lack of attention to the tribal women in colonial texts is because the voyeuristic colonial male gaze was already trained on caste women as the site of "erotic sexuality"; a particular fascination with sati and the selfless devotion of women it implied meant that nineteenth-century colonial texts dwelled less on the sexuality of tribal women (1997, 737–738). Rather, as was the case in accounts of the Bhil of the Dangs studied by Skaria, tribal women were thought to be equal and sobering partners in an overall commitment to family life evinced by tribal groups. The characterization of tribal women as sexually free, according to Skaria, begins as a (Bengali) middle-class, nationalist sensibility sought to re-masculinize men and ensconce women as paragons of motherhood and self-sacrifice.[6]

By the twentieth century, both the hypersexuality of the adivasi woman and her status as dependable helpmate were well elaborated, nowhere more than in the ethnography of Verrier Elwin. As a confidant and consultant of Jawaharlal Nehru's, he undoubtedly influenced approaches to tribal issues more than any other individual up to the current era (Guha 1999). Not enough has been made, however, of what Elwin's work can tell us about the *gendering* of adivasi citizenship today. At the risk of overstating, we might say that Elwin's texts and policies became both the model *and* foil for subsequent understandings of tribal organization, particularly gender relations. It will not be surprising that marriage figures largely in his discussions both because it was a common site of anthropological curiosity and because of Elwin's own controversial marriage to a young Gond woman from the village he studied in Chattisgarh.[7]

Echoing the form of nineteenth-century colonial arguments about the differences between tribal and caste groups, Elwin insisted throughout his career that the freedom of women in sex, marriage, and divorce was not only characteristic of India's aboriginal groups, but translated into an entirely different personality than that found among more restricted Hindu and Muslim women. He summarized this view in his 1943 work, *The Aboriginals*: "The woman holds a high and honourable place. She goes proudly free about the countryside. . . . She is not subjected to early child-bearing; she is married when she is mature, and if her marriage is a failure (which it seldom is) she has the right of divorce. . . . Her free and open life fills her mind with poetry and sharpens her tongue with wit. As a companion she is humorous and interesting; as a wife devoted; as a mother, heroic in the service of her children" (quoted in Guha 1999, 150). Elwin's romantic vision of the empowered tribal woman, with her "free and open" life is implicitly pitted against the more restrictive lives of caste Hindu and Muslim women, of whom Elwin had a lesser opinion. This "noble savage woman" was noble in part *because* of her liberated sexuality and independence.

Elwin's influence on the ethnographic representation of the Dhanka is obvious. His sentiments about the freedom of adivasi women are echoed—sometimes repeated almost verbatim—in P. G. Shah's 1964 ethnography *Tribal Life in Gujarat*. Consider the following set of quotations from the second chapter of his text, entitled "Women in Tribal Life":

> The woman who has enjoyed . . . pre-marital freedom remains a strong partner throughout life and sex relations are generally happy. Sex is seldom suppressed and soon leads to social and domestic independence . . .
>
> . . . [In my research since 1941,] I made out that the tribal population . . . enjoyed greater freedom than the Hindus. The position of woman among the tribes even at present is similar and she enjoys greater freedom in betrothal, age of marriage, in divorce, and freedom from compulsory widowhood than her Hindu sisters. . . .
>
> . . . A feature of the social life of tribal women in Gujarat is that there is no pardah either among the ordinary or tribal women in Gujarat. So her freedom in movement is greater and while her daily life may not be free from poverty and strain of life, she is on the whole happy. (29)

Shah's assessment reiterates Elwin's notion that adivasi women are more sexually free and, relatedly, enjoy more freedom in decisions about marriage, divorce, and widowhood than other women in India. In Shah's account, Dhanka women become everything that Hindu and Muslim women are not: in control of their sexuality, valued, and independent—even if they are poor.

Especially relevant for the consideration of Dhanka collective aspiration is the relationship that Shah draws between women's influence in collective life, domestic arrangements, and development. He comments:

> Attitudes towards women in ancient Hindu books has later on affected the standard of treatment of woman in tribal life. . . . In spite of these imposed social disabilities, the tribal woman has great importance and influence in tribal life; those tribes like Gamits, Dhankas, Dhodias and some Bhils, who allow woman to command great influence are more advanced than those like the Dublas and Naikas, and Bhillalas. Generally the tribal woman is more free from the limitations of the joint family system, as the new couple have no economic assets or joint property to prevent it from separating from the parents from as early a date as possible after marriage. (28)

What is interesting to note is that women's influence emerges for Shah in the formation of separate households upon marriage and not in women's participation in, say, an egalitarian political system. One suspects that Shah's insistence on this family formation as sign of development is part of the outlook of his generation, but also clearly derived from Elwin's anthropology.

Unnithan-Kumar's work on the rhetoric of freedom should caution us against simply accepting these historical assessments and their assumption that we can read "more" or "less" freedom from particular forms of marriage and kinship. And yet, at the same time, it is possible—indeed, likely—that Dhanka women had a different relationship to marriage practices and family formations in the early twentieth century than they do today and that some of the customary practices that gave them a certain room for maneuver in the arrangement of their intimate lives were eroded over time.

Such a shift would be in keeping with much of the social science about upward mobility in India. Let us consider M. N. Srinivas's famous description of Sanskritization again, this time attending especially to what it tells us about the implication of marriage and gender norms in efforts to rise in caste hierarchies. Sanskritization—or, we might say, Rajputization—is a process of upward mobility in which low-ranking caste and tribal groups begin to emulate the practices, and thus claim the rank of, higher-caste groups. Over time, the emulation of higher-caste habits allows lower-caste groups to make claims to a different historical positioning than that conferred on them by other communities.[8] We might, then, see Dhanka women's embrace of marriage and conjugality as an inherent part of the greater restriction that marks upwardly mobile communities—the "increasing harshness toward women" (Srinivas 1962, 46) we would expect to see.

What needs to be added to these accounts, however, is a consideration of what women are embracing when they take up such subject positions with heart and what it means for their day-to-day loves and labors. The neglect of women's dispositions in this regard results in part from not pushing Sanskritization theories for other, less obvious insights they might hold about gender relations. For instance, surely the fact that domestically based practices, such as vegetarianism and teetotalism, are central methods and symbols of upward mobility speaks to the essential contributions of women to these processes at a daily level. Who manages food stores and cooks? In Dhanka homes (and most others in living memory), it has been women. Thus we could say that the daily habits of aspiring groups like the Dhanka—their comportments and dispositions—that signal rising status implicate women not only as objects of boundary-marking to be exchanged but also as performers of the everyday *work* of group aspiration.

But the problem is also that the specific meanings of gender restrictions— the value placed on respectability, for one—are rarely examined on their own terms, for what such restrictions mean to women aspiring to respectability. Notice that Srinivas's theory of Sanskritization invokes women as the "ground" of status negotiation (see Mani 1998) yet seems to erase the possibility that women within these communities may have any response beyond blind acquiescence or utter dejection. There are historical precedents for such negotiations between caste groups. Not only British authorities and Indian nationalists struggled over the "woman question." As Sharmila Rege has recently shown, non-brahman counterpublics in the early twentieth century in Maharasthra used women as the ground to draw distinctions between brahmans and non-brahmans (2006, 43).

It is also important to remember here that the Dhanka are not engaging simply in a process of Sanskritization. Much of their vision for what it means to rise up and cease being backward would reject the very terms of Sanskritization. To be fair, Srinivas also recognized that rising in the caste hierarchy was not enough for Dalit groups after independence; rather, they chose to address their efforts in greater part to constitutional principles of equality (see Srinivas 1962, chapter six). Still, Sanskritization implies a model in which status is both structured and known. For an urban tribal group like the Dhanka who must balance and maintain multiple identifications in buoyant tension, it is not clear what "status" one occupies or should aspire to. The dream, however, is clear: a concrete home, a housewife, a government job. In this sense, it is an urban, statist dream and not about a return to an autonomous tribal past. *We were adivasis. We are now equal, unmarked national subjects.*

Yet, the question remains, what is one to make of all the ways in which the success of reservations seems to register in greater restrictions on women?

Respectability is the descriptor I have chosen to talk about a constellation of orientations and discourses through which Dhanka women are mobilized and mobilize in the effort to be good women engaged in the collective project of aspiration. It should not be seen as the opposite of male willingness or as representing a kind of natural complementarity between men and women. Rather, it seems to me that the promise of respectability is another kind of promise of security that emerges as the Dhanka struggle to fulfill the terms of legal definitions and distance themselves from certain aspects of ethnological definitions, notably the sexual freedom of women, while embracing other aspects of tribal-ness that are necessary to remain worthy and needy of reservations. It is different than, but not the opposite of, the security men seek in the form of concrete buildings and working taps, those monuments to the willingness to do what it takes to survive. It is a protective security, one that promises to undo the stigma of difference and low-ness, with tribalness now ironically the path to upward mobility that will bring Dhanka women in to the mainstream fold. It is thus just as important to the Dhanka as willingness; the two clearly overlap and interact.

A good woman . . .

. . . HAS A HOME

The fact of Dhanka male home ownership is also important for women. Though women do not own house plots themselves, familial home ownership gives women a certain kind of stability in the face of potential economic downturns. The seeming permanence of housing gives women as well as men a particular kind of assurance about their place in the world. Dhanka women whose families own their homes feel pity for those who must rent.[9]

In some ways, home ownership is more important for women than for men. Urban Dhanka life, as we have seen, is gender segregated; this separation maps onto the space of the neighborhood itself. Homes—their rooms, rooftops, and terraces—are women's terrain. Outer spaces and public areas like alleys, temples, and shops are for men and boys.[10] Women take pride in the size, cleanliness, and decoration of their house. It is, after all, the site of most of their sociality and labor. It is also the space where they may have female allies. A common relationship between women in Shiv Nagar Basti is that of sisters-in-law. When this relationship is friendly, looking after the house becomes a kind of collaborative project or mutual care. When this relationship breaks down, one is unlikely to find another friend or female relative to replace its potential benefit. The house and the division of its spaces are often the stage on which the drama of these relationships plays out; rooms are built or shut off or rearranged to mark the ending or strengthening of a relationship. Thus, closeness or distance in relationships can be conveyed by how much—or little—shared space two women retain in any given household.

Housework for Dhanka women is extremely labor intensive. There are no servants employed even part-time to assist with daily chores, as one might find in even lower middle-class homes—yet standards are high. There are few labor-saving devices like dishwashers or electric irons. One may or may not have other women or girls to assist with daily labor, depending on the age composition and personalities of a particular household. Chores include cooking at least twice a day, washing dishes, doing laundry by hand, sweeping, washing the floors, shopping in the market, bathing children, organizing stores and linens, and maintaining household shrines. The way that these chores are accomplished, the condition in which one's home and children are kept, are an extension of a woman and reflect on her heavily.

Even though women do not own and thus cannot pass on their houses, a home is also a legacy for a woman to give to her son. It is the place she will remain with her son(s) into her old age. When Rajendra and Lakshmi bought a new plot outside Jaipur, in Jhotwara, for their two sons, Lakshmi was the one who insisted we go out to the plot with a video camera to tape what was essentially a dusty patch of land. This was where she imagined her sons living together with their wives in the future. Its purchase brought her great comfort. Rather than reading Lakshmi's emotional connection to the new plot as a sign of the plot's importance as her insurance for old age—a functionalist reading that is common in narratives about north Indian mothers' relationship to their sons and sons' property—the importance of passing on a house to her son was more about pride in having been a good mother, in having been able to do right by one's son *regardless* of the outcome for the mother in the future. Like many communities in Rajasthan, Dhanka women and men express a great deal of concern that familial devotion has deteriorated since earlier times (see Gold and Gujar 2002; see also Cohen 1998). Sons will not necessarily look after parents. But a home is a permanent marker of the possibility of these commitments.

. . . ONLY WORKS OUTSIDE THE HOME IF SHE LIVES
IN A VILLAGE OR IS FORCED TO IN ORDER
TO CARE FOR HER FAMILY

Perhaps the biggest sign, for both women and men, of the Dhankas' changed status as a result of reservations is that many women in Shiv Nagar Basti stay home as housewives.[11] This is an acknowledged historical change from an era when Dhanka did not live in cities and thus both women and men worked. Rural Dhanka women work in the fields with Dhankā men; they are also solely responsible for housework. Urban Dhanka women sometimes marvel at the hard work put into farming by their rural relatives. It is understood that these women *have to* work because agricultural production would not be viable without their participation. (It is worth remembering here that the Dhanka are not "traditionally" farmers. Many Dhanka who today own farmland were the beneficiaries of land-redistribution programs in the 1960s). This is part of *gaon* ("village") culture and accepted, even admired.

Similarly, women who are in particularly poor homes, who have alcoholic husbands, or who have been abandoned are also understood as *having* to work and are pitied for what has been termed by Raka Ray and Seemin Qayum (2009) the "failure of patriarchy." Ray and Qayum's detailed exploration of domestic work in Kolkata is instructive for my case. They describe the emergence of an "astonishing consensus" in the nineteenth century that domestic labor and domesticity are essential to middle-class life. "The losers in this consensus were those women without protection and those who could not afford to stay at home—and were consequently excluded from the domestic sphere and proper domesticity—as well as the men who were unable to provide women with that protection" (122). Thus, in contrast to modernizing, or even feminist, narratives about women's ever-increasing liberation through education and work, Ray and Qayum found women domestic workers in Kolkata dreaming of a home, a husband, and a life in which they could work for that husband, not for unrelated outsiders.

In Shiv Nagar Basti, as in the cases described by Ray and Qayum, it is understood that women's commitment to their children means that they can and should do anything necessary to provide for them; "normally, they should be maintained by fathers and husbands as part of the latter's patriarchal familial duties" (125). But it is often not to be, especially when there are fewer jobs and more insecure contract labor. This means that women are required to find work in order to make ends meet. A woman working to bring up her own children is, to a certain extent, more respectable than a woman who would turn back to her natal family for support, though they may indeed be supportive.

Interestingly, as in Kolkata, the work that women take up tends itself to be domestic in nature, either working as servants in the homes of others or as sweepers in government offices. A few women have worked with the Reproductive and Child Health Project as helpers, and at least one woman has been employed in work with the state *anganwadi* program. Another woman was a primary school teacher, though her case was quite rare. In each case, women work in fields directly related to the concerns of other women and children.

Housewives are protected from the streets, where danger lurks. There is an overwhelming sense among Dhanka women in Shiv Nagar Basti that Jaipur City has changed in the last twenty years and not for the better. One fifty-year-old woman put it in simple, dire terms: "It was better before . . . because before there were fewer fights. Now there are more. There is greater *daco-ity* ["banditry"]. An individual, male or female, cannot move around alone. There are more criminals. Before it was not like this. Before you could move around [the city] even up until twelve o'clock at night. But now it is not so. That is why I don't like today's environment." Crowding and crime are cited as the two major deterrents to women and girls moving outside the house. In this sense, cultural expectations and urban space collude to restrict mobility. The southern gates of the Pink City along M. I. Road are indeed the most crowded urban spaces in Jaipur. Getting from one end of this stretch to the other, or getting from outside the gates to a particular destination in the Pink City, can prove difficult. The streets are noisy, girls are teased, and traffic is dangerous.

To some extent, discourses about danger in the streets among Shiv Nagar Basti residents are also about drawing distinctions between themselves and their Muslim neighbors as well as Bengali-speaking migrants with whom they feel they now compete for jobs. Many residents cite the rise in the population of "Bangladeshis" as responsible for the city's growth and decline (see Moodie 2010). The area in which Shiv Nagar Basti is located is generally considered a "Muslim part of town," and Dhanka are often mistaken for both Dalits and Muslims. To insist that Dhanka girls stay in the Dhanka neighborhood is also to be able to maintain distinctions that are often obscured to outsiders. This marking the Dhankas' distance from neighboring Muslims and Dalits is not done for outsiders but to shore up boundaries that are at once social and geographic for the community itself.

Perhaps it is this domestic orientation that explains the immense popularity of joint family dramas—soap operas, referred to as "serials" (in English)—among women in Shiv Nagar Basti. Other scholars have pointed to the reiteration of "traditional" Indian values in the face of cultural change and the negotiation of national identity that happens in these filmic contexts (Mankekar 1999). Less has been made of the way that such serials also make domesticity important. For women who have been excluded from national images of the good Indian woman, the shift to housewifery marks an important step toward domesticity. To see this domesticity celebrated—even in contexts like the shows, in which many of the leading ladies are actually employed and engaged in business—makes daily life more meaningful. Domesticity is a marker of freedom.

I had an interesting conversation about this with Ram Lal's daughter-in-law Nirmala. I was asking her when she feels really free, using the Hindi term *azadi*. She replied that she felt azadi when she was relaxing and watching serials on television. And then she made a very interesting observation. She said that while sometimes she wished she could roam around here and there—like her anthropologist friend who was always coming and going between one country and the next—that the life of a foreign researcher was hard. There was no freedom in it, because one was never free from worry about where the money or the next meal would come from. She, by contrast, did not have to bother about such things so that her free time, when she was watching *Kahani Ghar Ghar Ki or Kabhi sas bhi bahu ti*, was really her own. Domesticity, in this sense, is not a cage from which one must seek release, but a space of security and freedom from worry.

. . . WEARS THE VEIL

All of the married women in Shiv Nagar Basti practice *purdah*, meaning that they wear *ghunghat*, the veil, in front of their husbands' elder male relatives. Veiling practices are widespread throughout northern India. While the veil is often seen as the symbol par excellence of patriarchal control of women, it has also been rendered as a useful cultural prop for the maintenance of women's separate traditions or even seduction (Raheja and Gold 1994). While studies of the veil thus diverge from one another a great deal, one thing they agree on is that veiling practices must be seen in their cultural and historical specificity. Thus, though the fact that Dhanka women veil is nothing unexpected or remarkable, it is also a site for reflection.

The veil confers respectability in two important ways. First, it maintains respectable practices in the household. In order to protect the boundaries of approved sexual relationships, which are only between husbands and wives, fathers-in-law are forbidden to see their daughters-in-law. Similarly elder brothers. A woman who did not veil in the home would be seen as impudent and dangerous, imperiling the correct balance of gender and generational relations.

Second, veiling in the home aligns Dhanka women with other middle-upper-caste and class groups. One way to think about this is that the amount of time spent in ghunghat is a direct reflection of the high status of the family: women who do not work outside the home (where ghunghat is not required) spend much more time veiled. If one is at home and elder male relatives are present, one is veiled. It is the domestic male gaze that threatens familial harmony, yet it is the domestic male gaze that is coveted in the respectability complex. The veil, then, is seen to point to the ways that middle-class women are protected while lower-class working women are not.

The veil also aligns Dhanka women with Hindu traditions (and, to a lesser extent, Muslim traditions) rather than adivasi traditions. Recall the prevalent assertion discussed in previous chapters that tribal women were and continue to be freer than Hindu and Muslim women. This argument was made specifically about the Dhanka in P. G. Shah's ethnography: "A feature of the social life of tribal women in Gujarat is that there is no pardah either among the ordinary or tribal women in Gujarat. So her freedom in movement is greater and while her daily life may not be free from poverty and strain of life, she is on the whole happy" (1964, 29). It is interesting that Shah's initial remark on the "social life of tribal women in Gujarat" is that neither "ordinary" nor tribal women practice purdah; the "her" that emerges in the following sentence, however, is clearly taken to refer to tribal women. The reader is left to understand that tribal women really are different from their "ordinary" peers, but in this instance the basis of that difference is unclear. Nonetheless, Shah reaffirms the commonsense understanding that tribal women do not veil. The embrace of ghunghat, then, can be seen as a rejection of adivasi difference.

. . . HAS A LOVING HUSBAND AND LOVES HER HUSBAND

We now come to what is perhaps the most important characteristic of a good woman: she has a loving husband and loves her husband. For Dhanka women, the marriage relationship is paramount, but it is not just marriage per se that matters. Love, in forms of devotion, affection, and sex, is desired in marriage by all the Dhanka women I know. Protection and economic provision are extremely important, but without love a woman is incapable of expressing her own highest potential. Among the Dhanka of Jaipur, women prize love and seek it out. Ray and Qayum found love similarly valued by the domestic workers with whom they spoke in Kolkata: One woman in their account, when asked what she wanted for the future, commented, "Just some love. One can't live without love. Just like a plant or a tree, one withers and dies" (2009, 133). Another remarked, "All homes have their own sorrows. Mine is that the man who took my hand never gave me love" (133). Similar comments are made frequently in Shiv Nagar Basti. Gulabi, whose story I will relate in the next section, once said about her second arranged marriage to an alcoholic man "Everyone told me that he was good. He's good. Now who is wasting away to nothing [*ghusna*] inside [this marriage]? Who sees? Everyone just sees 'good-good.'" Her concern here is not so much that her husband does not fulfill his economic or social obligations because of his alcoholism, but that her soul has suffered because of the marriage. The verb she uses here, *ghusna*, can mean to evaporate or disappear.

One could attribute the importance placed on love to the dispersion of ideas about conjugal romance through Hindi films, romance novels, and discourses of development. A common assumption among historians and social scientists is that modernization brings with it a greater focus on companionate marriage. Yet as Perveez Mody (2002), Kriti Kapila (2004), and others have pointed out, the question of just what marriage is—what it does in any particular historical moment or for any particular community—must be asked; it cannot be taken as a foregone conclusion. I will elaborate this idea in the next chapter.

In the case of Shiv Nagar Basti, we must attend not only to modern or cosmopolitan forms of love but also to modern re-imaginings of traditional forms of conjugal love. In Jaipur, Rajput notions of women's bravery and fidelity are certainly implicated in this cultural complex, as is the specific question of sati and its relationship to regional notions of community. As noted by Lindsey Harlan, the fulfillment of the *pativrata* ("devotion to one's husband") role is seen as a special talent of Rajput women.[12] "Rajput women explain that just as sacrificing and giving have characterized the history of Rajput men, so they have characterized the history of Rajput *pativratas*" (1992, 121). This is why only Rajput women can become authentic satimatas, according to Harlan's informants; the strength and dedication it takes to become a satimata—sat—are a "caste-affiliated virtue and duty" (126). What is important for my analysis is that the husband-wife relationship is seen as paramount, superseding even that between mother and child, while at the same time women's emotional dedication and spiritual excellence is taken to be a sign of a particular caste identity. In other words, how a woman feels about a marriage, about her husband, is central to how her community imagines itself. These are not otherworldly concerns but, as Sangari and Vaid (1996) have shown, directly tied to caste formations in the state of Rajasthan.

In an exchange between Lakshmi (Rajendra's wife, Mona and Kanika's mother) and myself, the relationship of Dhanka women to this ideal is touched upon. As is clear in the below translation, Dhanka women venerate satimatas, even though their worship is not a central part of Dhanka religious life. While telling me the story below, Kanika was rummaging around, trying to find an old religious picture of a satimata that she had lost. While the specific trappings of satimata worship may not be the most important part of

Dhanka women's religious practice, the framework for understanding conjugality is, I argue, very important.

The conversation:

MEGAN: How does one become a sati?

LAKSHMI: Nowadays there is no sati. Fifty years ago there were more. Not every woman can do it; only if her husband loved her a lot and she loved him a lot. Only such a woman will become a sati—nowadays the government doesn't allow it. The police come and stop it right there. Even though the police come, sometimes a woman who wants to become sati does not cry. She tells all the other women "Calm down, calm down." She stands alone, she goes quietly into her room. She has a shower and dresses up. So when people get a hint that she will become a sati—the police or people from the village—they lock her up. But the door opens automatically and all over the walls are *mehndi hath* ("hands painted with bridal henna"). And other colorful impressions. Her baggage is magically full of nice clothes. She has *bindi, tika, roli, kajol*. She finds all these things in her bureau. So after a shower, she dresses herself up with all these things. And then the gates open, and so many times it has happened. The police don't believe in all this, but only one in one thousand [women] would become a sati. . . .

Even when we get burned by cooking food it hurts so badly. And she is burned all the way through. Do you know what she is burnt with? Not wood, coconut oil. With coconut she burns on her own. No one even puts a matchstick. She sits and burns herself. She burns herself with her husband's body.

MEGAN: She doesn't cry?

LAKSHMI: No, because the strength of the soul makes her very strong. She feels no pain. She doesn't cry. She just keeps walking. She finds a clean place and sits down to burn herself. She burns herself with the body of her husband. . . .

MEGAN: A woman would cry.

LAKSHMI: No, they cry for [their] children. But because the future depends on the husband, she feels more sad when the husband goes. Because, even when she looks at her kids, she thinks, "I have such small children. What will happen with him gone?" She wonders how she will feed them, send them to school, because the man used to go out to work, and she cared for the family. Now that is her biggest worry. And also, the children are nice to her now, but later they may change and abandon her. Earlier there were two people looking after the kids so they were scared of the father. Now their father is gone. So the children might *bigere* ("cross the limits"). They are capable of crossing these limits. What will be? Who can say what will happen?

MEGAN: So when a husband dies, it's harder [than when a child dies]? When the child dies, there might be more [children].

LAKSHMI: Sometimes when the husband dies young she may remarry. But if she has children who are old enough, fourteen, fifteen, where will she go? She can't remarry. She has no choice. She will look after her children. If a wife dies and he has a job, it doesn't matter how old he is—he can remarry.

In this description of modern sati, Lakshmi stresses that the act is illegal and unlikely to take place today. Even though she, her daughters, and many other women venerate satimatas, the ritual is seen mostly as a thing of the past. It is unclear from Lakshmi's narration whether she agrees with the legal proscription on sati, though interesting that she does not mention that the worship of satis—their "glorification"—is also illegal since the passage of the Commission of Sati (Prevention) Act following the Roop Kanwar case in 1987.[13]

Her own reverence for satimatas is obvious. Lakshmi stresses that the number of women who can become a satimata is extremely small. Like many women in Rajasthan, regardless of caste, however, she believes that sometimes the force of sat ("truth") in a woman's soul is so strong that she becomes a sati through means that defy human laws (the door flies open, the hennaed hands magically appear). In other words, the question of legality versus illegality is rendered irrelevant in post-1987 sati beliefs by a focus on the supernaturalness of the sati. Rather than focusing on a woman's volition, which would imply questions of law, sat is characterized as beyond volition. Sat for a woman emerges from the deep mutual devotion shared by husband and wife. What does it mean that a non-Rajput—non-high-caste—woman embraces this ideal so strongly? One interpretation is that it speaks to the hegemony of what we might call "Rajput gender ideals" throughout the region. In this reading, the differences between caste and tribe groups within Rajasthan may be less than those between all Rajasthani women and those from other regions. The attention to strength in Lakshmi's narrative is as telling as her reference to the love of husband and wife.

Another interpretation of the embrace of sati is that it speaks to the Dhankas' actual historical relationship to the Rajputs or to their embrace of Rajput traditions as an attempt to establish such a relationship in the more recent past. Satimata veneration may be part of the complex negotiation of an identity that must always be tribal, Rajasthani, and modern all at once. Because sati became central to Rajput community definitions in the late 1980s and early 1990s, it is a particularly potent way of aligning oneself with the regionally dominant caste. It is also important to remember that it was not only Rajputs who benefitted from the Roop Kanwar sati specifically. Sangari and Vaid have argued persuasively that sati is better thought of as supported by a caste coalition, which includes Baniyas and Brahmins; Jats, who have also historically practiced sati, are also regionally prominent. Thus we might think of it more as an alliance with regional conventions than a simple Rajput identification that attempts to, for instance, establish a Kshatriya heritage for the Dhanka.

The Work of Being Respectable

In Chapter 3, we saw that Dhanka masculinity was deeply entwined with the project of collective aspiration, especially as it entails the cultivation of willingness—to change and do what it takes to survive while retaining an orientation that recognizes one's own otherness from mainstream culture and history. In a similar way, the work of being respectable is the effort that Dhanka women bring to this shared project. As was the case in my account of willingness, the features that make up respectability, that mark a good woman, are rarely articulated as such, let alone compiled in a list such as that above. Rather, I have been reflecting on a constellation of social practices that tend to occasion comment and judgment among women in such a way as to convey the normative parameters for the narratives that follow.

No one can be a perfectly good woman. On one hand, this is simply because no one can be a perfectly good woman. On the other hand, as the following accounts will make clear, the conventions of good womanhood depend upon the security of men's employment, which is increasingly in jeopardy in Jaipur. In the stories of individual women below, it will become clear that this growing instability of employment resulting from privatization, government hiring cuts, and growing doubts about Dhankas' right to reservations requires that women undertake a great deal of narrative effort to maintain their respectability. It will also be clear that this effort signals a change for Dhanka women: women such as Richa, Gulabi, and Sapna were raised to understand themselves as having a particular role in the bargain struck by the Dhanka for inclusion via the ST category. Their domesticity (as a set of practices that includes the labor of maintaining a home and rearing children) and their commitment to domesticity as an inherent value—both of which are essential to respectability—were an important part of signaling and creating the daily affective experience of having "arrived." Conventional and constraining, their marriages and families were an integral element of collective aspiration.

RICHA

Richa is one of my favorite people to spend time with in Shiv Nagar Basti; most days in Jaipur I have spent at least a little time sitting on her roof, chatting. She has an open demeanor and laughs often. We are both a bit sarcastic and, though anyone else would probably not guess, almost exactly the same age, with Richa slightly my elder, even though I was a childless graduate student for much of our relationship and she is a mother of five. Richa clearly adores her three daughters and two sons—they are a tight-knit family.

Richa is always working: washing clothes, preparing food, combing the girls' hair for school. I imagine that this has been true for most of her life. Richa's mother died when she was very young. In her telling, because she never had a mother, she never really had any girlfriends either, and this is why she doesn't gossip and roam from house to house talking about all the other women in the neighborhood. She had to work in her childhood, too, which was spent in another Dhanka area of Jaipur, in the southwestern reaches of the urban area and far from the walls of the Pink City. Richa never went to school and is thus not *pardhi-likhi* ("literate"). Like many of her generation, Richa's upward mobility has registered in her ability to craft an apparently stable domesticity.

The last time I saw her, Richa complained that no one ever came to see her and that some women in the neighborhood wouldn't even speak to her. When I asked her why this was so, the answer was plain and straightforward. As she saw it, the husbands of those women had government service jobs and her husband hadn't gotten permanent employment yet. He, like many other younger Dhanka men, has been working in a government office on temporary contracts that are periodically renewed without his position being made permanent. The other women thought they were better than her because their husbands were in permanent service and because, unlike Richa, they could read and write. A tinge of contempt crept into her voice and she beat the clothes she was washing a bit harder as she told me "Those ladies never ever come into my house." She told me that this is why we are friends: I come to see her and stay for a chat.

But Richa tried to be positive about her life. She is so lucky with her husband, she told me. He doesn't drink, and on a holiday he prefers to stay home and fly kites with his kids rather than going into the market and drinking. He is a good son to his elderly mother and father. But he worries, too. They have three daughters and two sons—three weddings to pay for and only two dowries coming in. And as hard as he tries, he cannot get permanent work the way that his older brother and cousins have. He really tries, she assured me, because he is embarrassed that he cannot support the whole household on his own and has to take money from his parents. His boss has promised repeatedly to change his employment status, but so far it has not happened. With statewide budget cuts in many departments, it may not even be his boss's fault.

Richa said, "This is a difference between me and those ladies: they are *gundi* ('dirty'). Even if they are literate and their husbands have good jobs, they are not good women. Their husbands drink, and they drink with them. They are the ones who get the dirty *videos* from the bazaar." Richa told me she would not look at such a thing. "What goes on in the bedroom is between a husband and a wife and not for public discussion." Her husband agrees. "He doesn't go for this stuff either. He is a good man."

From Richa's perspective, being a good man or a good woman does not have to do with one's level of education or income but with comporting one-self in a particular way. Keeping away from things that are dirty—alcohol, public discussion of sex, too much time spent roaming about—is at least as important as having a particular kind of job. Her solution to the problem that her husband's unemployment and underemployment pose for her respectability is to focus almost entirely on her husband, children, aged in-laws, and natal family (also Jaipur residents). Kinship, its pleasures and responsibilities, is embraced wholeheartedly by this woman who grew up without a mother. It is the embrace of kinship that works to undo any possible stigma associated with her lack of education or her husband's unemployment.

Of course, Richa's focus on kinship does not necessarily lead to an entirely harmonious domestic sphere. Richa has an ongoing dispute with her sister-in-law, the wife of her husband's elder brother. The two sisters-in-law have built cement walls to partition off the large home that belongs to the brothers' parents. The parents, for their part, have chosen to live with Richa and her family. Being good, then, does not mean living without conflict. It does mean staying loyal to one's husband despite his weaknesses and rejecting dirty things, even if they seem to come hand-in-hand with the status of education. It hardly matters whether Richa's neighbors watch pornographic films or not. The point is that Richa is challenging both community hierarchies, in which she would be seen as below women with husbands who are employed full time, and older notions about sexually promiscuous, "free" tribal women.

For an ST woman, domesticity emerges as a complex positionality and not simply relegation to a predetermined structure.

GULABI

Girls sitting nearby muffled their laughter in the ends of their saris, hiding their faces so as not to be seen smiling. Gulabi began to sing into my tape recorder:

> Dono ne kiya tha pyaar magar
> mujhe yaad raha tu bhul gayi
> maine tere liye re jag chhodaa
> tu mujkho chhod chali
> Once we loved one another but
> I have remembered while you forgot
> For you, alas, I gave the world
> To me you gave lies

Gulabi liked to be taped and asked me to tape her singing more than once. She wrote her own songs, she said. I would not know it until later, but this song was not one of her own compositions. She sang in a shaky voice, but with complete earnestness. If she was aware of the smirking girls behind her, she did not let on. After finishing, she asked to hear the song played back.

It comes from a rather obscure 1969 movie called *Mahua*. (Though the song is well known, the source is not).[14] The plot of *Mahua* is simple and fantastical: A young man named Paramthesh is strolling around the grounds of a guesthouse on his wedding day. Upon arriving in a clearing, he hears hypnotizing *shehnai* (a reed instrument) music. Suddenly, a young woman appears before Paramthesh. He believes he has seen the woman before. She confirms his suspicion—they were together "in last birth"—just before he loses consciousness and begins to relive their previous life together. In this earlier incarnation, many years before, Mahua was the daughter of a priest on a feudal estate. The rajkumar of the estate, a Christian convert known throughout the film simply as "Rajkumar," sets his sights on Mahua, eventually killing her in a jealous rage. (She later comes back to life). Mahua, for her part, is in love with a young shehnai player named Palash (who is the same man as Paramthesh). Palash is also loved by another young woman, Tani, whom he saved from an attempted rape. Hearing of Mahua's impending Christian wedding, Tani swears to help Palash and Mahua wed. She is then killed defending Mahua from the rajkumar; Mahua subsequently kills the rajkumar to avenge Tani's death.

Midway through the film, Palash sings the song "*Dono ne kiya tha pyar*" to Mahua, who has died, as he cradles her head in his hands. Palash weeps and sings into Mahua's ear in an intensely romantic and intimate moment. Eventually Mahua wakes up and the couple is reunited.

Gulabi's own story does not echo this romantic tale. She is the mother of four children, two from her husband's prior marriage. Unlike most women in Shiv Nagar Basti, both Gulabi and her husband were married previously. Gulabi's first marriage, which lasted less than a year and a half, was to a young man who seemed fine at first and then turned out to have a very serious sickness. Gulabi's family felt that they had been duped and supported her in leaving this husband and making another match. By her own account, their new combined family got along well, and there was little conflict between stepchildren and stepmother; they thought of her as another mother.

Gulabi's second husband had a service job, like many other men in Shiv Nagar Basti, which afforded the family some measure of economic security. Yet there was one very large problem: Gulabi's husband was always drunk. In Gulabi's words, just as most people cannot live without water, so her husband cannot live without *sharab*, alcohol. Her account was confirmed by neighbors, who empathetically joked that he drinks alcohol for breakfast instead of tea and continues for twenty-four hours a day. Gulabi did not know what to do. Her husband manages to keep his job by showing up, signing in on the attendance register, and then leaving to get drunk. But he is not a useful or helpful mate. Her family, an older brother in particular, has tried to confront her husband and get him to change his ways, but this has had no visible effect on his behavior. What can she do? Even with a supportive maternal family, Gulabi has had to withstand two unhappy marriages—the second presumably because of the failure of the first.

Singing brings Gulabi comfort. Her rendition of "*Dono ne kiya tha pyar*," regardless of the judgment of her audience, expressed both heartbreak and the hope that even the most serious tragedy—death—could be overcome, even surmounted. It is worth noting that Gulabi's choice of "her" song puts her in the male position in the loving relationship between Palash and Mahua. Though the lyrics are passive (the singer has been forgotten and rejected), the act of singing makes Gulabi the agentive actor, whose love triumphs over the end of life.

There is more to her choice to consider, however. It is not incidental that *Mahua* is set in a tribal area, indexed by the presence of many Banjaras, including the only Banjara we meet, Tani, Mahua's rival for Palash's affections. The term itself refers to a flower that is often used by tribal groups to brew alcoholic beverages. In some ways, the film can be read as an allegory for the aggressive efforts to convert India's tribal groups to Christianity and the renegotiation of femininity that this entails. The rajkumar who pursues Mahua and eventually kills Tani is a Christian convert who augments his local authority with the trappings of a foreign religion, including an ornate church. Mahua herself is depicted as a rather idealized Hindu woman—the daughter of a *pujari*, whose integrity is protected in every way. Even if she does pursue a love marriage with Palash, this love is a love-through-multiple-births that gives it religious sanction. Tani is clearly "other" in her dress and demeanor— she is louder, more outgoing, and more overtly sexually aggressive. In the culmination of the film, with the murders of Tani and the rajkumar, however, it is clear that Tani is the heroine of the narrative. She is sacrificed, but is also the better woman because she gives herself to make Palash happy and support the natural dharmic order of things, foretold by the re-meeting of Palash and Mahua in their subsequent rebirths at the beginning of the film.

Thus, the film is about being able to preserve one's dignity in the face of external pressures. Cultural and sexual meanings become collapsed so that the preservation of Mahua's body for her love, Palash, also entails the preservation of tribal difference even if it is an ennobled difference. *Mahua* offers up the possibility of a modern Indian womanhood that embodies tribal qualities— bravery, independence, and self-possessed and devoted sexuality—but ultimately subsumes them into a larger Hindu-religious framing of respectability.

Gulabi's choice of song speaks to a similar relationship between cultural and intimate meanings. Her husband embodies long-held stereotypes of tribal peoples—that they are alcoholic and unreliable. The way for her to redeem her family for middle-class respectability is to both tolerate his behavior and maintain the marriage. Love, then, the fantastical possibility of its traversal across the time/space of lives and various incarnations, is very important. When Gulabi sings, she invokes the efficacy of that deep emotional register.

When Gulabi asks to be taped, does she actively recall the plot of *Mahua* and its delicate resolution of tribal and non-tribal femininity? It is possible, but doubtful. Rather, I would argue, the film is an index for history that flashes up in a moment of internal conflict. Its essence is that respectability cannot be judged by outcomes—whether or not one becomes the lucky, legitimate bride of Palash—but must be measured by the depth of feeling put into love.

SAPNA

The first time I met Sapna, my research assistant, Shally Vaish, and I were taken to her home by Ram Lal. He wanted me to meet her for several reasons. First, the basti in which she lived, which was a five-minute walk from

Shiv Nagar Basti, was, he said, a good likeness of what Shiv Nagar Basti had been twenty years earlier. Sapna's house, and the houses of her neighbors, were *kaccha*, built of mud brick and tarp, with small, narrow lanes and rudimentary sewers. It sat in the shadow of a Muslim holy site, near the cremation ground where the Dhanka *panchayat* often met. Its residents were not all Dhanka, though some were, but all were poor—noticeably poorer than their neighbors, the Dhanka and Dalits, of the abutting areas. I might have been skeptical of Ram Lal's narration—*This is just what our colony was like before*—as it reinforced a dramatic distance in space and time between these two bastis. And yet, I was also convinced: there were few televisions and radios like those found in Shiv Nagar Basti but more animals, as if this were a small corner of a rural village that had somehow been missed by the spread of the city. I could not help but think it is because it was so close to a site devoted to death. Polluted, before. *Before we got away from all of those associations. We were adivasis.*

Ram Lal also wanted me to meet Sapna because she was one of the widows that he said were most in need among members of the Dhanka Samaj. Sapna's husband had died in an accident several years earlier, leaving her with six children. The family was given temporary aid by the company her husband had worked for, but of Rs. 50,000, Rs. 15,000 went to a lawyer, and another sizable amount went for medical bills. Sapna was working as a cleaner in a school and hoping to get employment in another school closer to home to save on commuting costs. Ram Lal wanted me to see her plight, to help him think of things that might be done for women in such situations.[15] I regret that I was without particularly helpful ideas. Yes, a sewing cooperative would be good. Did anyone know how to sew? Was there some other kind of work that she could do? Ram Lal had clearly taken on the role of her benefactor, and when he mentioned that one of Sapna's daughters had recently been married in the samuhik vivaha, it was with obvious pride. The new bride had not yet shifted to her in-laws' place for the *gauna* (first sexual relation between husband and wife) and agreed that yes, the collective wedding had been a good idea and that she was very happy with her new situation.

Ram Lal and I departed after a time, making our way back home. It was one of the many moments in which I reflected upon my deep admiration for Ram Lal and other Dhanka elder men. He had improved the status of his own family, undoubtedly, but he did not forget about the others of his community and worked very hard to see that they were looked after. On our walk back to Shiv Nagar Basti, Ram Lal openly regretted that he couldn't do more for the graveyard residents who had to work as laborers because they were not educated like the residents of Shiv Nagar Basti.

I went to find Mona, who asked me where I had been. When I told her about our visit to Sapna, she said that there were rumors circulating about Sapna-ji's daughter. She was not home for a routine visit with her mother after all, but had fled an abusive husband and in-laws who were demanding more dowry. Mona used the word "torture" in English, and her own anxiety was palpable as she was only a few months from her own wedding. This report went against all the ideologies of samuhik vivaha, which was supposed to save women from the risk of rising dowry demands. Why didn't someone protect Sapna's daughter like they were supposed to? Why hadn't she told us, talked to Ram Lal about it during our visit? And what of Sapna who, with no status and protection, would be powerless to contest any marriage made for her daughter?

The next time I saw Sapna was several years later, during a visit to Jaipur. Ram Lal came and told me one day that she had been asking about me and wanted to see me. He and I retraced our earlier steps and arrived at Sapna's house, which had changed little on the exterior. On the interior, there were signs that things had improved for the family and less palpable anxiety about the future. Both Ram Lal and I were welcomed with exuberance, bellows of "Namaste, Tauji!" and "Namaste, Didi!" from the children. Sapna smiled. Yes, things had gotten better. She had a job as a sweeper in the nearby school now and made enough money for their survival. She was hoping to get a job in a factory eventually and bring in even more income. Sitting next to Sapna, I noticed new gold earrings of the kind that women wear especially when first married. They looked shiny and expensive. I realized what else had changed. Whether or not they had been sexually involved when I first met Sapna, it was clear that she and Ram Lal, who she still referred to as "Tauji," or "respected uncle," were lovers. When I quietly asked who gave the earrings to her, Sapna replied under her breath—and with a conspiratorial smile—"Tauji." Perhaps they had sanctified their relationship into some kind of permanent status— such practices are not unknown in Rajasthan and elsewhere—or perhaps not. I did not ask and she did not offer any information. What was clear was that Ram Lal's earlier sense of responsibility had grown. He was, in a sense, now the present-absent patriarch of the family, living nearby, visiting often, and yet, apart.

I visited Sapna once more during my time in Jaipur that winter, this time without Ram Lal. We chatted, the kids asked me about the United States. We never talked explicitly about her relationship to Ram Lal, but things between us had changed, a new level of familiarity had been reached. Was it because Ram Lal had told her about my own divorce and plans to marry again? I will never know. What was also clear, however, was that Sapna would probably never come visit me, or Ram Lal, in Shiv Nagar Basti. There was an invisible barrier that corresponded to the visible walls of the Dalit basti between her neighborhood and Ram Lal's, which would keep her from associating with his other female relatives, his daughters, daughters-in-law, sisters, and sisters-in-law. But this did not mean that Ram Lal's family did not know about Sapna. His eldest daughter-in-law asked me upon my return from visiting Sapna where I had gone. When I told her, she sucked in her lips a bit and got a quiet look. "How are they?" she asked gently, without malice, yet obviously curious.

Several days later, I came upon Ram Lal hosting several men who were obviously dressed in their best clothes. All were smoking bidis and drinking chai. "Meghnabai, come meet our guests from Gujarat!" he called. I entered the room and greeted everyone. Ram Lal was hosting these men because they were the relatives of a prospective groom for another of Sapna's daughters who would be married in samuhik vivaha that year. He told me it was his duty to take care of her and make sure she was settled. Later, I asked how old Sapna's daughter was. The answer: thirteen. By now comfortable enough with Ram Lal to argue, I demanded of him "Why are you marrying her? She's way too young." He responded that in her case, it was really the best thing for her. I do not know whether or not she was married that year.

The affection between Sapna and Ram Lal was obvious. They cared for one another, liked joking in each other's company, and clearly had a multidimensional, intimate relationship. Theirs was, I think, a collaborative project of respectability-building, one they both enjoyed. Recall that Ram Lal is one of the most prominent Dhanka men in the region—not only in Jaipur, but in Rajasthan as a whole. As a symbol of the possibilities of upward mobility, never too proud to tell people that he was a "third class fail," he is a community member who sets and interprets group norms. On one hand, this means that as a widower who still wants to have an intimate relationship with a woman, he must stay within accepted bounds of respectability himself. On the other hand, his choices also define what will be seen as respectable. Sapna is treated in many ways like a wife and in others like a widow. She is therefore a good woman on both accounts. Yet the hierarchies of gender and class are maintained between Ram Lal and Sapna. Women in Shiv Nagar Basti do not openly disapprove of Sapna—at least not to me—but they do not invite her into their homes either.

Sapna's case is an illustration of the fragile but often quite successful ways in which women and men negotiate group norms. Her ease and comfort with her community standing and her relationship with Ram Lal flies in the face of a simple Sanskritization narrative that might see this relationship as one more instance of the assertion of patriarchal authority: sexual access by a man of higher standing to a woman who has no choice. From another perspective, Sapna's ability to be both wife and widow is a position of strength, not a patriarchal bind. It is telling that perhaps the most public aspect of their relationship is Ram Lal's adoption of a fatherly role in the relationship to her daughters' weddings. Here his personal and public life seems to merge, but for Sapna, his commitment to her daughters' marriages is essential to not only her own respectability, but potentially her daughters' respectability in their own married lives.

Gender and Aspiration

All three of the examples discussed above gesture toward the importance of men's livelihoods for women's respectability. Richa feels domestically and socially compromised because her husband cannot convert his temporary, contract work with the government into a steady position. Gulabi can make ends meet because her husband is still able to show up to work to sign the attendance log, but her respectability comes from getting by under difficult circumstances, not from her family being especially "good." Sapna has had to cobble together several domestic strategies to survive without male economic support and in such a way that her respectability is maintained on a daily basis; the fact that she never visits Shiv Nagar Basti is perhaps as much her own choice as that of Ram Lal and his relatives. In all three cases, too, we see Dhanka relying on reservations and government service for their livelihood: government jobs are sought and coveted for both their economic and cultural resources. What men do or do not do in these arenas affects women. Aspiration needs the concrete of steady employment.

But seen from another perspective, the emotional work that women do to maintain their respectability in the face of hardship is also integral to Dhanka collective aspiration. If in an earlier era Dhanka women were more explicitly countering stereotypes about free and promiscuous tribal women by shoring up the domestic domain, today they are continuing this work but without the same guarantees for either upward mobility or social uplift. While narrations of samuhik vivaha, including my own, have thus far implied that the impetus for this arrangement comes from men, it is equally as likely that samuhik vivaha has been chosen and embraced because it also relies on the skilled cultivation of an orientation that is at once intimate and engaged in community uplift—an orientation that Dhanka women have developed over the past century.

Another way of making this point is to say that it is impossible for one gender to do the work of collective aspiration. Dhanka men and women have been waging a bet together in Jaipur City that investment in a particular kind of group life—a statist ST identity, an adivasi past, government jobs, properly arranged intimate relations—will yield something tangible: the protection of concrete. It takes a great deal of effort to maintain this dream.

A Traffic in Marriage

The first wedding I attended in Shiv Nagar Basti was for the large pipal tree in the corner of the temple courtyard.[1] It is a lovely tree, with a strong, white trunk and broad leaves. Throughout north India, pipal trees are revered for the shade they provide, which is thought to be especially protective. They are also symbols of conjugal love and happiness (Upadhyaya 1964). It is not uncommon for women to be married to trees to counteract an inauspicious astrological chart predicting early widowhood or multiple marriages. Nor is it uncommon for trees taken as daughters to be married to ritual grooms as a symbolic commitment to their ongoing care. Shiv Nagar Basti's *pipli ki shaadi* ("wedding of the pipal tree") was of this latter kind, with the pipal tree as bride. Trees and daughters seem to go together in Rajasthan, each capturing something of the joys and sorrows of the other: rooted in the familiar place of birth but vulnerable to forces beyond their control.[2] Daughters leave for destinations where they can no longer be sheltered; trees need cultivation and regular maintenance. Both belong to a place but cannot last without protection and care.[3]

This pipli ki shaadi was sponsored by Ram Lal, who had taken the basti's pipal tree as his daughter. Since she had grown up to full maturity, he told me, it was time to do the right thing and marry her off properly. The ritual would declare Ram Lal's dedication to the well-being of the tree, his commitment to taking care of this valuable resource in the future. There would be many guests attending and a *pandit* ("priest") was called for the occasion. If it was unusual for a Scheduled Tribe to host such a ritual, no one commented on it. One older man explained the ceremony to me as a form of "environmentalism," using the term in English.

The women of Shiv Nagar Basti began singing songs, as they would for any other woman's marriage, sitting in the alley, faces veiled. The song's lyrics

(*What will my new husband be like?*) were slightly odd and strangely moving when being sung for a large old tree. As was often the case, the songs were led by Uma, Ram Lal's sister, who still lives in a rural village outside Jaipur, where she keeps goats. Uma was always called for such events, in part because she seemed to know more about the proper execution of rituals than other women in the basti and in part because she held a position of honor in such ceremonies simply by virtue of being Ram Lal's sister. When singing died down, Uma would begin again in a loud voice, encouraging other women to sing. Eventually, the bride's party, led by Ram Lal's human daughter, began the procession to the *mandir* ("temple") grounds carrying the water pots, neem leaves, and drums typical of Rajasthani weddings.[4]

Having not known that the ritual would take place on this particular day, I had not brought a camera. I have no pictures of the bride, which at the time I regretted. I wanted to remember her. She was both sweet and haunting, with pink and red *dupattas* ("scarves") spread from her branches and a basket for her head. The weave of her face was demurely framed in yellow. She was fragile, a bit funny, and immediately compelling.

It was then time for the arrival of the groom, whose procession included wildly dancing little boys and a brass band. The groom, seated on a small dais covered in yellow cloth, was represented by a series of slightly disassembled signs: a coconut, garlands, a brass bell, a miniature turban, and many flowers. The priest, a dedicated smoker, sat under the tree puffing on bidis, while elder men from the crowd came forward to present the gifts. The bride's gifts were given to Ram Lal's relatives, with the greatest share going to his daughter-in-law, Nirmala. These included saris and *lehngas* (skirt and blouse; traditional rural Rajasthani dress for women) and, I suspect, jewelry, though the jewelry that had been shown around earlier as part of the dowry was not publicly presented. After the gift distribution, the priest began his prayers over the couple on the loudspeaker. Nirmala and her husband, Ram Lal's eldest son, were called forward to also, it seemed, stand in for the pipal tree and her coconut groom. At the end of the puja, they circled the tree together in a manner similar to the circumambulation of a wedding fire and wrapped her with blessed thread.

After the ceremony, vast amounts of food were served to all the guests present. Mona turned to me several times and said "lots of guests, no?" to which I readily agreed. There was a large crowd gathered in Shiv Nagar Basti. It occurred to me, then, that all day people had been calling the attendees "guests" in English.

✱

In some ways, I want to make a very simple point in this chapter: we cannot presume that we know what marriage is or does. Without sustained attention to its specific forms and histories, as well as the kinds of attachments it makes possible, we cannot know what any social formation, including marriage and family, is about. Marriage is not only the exchange of women; the control of women's reproduction; the nexus of state, community, and familial patriarchy for the preservation of private property; the social institution necessary for capitalism; or the public assertion of compulsory heterosexuality, any more than it is the coming together of two souls joined to one another by kismet. Marriage can work as one or many aspects of each of these now-classic explanations for its existence. One of the weaknesses of most approaches to marriage (and perhaps the cause of the fatigue with the topic found in anthropology and feminist theorizing) is an implicit functionalism and universalism—including the colonial anthropological common sense that marriage is a good place to see culture at work[5]—that has carried over into feminist analysis. Surely marriage does things besides either sanction reproductive couplings or publicly acknowledge "private" emotions. But what this is varies widely across time and space. It is as if even in our critiques we are seduced by the rhetoric of modern marriage that proclaims it a social institution, and therefore bounded, obvious, and knowable. We "know" marriage before we begin. Yet, it is the flexibility of marriage, rather than its permanence as an institution or tradition, that makes it such a generative social formation. Here is a transfer point for myriad relationships and kinds of relationality, all brought to the scale of the intimate. Marriages draw insides and outsides—how these are drawn and to what end is an ethnographic question.

In this chapter, I consider the emergence of collective weddings, in which multiple brides and grooms are married in a single ceremony, among the Dhanka in Rajasthan since the year 2001. I opened my discussion with a description of Ram Lal's pipli ki shaadi because I think it raises many of the issues that I will explore below. It would be very difficult to say definitively what the pipli ki shaadi was about. Several explanations were explicitly and implicitly suggested by participants: the protection of a beloved resource and daughter, environmental stewardship, the expression of Ram Lal's status as the wealthiest and most respected man in Shiv Nagar Basti, the dedication of resources and public affection to his daughters and daughter-in-law, and community building through collective celebration and feasting. Any one of these might be highlighted as the real explanation for the pipli ki shaadi, yet none is, on its own, sufficient to represent the density and complexity of this small community event.

And so it is with other Dhanka marriages. While most Dhanka couples are now married in private ceremonies arranged by parents and involving

dowry given to a groom and his family (the form of marriage that remains
the community ideal), since 2001 the annual *Dhanka Samaj Samuhik Vivaha
Sammelan* ("The Collective Wedding Festival of the Dhanka Samaj," often referred to simply as the "sammelan") has become a centerpiece of community
identity and organizing. The samuhik vivaha sammelan is tied to issues I have
raised throughout the previous chapters: tribal identity, collective aspiration,
intragroup politics, and intimate gender relations, yet it cannot be reduced
to any of these. Rather, in this chapter, I suggest several different meanings of
samuhik vivaha that emerge independently and reinforce one another. I show
that these annual events allow the Dhanka of Jaipur to do several things at
once, in a heavily saturated symbolic environment: demonstrate their electoral relevance by convening a large gathering of tribe-mates and attracting
the attention of political leaders and parties, especially the Congress Party;
boldly embody Dhanka men's willingness to undertake community service
in the interest of group uplift; distribute literature describing Dhanka history and culture, such as the *Smarika* referred to in previous chapters; and
prove Dhanka difference (their tribalness) from caste Hindus in their superior treatment of girls and women, while at the same time controlling girls'
choices about their movement and future.

This last point is extremely important because the dominant rhetoric of
samuhik vivaha is that it is a community service undertaken for the benefit
of girls and their families who might be harassed for impossible dowry payments or, without access to sufficient funds, be unable to marry. Yet the event
itself—from the selection and matching of couples to the collection of community contributions—is organized by an entirely male wedding committee.
It is arguable that the political benefits of the sammelan accrue to Dhanka
men since it is their right to, and need for, special benefits that are reinforced
in public enactments of identity. There is, then, a traffic in marriage, as couples (particularly women) are ideologically central to forms of affiliation and
claim-making but are themselves kept outside the social relations that determine their futures.

My intention, however, is not simply to blame Dhanka men for using
Dhanka women for their own benefit—to unmask patriarchy at work. The
majority of Dhanka women are supportive of samuhik vivaha and accept it
as an important centerpiece of Dhanka culture, despite its rather recent ap-
pearance. I do not want to repeat the mistakes of the traffic in marriage debates, from which my argument obviously draws material and inspiration,
by positing either wholly oppressed or entirely free women or men. Surely
I do not argue that Dhanka women are, as Marilyn Strathern put it "always
the objects of others' transactions" or, on the contrary, free to act as "subjects

or agents" (1988, 331). Rather, I want to argue that the specific ethno-legal construction of Scheduled Tribe communities and the vagaries of Rajasthani caste politics have created a situation in which marriage is *necessarily* the site of community articulation and consolidation.

Dhanka men do not control the terms of the traffic in marriage of which they are a part; they have adapted quickly and effectively to the social and political changes arising from the erosion of reservation benefits. Dhanka men did not choose marriage as the site of their community agency in any simple sense, but it has become the site in which they work on the ongoing project of collective aspiration. In samuhik vivaha, then, we can see the double bind of *jati* ("caste"; see also A Short Glossary) and gender as it plays out for this urban tribal group: as subaltern men, Dhanka men feel compelled to protect and shore up their control over women in order to establish and mark the boundaries of community. The ability to do so is read as success—by both women and men—because it confers dignity and status on the group as a whole (see Gupta 2010). Thus, there is not a simple ground from which to stage a feminist argument about samuhik vivaha sammelan. I choose, rather, to put this practice in historical context and unpack its many meanings to convey its complex and sometimes contradictory role in contemporary Dhanka life.

Why Collective Marriage?

To begin to understand why samuhik vivaha has become the most important and visible site for the consolidation and articulation of Dhanka identity, we might start by considering the way that marriage has figured into the construction of "community" in postcolonial India. Such constructions demand particular understandings of—and practices to recreate—the proper arrangement of marriage, which is seen to determine the quality and sanctity of a group's ethno-legal life. From debates about the Hindu Code Bill in the 1950s to the public furor over the Shah Bano case in the mid-1980s, it is clear that the ability to control women and their marriages is seen as essential to community identity.[6] Efforts to reform the religiously based personal laws that govern every Indian citizen in matters pertaining to family life (marriage, divorce, inheritance, and so on) are repeatedly met with resistance based on the argument that such reforms contradict ancient religious tenets and violate a group's right to its own sacred cultural practices. Family practices, and especially marriage, are seen as a terrain into which the state should not tread as they are the proper domain of the community; feminist arguments against discriminatory personal laws are thus frequently met with the charge that they are a result of "Westernized" thinking.

Nowhere has a community's right to legislate marriage and family life been more strongly articulated than in Rajasthan, where debates about the immolation of widows (often referred to as "sati") have starkly divided public opinion and provoked widespread feminist protest. These conflicts have in fact been most pronounced in the immediate environs of Jaipur, where most of the modern cases of widow immolation have occurred.[7] The Rajput communities in which widow immolations have taken place have repeatedly asserted their right to venerate satis as embodiments of a noble, martial strength and loyalty; they also argue that support for a voluntary sati is a religious act and should not be subject to criminal law—though few, if any, witnesses to immolations ever come forward for fear of being prosecuted as abetting in suicide.[8] Such ideological weight on marriage has created a situation in which there is arguably no other social phenomenon that has the potential to impact a group's public recognition as a rights-bearing group in the state.

Equally important for understanding why collective weddings have emerged as a centerpiece of Dhanka social life is the history of subaltern reform movements that have focused on marriage practices. Unlike upper-caste reforms, which centered on greater permissiveness in marriage—for instance, allowing widow remarriage or raising the age of consent (see examples in Sarkar and Sarkar 2008)—subaltern efforts for internal reform often involved more restrictive, Hinduized marriages as part of a total alteration of society (other common themes have been teetotalism, vegetarianism, and the observance of Hindu ritual; see Chapter 2).

The reform of marriage practices has been a frequent theme of adivasi-empowerment movements since at least the nineteenth century. This is likely because the difference of tribal gender and marriage arrangements was one of the defining markers of tribe versus caste, as we saw in the previous chapter. To be "less" tribal, marriage reform is a good place to start. Such reforms have often been read in the social science literature as indicative of a process of Sanskritization. As I previously noted, Srinivas argues that "the institutions of the 'low' castes are more liberal in the spheres of marriage and sex than those of the Brahmins. Post-puberty marriages do occur among them, widows do not have to shave their heads, and divorce and widow remarriage are both permitted and practiced. In general, their sex code is not as harsh towards women as that of the top castes, especially Brahmins. But as a caste rises in the hierarchy and its ways become more Sanskritized, it adopts the sex and marriage code of the Brahmins. *Sanskritization results in harshness towards women*" (1962, 46; emphasis added). A common theme of such arguments is certainly that adivasi women lose out in this tradeoff, with their freedoms sacrificed in the name of upward mobility. In his reading of the early twentieth-century ethnography of the Bhils across western India, for instance, Robert Deliège argues that there is a clear pattern of hierarchization that takes place within formerly egalitarian tribal marriages and that this has unfortunate consequences for Bhil women: "The submission of wives to their husbands is the cost of status improvement paid by Bhil women" (1985, 157).

While I have already noted that it does appear that Dhanka women have probably lost some of their rights in choice of marriage partner, divorce, and other arrangements of intimate life, it would be too simple to read all changing marriage practices as Sanskritization. The array of Dhanka marriage practices today not only references reform movements demanding more Hinduized marriages but also a history of resistance and assertion. Marriage has also figured centrally in subaltern critiques of upper-caste domination. This is because endogamy—the strict exhortation to only marry within socially specified groups—has been identified as a key element in the perpetuation of caste inequality. The operation of endogamy was a central insight of Dalit leaders in the early twentieth century. B. R. Ambedkar, India's first law minister and author of the Constitution, for instance, saw endogamy as the central way in which caste "purity" was maintained. As Anupama Rao puts it, "Marriage was a hinge, articulating the social and sexual orders, but it also regulated sexuality through caste norms" (2009, 232; see also Ambedkar 2013).[9] Ambedkar argued vociferously for the importance of gender equality and intercaste marriage in any project of social justice for Dalits, declaring in 1951 that the Hindu Code Bill, which attempted to reform many aspects of marriage, divorce, and inheritance, was "the greatest social reform measure ever undertaken by the Legislature in this country" (quoted in Pandey 2013, 68).[10]

Closer to the regional and historical provenance of the Dhanka of Jaipur, the famous Bhagat Govind Giri espoused a message of reform that had a critique of the upper-caste treatment of women at its heart and argued that adivasi marriage practices were much better for women.[11] Historian Vijay Kumar Vashishtha argues that Govind Giri "infused confidence among his followers by encouraging them to consider themselves as equal to the upper-caste Hindus and even higher on account of the flexibility of marriage customs among them" (1997, 24). In this vein, Govind Giri harshly criticized Brahmins, Banias, and Rajputs for forbidding widow remarriage and practicing female infanticide. He thus sought to undermine their hegemony and symbolic power in the region.

It is difficult to know what Dhanka marriages were like prior to the twentieth century, making a historical shift from one kind of marriage to another

almost impossible to trace.[12] The turmoil created for the Bhil and its subcom-
munities by the famine of 1899, including widespread migration, as well as
the proliferation of reform movements connected to local *bhagats* ("ascetics"
or "the religiously devout"), make it likely that within any given community
there were segments practicing different kinds of marriages, a situation that
continues today. As noted in Chapter 2, the Dhanka were rarely considered
worth ethnographic description themselves, being a low and stigmatized section of an already stigmatized tribal group.

If we look at ethnographic accounts of Bhil marriage, we find that there
were several different marriage practices in the past. R. E. Enthoven's 1920
The Tribes and Castes of Bombay, for instance, reports that marriages were
arranged by relatives, with the groom's family seeking out the bride's, and
bride-price paid to the girl's family. But he also records that in Mahi Kantha
Bhil women chose their own husbands, while at Tosina it was common for
men to take their brides by capture ([1920] 1975, 160). K. D. Erskine (1908)
also describes marriage by elopement and panchayat settlement in Rajputana
in addition to arranged marriages with bride-price. He further remarks that
while bride-price in Udaipur was paid to the bride's family, in Jodhpur the
bride-price was paid to the local ruler (239). By the time of Deliège's review
of the literature, there are a multiplicity of marriage forms recorded, including sororate, levirate, cross-cousin, arranged with bride-price, arranged with
dowry, elopement, civil (i.e., presided over by community), or conducted by
a Brahmin priest (1985).

In a similar way, several different options were available to the Dhanka
by the 1960s. While P. G. Shah records the prevalence of bride-price paid by
grooms themselves to the father of their chosen bride, he notes the increasing
cost and growing size of Dhanka weddings starting in the 1930s as well as a
shift toward employing Brahmin priests which, he notes, also tends to bring
down the age at marriage (1964, 32–38). However, love marriages through
elopement were reportedly not rare. At the same time, Shah describes the following intriguing development

> The group solidarity and sense of unity [among the Dhanka] is now growing,
> and the tribal families of certain villages combine and regulate the marriage
> date en masse. The new practice is to fix three or four common dates of mar-
> riage throughout all the villages and their priests meet and fix a number of
> suitable dates for the wedding of all the members of that village. . . . There is a
> growing sense of solidarity and faith in the leaders who fix the dates; and also
> a confidence in the priests who select the dates and whose skill is supposed
> to ward off all evils. . . . The transition is, however, slow and partial, with the
> result that both the old and new systems are in force simultaneously. The old

social structure is slowly adjusting itself to the new ideas and a new transition is observable. This change is evidently based on the mutual convenience
of the priest and of the community, who are saved the time and expenses of
individual feasts, and who are satisfied with a single common dinner for each
group or village. (1964, 133)

Is this an indication that samuhik vivaha or some precursor of the sammelan
was already in practice in Gujarat in the 1960s? It seems possible, though
none of my informants explicitly made this historical connection. In their
telling, the samuhik vivaha was a very recent undertaking of the Dhanka.
What is interesting is that Shah records several possible forms of marriage
being available to the Dhanka in the mid-twentieth century and that the "new"
form is clearly marked as an improvement on the earlier forms. Shah's description foreshadows the message of social service that has become deeply em-
bedded in the annual samuhik vivaha sammelan: the collective marriages are
convenient and save the Dhanka time and expense. There is also the intimation that these collective weddings signal a growing conservatism and austerity in marriage practices and as such represent a positive development for the
tribe. The "regulation of dates of mass marriage" is thus described in a chapter
on cultural change. In other words, changes in marriage practices are taken
to signal aspiration, but they are not a means to individual upward mobility;
Dhanka aspiration as demonstrated in mass marriages is decidedly collective.

The Dhanka Samaj Samuhik Vivaha Sammelan

2003. February morning in Shiv Nagar Basti, outside the walled city of Old
Jaipur. There is a charge in the air—the morning routine is broken today.
Garbage trucks are scooping up the trash that usually sits at the northwest
entrance to the basti, where I arrive, crossing the yard of the nearby Blessed
Mana Convent School, sending the pigs into wild screams and retreat. People
are out in the alleys, where webs of silver and gold tinsel strung from balcony to balcony create a festive canopy for the neighborhood. There are more
men in the alleys than usual at this hour; they have taken the day off from
work or from looking for work. I arrive at the home of my friends, Mona and
Kanika Solanki, where the morning meal has just ended. I am especially fond
of Mona, who is mature beyond her age, several years younger than my
own. She and her younger sister, Kanika, a much more tempestuous young
woman, are charging around their two-story brick-and-cement home, trying to rush through morning chores like washing dishes and dressing themselves for today's special occasion. There is a great flurry of pastel shawls and

FIGURE 3. Garlanding newly elected members of the Samuhik Vivaha *Sammelan Samiti*. *Photo by author.*

FIGURE 4. The grooms' parties prepare to depart Shiv Nagar Basti in 2003. *Photo by author.*

FIGURE 5. A groom in 2003. *Photo by author.*

FIGURE 6. The brides of 2003. *Photo by author.*

FIGURE 7. The stage at samuhik vivaha. At the end of the day, it will become the site for political speeches. *Photo by author.*

trading of clothing before each young woman is happy with her outfit. I sit and watch the chaos, occasionally offering an opinion about a color choice or helping to braid someone's hair, with my shoulder bag—camera, notebook—in my lap. Today is samuhik vivaha, the Dhanka collective wedding.

The horses begin to arrive. Shiv Nagar Basti is the grooms' side today, and the horses for the wedding procession will depart from the basti. They are white, pure white, with fancy costumes and calm demeanors. Seventeen grooms arrive, one by one. They are all dressed in the same white tunic and pants, the same red turban, each one with a number from one to seventeen pinned to their chests. They all carry a plastic sword, and the lucky ones wear garlands of Rs. 10 bills. Mona and Kanika are proud of the grooms and point out all the important details. "*Look, they're old. [Or very poor.]*" "*That groom over there, see his leg, he has polio.*" All these boys will get married today. We are happy for them. A brass band arrives, and the drummer, and soon everyone is dancing in the alleys. There is suddenly a big crowd—the grooms' female relatives are dancing, laughing, asking for photos. The drum rhythms are booming, expansive. They pick the crowd up and carry it into the street, where the procession winds through the back lanes of the middle-class colonies of Jaipur City that lie to the south of Shiv Nagar Basti. We walk for an hour and then arrive at the Daessera Maidan, a civic fairground of sorts where every year *Ram Lila* is played and enormous demon Ravanas are burnt to the delight of the Hindu crowds.[13]

Today instead of one towering blaze there are seventeen separate fires and marriage tents erected on the grounds, each labeled with a number so that the proper bride and groom can be seated for their ceremony. The colors are bright red and yellow, vibrant blue and green. Colors of good luck, auspicious beginnings. There are seventeen pandits, Brahmins, marrying tribals who a generation earlier were not even allowed to worship in temples. There are seventeen dowries laid out for inspection: beds, linens, cooking pots, clothing, jewelry. All the dowries are the same. Each couple will leave with identical tools to set up a life together, for which the family of each bride and each groom paid Rs. 4,500. The rest of the money for the dowry and the priests came from community donations; each Dhanka family is expected to donate what they can every other year. The collective wedding, the samuhik vivaha, is seen as a social service. The organizers assure everyone that these seventeen girls will not be harassed or abused by in-laws demanding that they bring more dowry than their families can afford. The boys will not make ever-increasing demands for dowry because the eyes of the entire community are on them. Families do not have to worry about going into irredeemable debt to marry their daughters.

We join the others working at the event. Mona and Kanika grab ladles and begin to dish out hot potatoes and fried bread to the hundreds of women seated in the women's tent for the wedding feast. I am whisked over to the expectant brides to take pictures: seventeen young faces. Meanwhile, the men of the Dhanka Samaj Samuhik Vivaha Samiti, the community leaders and organizers, have gathered on a stage erected for the event in lecture-hall style.[14] They make impromptu speeches about the future of the tribe and the benefit of collective marriage for everyone's development. The purpose of the speeches is clear: Samuhik vivaha communicates important aspects of who the Dhanka are. It tells the Dhanka who they are becoming. It shows that the Dhanka are modern and no longer backward. It shows that they are taking state messages to heart, marrying girls at the legal age and rejecting the burden of dowry. It shows that they can take responsibility for themselves and not rely on government to do things for them. It is "self help" and welfare blended skillfully in an effective ritual. The men on stage read off the names of this year's donors. They call out the couples' numbers and "match" them, sending them to their respective wedding fires where the priests preside. Afterwards, the community leaders speak to the couples, exhorting them to work for the benefit of their people, their tribe, their samaj. The marriages are complete, but we in the crowd of several thousand are still waiting for the event's important finale.

In the late afternoon, a cavalcade of white Ambassador cars pull up at the entrance to the fairground. A Dhanka Member of the Legislative Assembly, Kuldip Indora, and his son, dressed in the white cotton of north Indian politicians, arrive and are channeled through the crowd to the stage. They are what we have been waiting for. The crowd, dispersed in its various activities celebrating the marriages, eating, or visiting with relatives, gathers into straight rows to hear their speeches. The politicians wear the green, white, and saffron badges of the Congress Party, and I notice that the men on stage are wearing them as well. The speeches are passionate: "We must work for the development of the Dhanka Samaj!" "This samuhik vivaha is of great benefit to our people!" The son, the more gifted orator of the two, works the crowd into a chant for his father, "Jai Kuldip Indora!" The futures of the brides and grooms, those least fortunate of the community and today's beneficiaries, are linked to the future of the whole. Dhanka development, Dhanka futures.

The Emergence of Samuhik Vivaha

An ideal Dhanka marriage follows a familiar ritual sequence for weddings among Rajput-influenced segments of north India. Extended male relatives begin to look for suitable brides and grooms when girls reach the age of about sixteen and boys eighteen or nineteen.[15] Boys and girls do not meet each other before they are married, but they are sometimes allowed to talk on the phone and carry pictures of one another—posed studio shots that are arranged with great care, modeled on film heroes and heroines. The bride and groom are formally engaged when the male relatives of the boy are received and fed at the home of the girl. The girl is presented with jewelry, dressed in fancy clothing, and "shown" to the boy's relatives. If both sides agree, the match is blessed by a Brahmin priest and gifts are sent with the groom's party for the boy. Several weeks to months later, the actual wedding will include a *mahila sangeet* ("women's ritual singing"), the arrival of the *barat* ("groom's procession") and subsequent *pheria* ("circumambulating the marriage fire") at the girl's home, and a *vidhai* ("farewell") ceremony for the girl the next morning. Dowry items are displayed during this last ritual.

Individual weddings, with dowry given to the groom and his family by the bride's father, remain the preferred form of marriage among the Dhanka community. If a family has the means, they would much rather marry daughters off themselves, without outside intervention. At present, however, an individual wedding usually costs between Rs. 100,000 and Rs. 200,000. In an area where the average monthly family income is around Rs. 3,000, this represents a huge outlay of money—much of it borrowed—for any family. In local accounts, collective weddings were initiated to help families deal with the rising costs of marriage by transferring the financial burden to the community and to protect girls and their families from rising dowry demands and possible violence.

The Dhanka Samaj's annual samuhik vivaha sammelan began in 2001 and has been held every year since sometime in the spring months from February until May. Major decisions about the event, including its date, are determined by the Samuhik Vivaha Samiti ("Collective Wedding Committee"). Though attendees at the event include Dhanka from all over Rajasthan and as far away as Gujarat, the event is always held in Jaipur; the Samiti members are always Jaipuri Dhanka, and men from Shiv Nagar Basti are especially visible in the activities. All Samiti members are men, though some women do take on important roles in the event planning (particularly around the food to be served to thousands of attendees). Elections for Samiti officials are held several months prior to the event. Elections represent a chance for new volunteers to step forward to take up leadership roles, but in general the outcome is already given: Ram Lal Solanki is nearly always named the committee president (adhyaksh), with important supporting roles going to other prominent Shiv Nagar Basti men, including Ramesh Moriya and the pujari, Kaluram Dabi. Even though the results are somewhat prearranged, a secret vote is still taken. Samiti officials are garlanded in a special ceremony, in a manner reminiscent of many political occasions, as a sign of esteem and respect and also to mark the officials' commitment to the constituents they serve.

Funds for the samuhik vivaha are collected from the wider community before and during the event. Each Dhanka household is expected to give at least once in three years; individual donation amounts are recorded by the Samiti and also announced during the wedding. Monies are also collected from each bride and groom's family in order to participate. The amount has increased a bit over the years, but in 2003, the year I attended, the cost to each family was Rs. 4,500. These fees, along with the donations, go to paying for the ceremony itself, which necessitates rented tents, chairs, and loudspeakers; the priests who attend to each wedding fire; the food for thousands of guests, served in multiple, gender-segregated seatings throughout the day; and the items presented as gifts to each couple: a bed, pots and pans, some clothing, and a small amount of jewelry.

It is this last category that draws the most comment and praise. Samiti members and the Dhanka community at large are quick to point out that the real benefit of samuhik vivaha is that families do not have to go into great debt to pay dowry for their daughters. Girls who are being married in the collective ceremonies, it is said, will be safe from the kinds of harassment that have begun to plague other poor communities who have taken up dowry practices. And while the focus of the committee is clearly on the well-being of girls, it also implicitly acknowledges the costs and difficulties that face some grooms' families as well. There are expenses for both sides in a typical Rajasthani wedding, and these cannot be borne by poor boys' families any more than girls'.

Samuhik vivaha is meant, then, for the poorest of the poor—those Dhanka who cannot get married in solitary ceremonies either because of poverty or, in some cases, because of physical conditions or age. For instance, in 2003, one of the grooms had suffered from polio as a child; one of the brides was considered well beyond proper marriageable age. Girls and boys are put forward as volunteers by their families, and the ideology of the events proclaim them entirely voluntary. In practice, Ram Lal and other committee members are known to approach particular families, particularly girls' families, and encourage them to participate, arguing that it will be the best thing for the girls since the families have few other options, as well as the best thing for the community because it discourages wasteful spending.

Samiti rules (see rule four below) state that girls and boys must be of legal marriageable age and provide proof of this age in the form of official documents. The reference to age is an extremely important gesture, for it is quite clear that not all of the participants are, in fact, of legal marriageable age, which was set in the Hindu Marriage Act of 1955 as eighteen for girls and twenty-one for boys. The explicit demand for age verification, however, shows that the Dhanka, unlike other caste groups in Rajasthan, respect the law and do not marry off their girls as children. This distinction communicates the worthiness of Dhanka as recipients of the largesse of the state, proclaiming their allegiance to legal, modern practices as I discuss below. Whether these age restrictions are observed in practice matters less than the way in which the rule acknowledges a broader context in which other, more powerful, communities such as Rajputs and Gujjars are often portrayed in the media and elsewhere as non-modern and retrograde because they marry their girls too early.

Samiti members are clear that the gifts given to the couples are not a dowry per se but a gesture of goodwill from the community to help poor young people set up household properly, even if they tend to be seen as gifts to the girls. As one Samiti member told me, the jewelry, linens, and kitchen items are given to the brides so they can "go and set up home anywhere."

It does not appear that the Dhanka of Rajasthan practiced samuhik vivaha prior to 2001, though residents may have been familiar with the practice via Gujarati family members. It is also not clear if it descended directly from the practice referenced by Shah, or if it is more closely related to the recent rise of mass marriages among many groups, from Sikhs to Rashtriya Swayamsevak Sangh members. Residents of Shiv Nagar Basti from the era of service (in their forties and fifties now) reported celebrating simple weddings that, while not without dowry, used money as mostly symbolic tokens. Marriages were arranged by parents, and prospective grooms and brides were allowed to see each other, if not officially "meet" before the ceremony. Women were given jewelry by their parents, but, again, the value of this gesture in monetary terms was not stressed by the Dhanka women and men I spoke to, in contrast to their description of weddings and dowries today.

Samuhik Vivaha Rules:

1. Please send biodata and an application for the son or daughter you want to marry by December 31, 2003.
2. If the marriage has already been arranged, then please send a registration letter up to January 20, 2003.
3. You must pay Rs. 500 for the registration letter and the remaining Rs. 4,000 before the date given.
4. The groom must be 21 years old and the bride must be 18 years old and a birth certificate must be submitted. Age certificate, school or college certificate, father/mother/guardian's sworn statement must be given.
5. Yellow rice, milled rice should be placed at your residence.
6. All wedding rituals, such as the *torun*, *siyala*, *pheria*, and *vidai*, will be done in a manner conforming to custom.
7. The marriage will be held in the afternoon, the horse and band will be managed by the Samiti.
8. All grooms should be dressed the same. *Shervani, churidar pajama, safar,* etc. will be managed by the Samiti.
9. All the gifts, jewelry, etc., are given to the groom by the Samiti.
10. Wedding guests will let the groom's relatives lead the way.
11. All alcoholic drinks are completely banned.
12. The Samiti will make all food etc. arrangements for those who come from outside Jaipur

Marriage for the Samaj

I now turn to the political effects of the samuhik vivaha sammelan, which include demonstrating Dhanka electoral relevance and making links with political parties, communicating male willingness, distributing written literature on the history and culture of the samaj, and showing that the tribal difference of the Dhanka lies in part in their superior treatment of girls and women compared to upper castes in Rajasthan—while at the same time maintaining control over girls' marriage arrangements and imaginations of their possible futures. None of the meanings described below should be taken as the singular explanation for Dhanka collective weddings; less so should they be considered the explicit functions of the event. Rather, what makes samuhik vivaha so successful as a political strategy is that it brings together many disparate and sometimes contradictory agendas in a visible ritual that does not *seem* to be about politics. The typical figurations of marriage for Jaipur's Dhanka are not love and intimacy, though it is expected that these will grow when carefully nurtured under the watchful eye of the community, but rather of domestic peace, individual happiness and fulfillment, and community continuity and protection. Thus, the oft-repeated message of the sammelan—that it exists for the benefit of poor Dhanka and especially Dhanka girls and their families—takes on a connotation of social service rather than political intervention. But again, I am less interested in exposing the samuhik vivaha as being "really" about something other than its stated purpose and more in showing how multiple meanings accrue to an event that is now the centerpiece of Dhanka organizing.

SHOWING THE NUMBERS

In Rajasthan, no one group, caste, or tribe comprises even 10 percent of the population of the state (Björkman and Chaturvedi 2001, 138). In 2001, the STs made up about 12.6 percent of the state's population, with Minas and Bhils together comprising 93 percent of that number. The Dhanka, who number 77,079 according to the 2001 census, together with Tadvi, Tetaria, and Valvis, make up 3 percent of the state's ST population, but a mere 0.14 percent of Rajasthan's overall population.[16]

While Rajputs remain the most symbolically powerful caste group in the state, they constitute only about 6 percent of the total population.[17] Recent years have also seen challenges to Rajput dominance. The successful reservation bids of middling farmers in the region have changed more traditional political demographics and voting patterns in the last two to three decades (Jaffrelot 2003; Michelutti 2008). The Jats, for example, have been included on the list of Other Backward Classes (OBCs) and have thus been able to bring together considerable landholdings with greater electoral visibility; they are also the largest caste group in the state, with about 9 percent of the population. Gujjars, too, have consolidated power in some areas, though their most recent strategy has been to claim Scheduled Tribe status and attempt to thwart competition with the Jats, a maneuver that has changed Rajasthan's political calculus.

Animosity between Rajputs and Jats has a deep history, stemming from mid-twentieth-century land reforms that took traditional Rajput holdings and distributed them to landless peoples, allowing Jats to increase their shares. Their displacement, temporary as it was, actually served to join formerly disaggregated and factional Rajput lineages into a "Rajput" identity; thus, all other identities in the state, particularly those of tribes who sit on the margin between Rajput and non-Rajput, become conversely solidified (Unnithan-Kumar 1997). This has been the case among the Minas.

In this electoral scenario, the Dhanka are a very small group; however, any group's collective votes can make a difference in any given election because the margins between communities are so small. As many political scientists have shown, caste and tribe groups tend to vote together, constituting what have been called "vote banks" in South Asian politics.[18] Vote bank calculus is charged in an especially electric way in Rajasthan because no one group has a clear electoral majority. Coalitions are frequent and fragile and small groups can make a difference. Therefore, any moment in which a small group like the Dhanka can impressively demonstrate their numbers needs to be seen as a moment of political import and potential recognition of the tribe's relevance to Rajasthani elections. It can, therefore, attract the attention of political parties. Coupled with a long history of anticolonial and postcolonial demonstration politics—a politics of presence in which the visceral effect of being able to draw a huge crowd is an important part of demonstrating will— the statistical meanings and interpretations mobilized in electoral politics make it important to get groups together in public places, no matter what the event. Indeed, it is arguable that demonstrating the numbers of Dhanka in the city is more important than the social service of providing weddings for poor families and girls. While the politically minded Dhanka elders I know vehemently insist that the Dhanka are free to vote as they choose as individuals—they are adamant that the community does not have a party link—they also know that groups are more powerful when voting together and that it is useful to be courted by political parties when wanting to get something done in the state. Along these lines of reasoning, they have had a long relationship with the Congress Party that continues to this day, despite recent overtures from the BJP.

As becomes clear in my description of the 2003 samuhik vivaha, once the politicians departed, the wedding festivities began to dissipate. Indeed, it was the arrival and speech of the Indoras, and not the individual marriage rituals of the seventeen couples, that was the climax and highlight of the celebration. The Indoras, it should be noted, are not Dhanka, but Dhanaks, and therefore Scheduled Caste. As I discuss in Chapter 2, the Dhanka of Rajasthan claim Dhanaks as their historical tribe-mates, but it is possible that such a claim would be unpopular at the time of writing, nearly eight years later, because Dhanka ST status has recently been challenged.

The reverberations of the event lasted for several days, not only for the families and couples involved. The most prominent regional, vernacular-language newspaper, *Rajasthan Patrika*, ran a picture of the samuhik vivaha the next day with a short description of the event; it reported the presence of thousands of Dhanka from eastern Rajasthan.[19] The Dhanka Samaj newspaper ran a full story in its next edition that again linked the success of samuhik vivaha to its ability to convene a large audience of samaj members. As with many ritual events such as weddings and lilas, the success of samuhik vivaha for those involved was articulated in terms of the crowds it was capable of drawing. In the time leading up to the 2003 samuhik vivaha, my frequent invitations to attend were usually couched in terms of how many Dhanka it would bring together.

The samuhik vivaha can, then, be seen as an opportunity to remind residents of Jaipur and political parties that they are a relevant community to consider. Holding their event in a large *Ram Lila* maidan, parading through the streets of wealthy colonies, and getting an unusual amount of press coverage are all effective in garnering outside support and attention. Though rarely described in these terms, the event is then a political rally that is meant to have an impact beyond the families it seeks to assist.

COMMUNICATE WILLINGNESS

To summarize an argument I put forth in the preceding chapters, because urban tribals like the Dhanka can no longer call upon those features of life previously used to mark tribes as distinct, such as culture and land, they must utilize new strategies and inhabit new political subjectivities to demonstrate themselves as deserving of their special benefits under the law, especially reservations. Willingness to be developed and adapt to new conditions is the key to understanding the Dhanka articulation of themselves as political actors in this interstitial space. At the same time, willingness is important under the political economy of *thekadari*, or free market contract labor, which emphasizes "self-help." When male political leaders occupied the stage at samuhik vivaha and later when the Indoras arrived to lead the Dhanka in collective cheers, the theme of their comments was very much the willingness of the

Dhanka to do what needs to be done to help their community "progress." Samuhik vivaha is thus a project belonging to a new era of development, one that does not totally reject the earlier statist model but that emphasizes individual and collective initiative in the pursuit of collective goals.

Speeches tended to reiterate variations of the following messages:

> The samuhik vivaha is a great undertaking for the Dhanka and shows how much they are willing to do to help their tribe-mates. It shows that they recognize that the youth are the future and must be developed with right habits so that they can have successes. It speaks to the unity of the group and the special identity of the Dhanka, as those who are willing to take on challenges to make things better, who are resilient and have always adapted to new situations. The Dhanka embrace self-help and always work together, as one, for the benefit of their community and their young people.

The centrality of samuhik vivaha to contemporary Dhanka political strategies in Jaipur demonstrates again the cultural work that goes into fulfilling the tribal role and being simultaneously different, backward, and in need of assistance but also (potentially) modern and eager to do what it takes to get by in their current circumstances. Because the event cannot be construed as a realm of "tradition"—in ritual and trappings, the weddings are Hindu and upwardly mobile—the event rather evokes a kind of abstract quality of collectivity oriented toward willingness. *We were adivasis.* Tribalness is not engaging in unfamiliar practices on remote tracts of land, but is rather a positive inclination toward the state and its messages. Samuhik vivaha thus indexes a difference not only from upper-caste groups, which I will discuss below, but also difference from other tribal groups. If the Dhanka are willing to embrace self-help and community development they cannot be the stereotypically defiant, recalcitrant, or hopelessly primitive other to Indian modernity. Indeed, they stress that this spirit of social service is a kind of inherent quality of the Dhanka as a people. As we saw in the historical essay, "Our Society," in Chapter 2, many Dhanka commentators stress that the group has *always* worked for social uplift and group benefit. In this way, they can also index the supposed egalitarianism that is thought to characterize tribes as opposed to castes, without drawing unnecessary attention to the decidedly caste-like way in which community life is organized.

These themes are nicely summarized in a letter to the Dhanka Samaj published in the souvenir booklet of the samuhik vivaha. The letter was authored by Dr. Dabi, who is a famous figure for the Dhanka of Jaipur. A local psychiatrist and Dhanka himself, Dr. Dabi is reported to have once held the position of head of psychiatry in the Jaipur Psychiatric Hospital. Legends about his childhood are often used to impress upon children in Shiv Nagar Basti the value of education: he was so committed to his studies, he would study under a streetlight when there was no electricity in his home. Dr. Dabi inhabits his role of local hero with pleasure and dedication. In the following letter, he explicitly links marriage, community willingness, and Dhanka development.

A Friendly Request

Service for humans is service to God. I feel that this is also true of service to society. A prosperous society will make a prosperous nation. Any work done towards the betterment of society can never be unfruitful. A society is made up of families and everybody is responsible for the family and the society. Along with education, there are many more social projects that need to be undertaken and we cannot deny this. A sacred tie, like marriage, is a must for the family in the society.

In fact, Indian society is full of misconceptions and social ills. We hear of the film stars and the wealthier groups spending *crores* of rupees in each of their marriages every day in the newspapers. And on the other side, there is one section of this society who cannot afford to spend anything in their marriage. The increasing expenditure in marriages has caused so many young men and women to stay unmarried all their lives.

Being a psychiatrist, I can say that staying unmarried can be a detriment for any human. Not being married, in both men and women, can cause many ill effects in the body that can also cause bad effects on the mind. In this way, [a] *manurogi* [mentally ill] family can [emerge and] be a challenge to this society. Samuhik vivaha is a solution to many of these problems. So, like many of the more developing sectors of this society, even Dhanka Samaj has not hesitated in adopting it.

In fact, being the head of the Dhanka Samaj Samuhik Vivaha Committee, it has been my experience that in a hard working society such as ours, samuhik vivaha is a boon. In response to this committee's various samuhik functions, all together 52 couples have been married and are leading a healthy and successful married life. This is not only an achievement of this committee, but also of the whole Dhanka Samaj. In fact, I would say that it is the responsibility of all of us to organize such samuhik vivaha. Come, we should utilize the energy and the excitement and the success achieved for the future and give a new color to it. To gain *punya* [attain good] people marry the plant basil, but we organize marriages for our own people. And probably there is no higher good than this. Being the head of this marriage committee and incorporating such work has given me deep satisfaction, but the truly deserving are the working members of this committee who have worked day and night for the success of this occasion, and I thank all these people and also the future members who

help us in this good deed—and the tree that we have planted with our immense efforts—not to destroy it with your selfish acts. To think of it as their
dharma and maintain it.

My heartiest best wishes to all the new members, and I also request that you
not disrespect any of the elder members of the society and not to bring casteism, groupism, and rich or poor, big or small, -like things into this society.

Once again, I thank all the brothers in the society and all the working members for their support.

Dr. Dabi

(*Smarika*, 2003, p. 10)[20]

What might be most immediately striking about Dr. Dabi's letter is its
strong exhortation to heterosexual marriage. In his analysis, which surely
carries an aura of authority since he is a practicing psychiatrist, not being
married causes physical and mental defects from which young people must
be protected. Samuhik vivaha, then, is not just an uplifting social service for
those who organize it, but a necessary intervention in social trends that could
undermine Dhanka collective life. These two themes interweave in Dr. Dabi's
plea: marriage is a necessary institution and samuhik vivaha is the means
to make sure that all Dhanka are properly married. His letter embodies the
notion that is prevalent among sammelan organizers, that marriage is understandably the highest goal that any young woman can have. Though he does
not specifically address his comments to Dhanka women, the very fact that
he and all the organizers are male but half the participants are female means
that such attitudes set the horizon of female expectation.

It also gestures toward the gulf that exists between different "kinds"
of Dhanka men. While Dr. Dabi may be one of the most highly esteemed
Dhanka man in Jaipur, he is identifying himself here with the samuhik vivaha sammelan committee, including Ram Lal and others, in the creation of
an "us" versus "them" within the Dhanka community. "We" put together the
ceremonies; "they" need them because they are poor, backward, and a risk
to a properly functioning society. His attribution of the events' success to
the "whole Dhanka Samaj" would in fact not be necessary if every Dhanka
felt included in the event equally, nor would his appeal to leave aside intra-
community differences of subcaste and class.

The final paragraph of Dr. Dabi's letter speaks directly to the themes of
willingness I have been developing in the last two chapters. Dhanka society is called "hard-working"; he lauds the "immense efforts" of the committee members in carrying out the weddings. The impetus for such efforts is,

importantly, located squarely within the community: *we organize marriages for our own people.* His letter communicates the message that "we" see there is a (potential) problem in our community and are willing to get together to do something about it. "We" care deeply about our own people but also, implicitly, about society at large, which we might threaten if we did not comport ourselves and arrange our family life in the correct way.

PUBLISH COMMUNITY, DISTRIBUTE HISTORY

Throughout this book I have made reference to the *Smarika* ("Souvenir") of the Dhanka Samaj Samuhik Vivaha Sammelan. I have referred to essays, such as "Our Society," in which Dhanka history is narrativized despite difficulties with historical evidence, and in which the problem of the multiple names for the Dhanka is explained. I have described Dr. Dabi's letter to the community above. There are many other interesting pieces contained within the booklet, including a history of a local guru known as Garib Das Maharaj and a story about a famous Dhanka athlete. But it also contains photos of all of the Dhanka Samaj Samhik Vivaha Sammelan committee members, photos of the event itself, and a directory of notable Dhanka of the area, with their job titles, photos, and contact information. It is, thus, simultaneously a history, a photo album, a phone book, and a souvenir of the sammelan. Its very publication speaks to the literacy of the Dhanka and their vibrant existence as a community.

The Smarika also provides a chance to reflect explicitly on the samuhik vivaha itself—on its successes and its meanings for the participants. Consider the following comments, entitled "The Advent of Spring in My Life":

The boys and girls who got married through the collective marriage Samiti were very happy about their marriage and their views are described below:

> We both are happy.

> Initially, my parents were hesitant to get me married through this samiti as they wanted it to be a big affair. But my in-laws insisted on getting the marriage through this committee. We both are very happy with this marriage. I hope that other couples get married through the samiti, so that there is no extravagance and they can economize.

> Sita, Polo Victory, Jaipur

> Our family is very happy.

> We got married on 7.2.03 through this samiti. We are very happy with this marriage. Even our family is very happy.

Pritham and Suresh, Polo Victory, Jaipur

Collective Marriage Samiti has shown us the way.

After my father's demise, the financial condition of my family was not good. The committee members encouraged my mother to get me married in this committee and they have saved my mother from financial problems.

Meena, Ghat Gate, Jaipur

Great Work.

I got married in this sammelan. Everything was great. The celebration was so good that perhaps my family could not have done it better than that. I, my wife, along with my family members, are all obliged to the person who got this sammelan done.

Vijay, Atroyi Bawi, Jaipur

(*Smarika*, 2003, p. 11)[21]

The statements of the individuals and couples serve to legitimate all the claims made about samuhik vivaha. Meena's statement, for instance, assures readers that the collective wedding saved her widowed mother from the burden of dowry. Sita records the "progress" in the view of her own family from the desire for a lavish wedding—and the willingness to give a dowry it implied—to the more community-appropriate view that extravagance is not in the best interest of any family. Her in-laws become especially virtuous in this telling, as it is they who would have stood to gain from a private wedding with dowry. There are several references, as well, to the Samiti, which again speaks to the prestige of the men who organize the event. As a whole, "The Advent of Spring" works to tie the welfare of the couples to the welfare of society. Its distribution in the Smarika makes this the official narrative of samuhik vivaha, whatever the realities of the private feelings of the commentators might be.

MAKE DISTINCTIONS: THE DHANKA VERSUS THE GOLDEN CASTES

It is an important part of the rhetoric around samuhik vivaha that it is a social service for girls and their families. I have already discussed how this message communicates the willingness that Dhanka men embrace as the quality of collectivity that makes them a unified tribe, in place of more familiar kinds of "indigenous traditions." This rhetoric sends another important message, however: that unlike upper castes in Rajasthan who may harm or even kill women in the name of tradition, the Dhanka have both respected women in the past and work hard in the present era to provide for their well-being.

We might think of this respect for women as the "positive" side of the image of sexually free tribal women—seen in another light, their license and moral laxity can be empowerment and self-determination. Dhanka men do not stress this freedom, however, as it is the *stability* of marriage and family and not the freedom of women that signals their upward mobility. Collective aspiration in this sense is aimed at properly arranged companionate marriages that do not set the Dhanka apart except in their obvious willingness to better their own lot. Along these lines, consider the following statement, made to me by an elder named Hemat Lal at a Dhanka panchayat meeting. While talking to a group of older men, I had asked him how the samaj approached female education, to which he replied that women got equal education among the Dhanka. Knowing this to be patently false, I asked him to say more. He continued:

> We are interested [in educating girls] and we give a lot of importance to the girls. We don't have the dowry system. We have nothing like the dowry system. We don't take any money et cetera from the girls. We have started group weddings. It has been going on for the past five years. In [these weddings] we take three, four, or five thousand rupees and do a group wedding. Nowhere do the girls have a better place in society. And whatever stories of murder et cetera that you have heard are in other communities. We have made an announcement in the Delhi Court Club about this. I am the president of the All-India SC/ST Organization. We have declared that the brides and grooms are not sold in our society. All this happens in the golden castes. . . . We always say that we only have a girl and a water pitcher to give. And we don't have anything else. And our society accepts it. So there is not dowry in our society. . . . We never give our girls any trouble. We don't have murder cases and we respect women a lot. Beating women and dowry are not a part of our society. Otherwise, it's fine. And group marriages are taking place.

As stated above, the Dhanka do in fact practice dowry marriages today and domestic abuse and dowry demands are not uncommon. In other words, Hemat Lal's representation of Dhanka social life as outside the norms of a more general Rajasthani culture that sanctions violence against women is at best an exaggeration and at worst an outright lie.

Here, I am less interested in contesting the comment's veracity—though it is certainly an important question—than I am in what Hemat Lal seeks to do with this representation. To me, the salient message here is that the "golden castes," which we are expected to read as Rajput and perhaps Brahmin castes, are not superior to low castes and adivasis but, rather, engage in retrograde cultural practices such as murder (implicitly referring to sati) that make them backward in comparison to these seemingly lower groups. It reverses the typical hierarchy of caste and tribe and reframes the relationship between time and tribalness so that upper castes, not the Dhanka, are stuck in the past. *We were adivasis: we respected our women and did not murder them.* Hemat Lal speaks to the ongoing symbolic power of sati in the gender imaginary of Rajasthan by contesting it.

We may think of Hemat Lal's rhetoric and the more general sentiment it coalesces as a similar effort to those undertaken by reformers like Govind Giri and others discussed above. Hemat Lal questions the political status quo and ties together the treatment of women and the Dhanka embrace of samuhik vivaha. He references samuhik vivaha, self-help, and Dhanka futures in such a way that Dhanka willingness to be different from those around them in pursuit of modern goals and aspirations is affirmed. Whatever they might have been in the past, they were not, he seems to say, among those groups that are causing problems not only for women but also for the nation-state as a whole through their insistence on backward practices. Hemat Lal thus works against the hegemony of the Rajputs while still functioning largely within its terms—community status is indexed through the status of women and, importantly, men speak *for* women. It is not proposed that women start debating these things themselves, and Hemat Lal's assertion that the Dhanka give "a lot of importance" to the education of girls is contradicted by the available statistics and by my own sense that young girls feel thwarted in pursuit of alternative goals.

The traffic in marriage is not, then, uncontested. I discuss girls' responses and relation of ambivalence to the community projects undertaken in their name in the next chapter. It is also not clear that the traffic in marriage has immediate, *discernable* benefits, and this is the point with which I would like to conclude. What is clear is that samuhik vivaha allows the Dhanka to make particular kinds of assertions of identity in an era when the security—and political viability—of reservations are being steadily eroded and when the criteria of identity are more in crisis than ever—thus the need to undertake multiple strategies at once. It is a prescient step, I think, because it effectively privatizes community concerns into the communal ceremony and private, everyday interactions of marriage that result. Collective marriage is about a particular kind of inclusion in a social and political terrain that is shifting—it is an embodiment and signal of a new kind of aspiration, which may be what it takes to keep the project of collective aspiration alive. The next chapter asks about the costs of this inclusion.

6

Wedding Ambivalence

What do the young women who are proclaimed the beneficiaries of the Dhanka samuhik vivaha sammelan think about the activities undertaken in their name? How do they view marriage and how do they conceive of its relationship to something like a broader "Dhanka identity"? Aside from "The Advent of Spring in My Life," the essay in the sammelan *Smarika* declaring the joy and merit of the event, the voices of the young women who are potential brides are largely absent from the design, planning, and enactment of the annual ceremony. They are, in many ways, objects in a traffic in marriage, rather than subjects whose desires and concerns are taken seriously by sammelan organizers. Or, to put it another way, their desires and concerns are not interpreted as *claims* by the male organizers, who assume they know what is best for the girls. For elder men, young women's marriage, either in a private ceremony or in the samuhik vivaha sammelan, is a given and seen as the only viable future that Dhanka women have. Despite male assertions that the Dhanka are working hard to educate girls, very few Dhanka women have a hope of supporting themselves outside the context of arranged marriage. And while marriage may not offer Dhanka women today what it offered the women who are the wives of Dhanka elders, it is the only site of aspiration available. As such, it is, to use Lauren Berlant's term, a site of "cruel optimism," wherein that thing that holds out the promise of a better life is exactly what limits girls' lives (2011).

But surely there are other ways of looking at contemporary Dhanka marriage practices besides simply as a traffic in marriage. As I learned about the samuhik vivaha and Dhanka identity concerns from esteemed men in Shiv Nagar Basti, I also learned about how young Dhanka women think about their lives, from their stories about educational goals thwarted or deferred, to their dreams for a "smart,"[1] kind husband. As I mentioned briefly in Chapter 1, the generosity and openness of two young women in particular, Mona and Kanika Solanki, facilitated my ethnographic work in Shiv Nagar Basti from the very beginning. Their interest in and respect for my efforts and our growing friendship encouraged others, including elder Dhanka men, to talk with me.

When I first began visiting Shiv Nagar Basti, Mona picked up right away on the most obvious similarity between us, despite very obvious differences of nationality, education, and economic status: we were unmarried but likely to be married within the following two years. I had a serious boyfriend who I planned to, and eventually did, marry, and Mona's parents were actively looking for a groom for her. Mona's anxiety about this process was palpable for much of the fall and winter of 2002 and 2003 and led to many questions about the trajectory of female-male relationships in the United States. She also expressed more private worries about the imagined groom's looks, personality, and financial prospects. Mona was excited but afraid. She accepted her imminent marriage but mourned an education that, she hinted, ended too quickly.

Over the years I have tried to find the right term or phrase to describe the complex affective register in which Mona comported herself in those days, to give her disposition a literary life. I am afraid that the best I can do is to talk about Mona's deep ambivalence. Dhanka girls are staked in a political gambit by Dhanka men. This is different than the project of marriage and respectability of which their mothers and grandmothers were a part in an earlier generation because the stability that underlay this project of collective aspiration—the security offered by reserved, albeit low-paid, government jobs—has been steadily eroded in the last ten years. When middle-aged Dhanka women married, they were part of an aspirational political project, one that sought to use the concrete of their houses and security of their properly arranged families and intimate lives as a base for making claims of inclusion. Dhanka girls today face a very different political, social, and emotional terrain. But they are not muted objects of exchange in the new forms of marriage. They are engaged in a complicated personal process of resistance and acquiescence during which they learn difficult lessons about love, aspiration, and, sometimes, violence. The world described by most analysts of marriage exchange—whether Marxist or structuralist or even feminist—looks very little like the world—sometimes fantastic, tragic, or even enchanted—that girls inhabit as they face the prospect of marriage to a man they do not know. It is perhaps partly their age, betwixt and between the social status of girl-daughter and woman-wife, that provokes the continual movement back and forth between knowing and not knowing, between a frighteningly unknown

future and a comfortable present, or between the joy of unimaginable possibilities and the constraint of routine. This liminal time is especially charged
for Mona and other young women I talked to because it will determine a
great deal about their unique destiny. But it is also important beyond any one
girl's future because the tethering of Dhanka marriage to the community's
collective aspiration implicitly tells girls that there is something else going
on here, that tradition, *parampara*, is not fixed, but can be changed. *We were
adivasis. We were something that we are not now. Could we be something new,
again, in the future? Could it be otherwise?*

"Ambivalence" is not the object of traditional political analysis as it defies
the possibility of individual or collective decision-making in the name of a
particular goal or view—there is no set position from which to make judg-
ments. It can also seem like an ethnographic cop-out to the extent that it
points to the kinds of complexities that anthropologists *should* expect when
dealing with complicated processes of social life. Yet I think it is central for
understanding the negotiation of freedom and unfreedom, those moments
of contingent choice and acquiescence, in which much of intimate social life
occurs and in which particular visions of the future are elaborated, changed,
and abandoned. The truth is that it requires a great deal of effort to maintain
the emotional buoyancy that allows one to be part of a project one is not
entirely convinced of. We need not necessarily call this effort "politics" but
would do well to think of "the flourishing of the social to one side of the political as something other than a failure to be politics" (Berlant 2008, 25).[2] It is
interesting to note that "ambivalence" recurs as a descriptor for the positioning and disposition of young women in contemporary India, but has yet to be
theorized or unpacked as such. Ritty Lukose, for example, notes the deep ambivalence of young women at an OBC college in Kerala when discussing their
feelings about romance with young men at the college, particularly relationships that cross caste or class lines (2009).[3] I think of ambivalence as the nurturing of the otherwise I referred to above. It is an orientation to the world
that keeps one's life narrative open to the possibility that something different
could have happened but that remains faithful to what has happened.

Young women's ambivalence, then, cannot be seen outside the context of
a social life defined by marriage as its horizon. Indeed, the language of the
horizon has also been used by Lukose to describe the normative "ideas, imaginings, expectations, and structures" that inflect college women's negotiations
of romance (121). Young women are ambivalent in part because they do not
reject or throw off this social boundary. Their agency here is not one of rebellion or resistance, but of refusing closure. In this sense, Saba Mahmood's
(2005) highly influential account of women in the Egyptian piety movement

is relevant and useful for understanding young Dhanka women's tendency to acquiesce to social conditions. Mahmood has cautioned Western feminists against assuming that agency is only present when manifest in acts of resistance and rebellion, noting a decided tendency to only recognize agentive action when it conforms with a particular understanding of the individualized subject who must throw off constraint. She argues that we need to see agency, rather, as a mode of embodiment which can also include the inhabitation of norms—the training of the body and the faculties—toward a particular goal that may not appear "liberated."

I am in complete agreement with Mahmood's assessment that there is a strong tendency to locate women's agency only in acts of resistance; this often results in feminists not wanting to tell stories about how the conventional and the mundane are created and sustained, which has limited our view to be sure. But it has also often seemed to me that very few women have the supportive context, emergent and changing as it may be, of a collective piety movement to provide a framework for their agentive embodiment. In other words, norms are usually not so clearly articulated as they are among the Egyptian women studied by Mahmood, who strive to pray five times a day, wear the hijab comfortably, and learn an active, affective response of shame that is signaled in particular bodily comportments and responses. And further, even when norms are understood, they are not always inhabited with dedication; rather, they are strategically occupied, for a time, and often while someone is of two, or three, or four minds about it at that. I am not certain that any working model of agency is yet able to capture this ambivalence. Here, I have found the work of Lauren Berlant helpful precisely because her concern is with the promise offered by the conventional, but her attention is often to how this promise is disappointed and ambivalently experienced. Clearly there are important differences between the contemporary Euro-American context that is Berlant's site and context and the political terrain I have been describing here, but, on the other hand, marriage, with its promises of love, security, reproduction, and futurity, is exceedingly important in both and surely constitutes a "conventionality" in Berlant's sense. She says, "To love conventionality is not only to love something that constrains someone or some condition of possibility: it is another way of talking about negotiating belonging to a world. . . . The convention is not only a *mere* placeholder for what could be richer in an under-developed social imaginary, but it is also sometimes a profound placeholder that provides an affective confirmation of the idea of a shared confirming imaginary in advance of inhabiting a material world in which that feeling can actually be lived" (2008, 3; italics in original). In an earlier chapter, I showed how older Dhanka women narrate their lives in such a way as to create themselves as respectable women who take seriously conventions of good womanhood even as the material conditions for the inhabitation of these norms is impossible—an act of love. But young women also love the conventionality offered by marriage even as, for them, it cannot yet be a site of cultivation but remains a hope, fear, and fantasy.

The definition of ambivalence I am working with in this chapter is all the more important in the realm of young women's dreams about marriage because these are so heavily inflected by the language of "karma" and "kismet" in the north Indian context. This latter term was frequently invoked in young women's discussions of their upcoming weddings: the happiness of domestic life is defined by one's kismet. The ambivalent disposition of many young women stresses the arbitrariness of kismet, rather than its intractability. By insisting that things might have been otherwise than they are, girls insist on a notion of fate in which any given reality could yield many possible futures. A girl's kismet in marriage might uncontestable, but it is also singular.

*

Dhanka girls are in many ways constructed as a ground from which Dhanka male leaders stage a series of negotiations with the local political system; yet, as critiques by Marilyn Strathern and others have alerted us, we must be careful about accepting the absence of a subjectivity of the gift. Do girls benefit from samuhik vivaha and view it as in their interests? How do they think about marriage more generally? Since Dhanka girls are not consulted at any stage of the process, at least not officially or in overt ways, one answer to these questions would be simply that they are simply being exchanged as currency in the political trade of Rajasthan. As I argued above, this is a common end for analysis in feminist and anthropological approaches: marriage practices exchange women, with value accruing in patriarchal fashion to the men who control the trade. And, on one hand, girls *are* being used as markers and creators of social value in the familiar north Indian dowry system of regular Dhanka weddings. Girls' public exchange in samuhik vivaha is certainly potent political currency.

Girls are, for obvious reasons, deeply invested in the ideologies and social relations that arrange the situations in which they marry, love, and bear children. They are not merely exchanged, nor do they necessarily accept that marriage should be the one path to social status open to them. They actively engage in processes of narration and negotiation—fragile moments in which they open creative possibilities for imagining that the world might be different. Below, I do not present simple stories of refusal in which girls throw off community expectations because this is something they rarely do. Rather, I try to give a sense of the kinds of intimate conversations—the languages—in which girls come to think of themselves as part of the wider worlds of family, tribe, and even, sometimes, nation. I characterize girls' subjectivity in these conversations as "ambivalent" in order to highlight the extent to which they do not easily occupy a "position," and thereby throw into relief the undecidability of subaltern speech "in the face of which we must risk the decision that we can hear the other" (Spivak 1999, 199). My account should be thought of as a gesture as much as reportage, a mode of attention to that which is said and that which is held back by my young interlocutors. I am undoubtedly telling stories where there is often silence.

My analysis focuses on two important themes in these conversations, love and education, both of which continually reemerged as areas in which Dhanka girls had deep and conflicted investments. Many of the conversations that are discussed below took place in the Reproductive and Child Health Center, in the front room of Ram Lal's house, while the auxiliary nurse midwife, Priya, was sitting at her post. A young, unmarried woman herself, Priya provided a comfortable atmosphere for the girls to discuss and debate their personal struggles. I was privy to many of the discussions, though there were some topics—such as the particular identity of a particular girl's boyfriend in the neighborhood—that were off limits to me, ambiguously positioned as I was between the older and younger generations of women in the basti. I couldn't easily be trusted. I might not understand.

It is important to remember at the outset that Dhanka girls do not work, aside from the occasional sewing piecework, and do not aspire to have jobs outside the home. During the years between when they normally leave school (sometime around eighth class) and when they marry (between ages sixteen and eighteen), girls spend a great deal of time doing house chores and socializing with one another. It was not a coincidence, I think, that issues related to love and education frequently arose in this particular setting. On one hand, marriage and school are frequently the subject of interventions by the Reproductive and Child Health Center, whose publications, as we will see below, routinely prescribe the trajectory of these social forms. Marriage and school are presented as foils to one another: girls' early marriages thwart their education. On the other hand, the plots that are available to girl to imagine their futures are in large part drawn from the domestic world of mothers and fathers, aunts and uncles, and neighbors, and from the fantasy domestic worlds presented on popular serial television shows. In short, these plots are about love.

Love

It was all the news when I arrived at the health post that morning: Mona and Kanika's cousin, Aparna, who lived in another neighborhood and had been engaged several weeks earlier, had received a picture from her groom-to-be. "Well, how is he?" [*Woh kaisa hai?*] I asked in the casual manner I had learned was appropriate for such occasions—both curious and indifferent, bordering on sly. "He is *smart*" [*Woh* smart *hai*]. But, I was told, I could see for my-self, since Aparna was visiting and had been looking for me all morning to share the photo. The more important thing was that the boy had also sent gifts—a plastic kewpie doll being the "sweetest"—and called on the telephone at Aparna's uncle's place. "What did he say?" I asked, more enthusiastic. The girls smirked; the boy had apparently told Aparna that he could not wait to come and get her. "I'll be coming for you soon," he said. The girls were clearly a bit envious of the budding relationship.

When I saw her later that day, Aparna seemed excited and scared, vaguely pleased to be the object of her cousins' jealousy. She had gotten lucky, it seemed, because the boy had a sense of romance. Aparna might have a chance for something the girls spent a lot of time imagining and hoping for: a hus-band that loved her, whom she loved.

There were rumors in the air throughout my fieldwork in Shiv Nagar Basti that girls sometimes got upset about the impending marriage in part because an engagement had broken up a secret relationship with a boyfriend in her neighborhood. Not only are urban Dhanka quite strict about arranged marriages, any boy from the same basti, even unrelated, would have been completely off limits as a marriage partner. When I asked Dhanka girls about how one meets a boyfriend initially or encounters him subsequently, they often responded in language reminiscent of the Hindi romance films that are popular in north India. They told me, "Didi, maybe you just see him across the bazaar. Your eyes meet. You might go back to that place to look at him again. He might try to call you." In other words, these relationships happened at a distance, did not involve sex or other physical contact, and were highly emotionally charged.[4] Relationships were about the intimacy of talk, rather than physical closeness. One engaged Dhanka girl said that boyfriends and girlfriends got together to talk: "You tell them how you feel, tell them that you miss them. You just talk."

When I asked why no one ever married their boyfriend, either by getting their parents to arrange it or by eloping, I was told, "It is not to be, it cannot be. You love your *lover*, but you marry your husband. It's not like where you come from—here, mummy-papa choose." Again, the explanation was equally a lamentation about the ways in which true love was thwarted by the conventions to which one must necessarily submit. When girls said "where you come from," they presumably meant the United States. Though I tried to explain that social expectations, class, education, and race all seriously impacted who Americans "chose" to marry, the contrast was an important part of the story about the value of the fantasy of one's lover and about the necessity of accepting fate. If my choices were also constrained, or theirs were equally free, the contrast—and therefore the bargain made by Dhanka girls—would no longer hold.

Laura Ahearn (2001) has written extensively about the ways in which discourses about selecting a mate as a "life friend" and subsequent companionate marriage have spread in Junigau in rural Nepal, with the result that elopement is now seen by young people as the best form of marriage and has recently seen a dramatic increase. Ahearn traces this new concern with romantic love to the pervasive rhetorics of development, greater literacy, and increased mobility to regional centers where boys and girls go for studies, meet with less supervision, and see movies that are often about star-crossed lovers. Clearly, an element of Dhanka girls' discussions of lovers and husbands grows from similar circumstances

I have stressed the extent to which "willingness" is the Dhanka strategy for group identity and development, and girls sometimes exhibit this willingness as well. While Dhanka elders do not expect girls to graduate from secondary school, they do expect them to be literate, and, as I argued in the previous chapter, Dhanka elders go to lengths to demonstrate that they are committed to the well-being of young women in a way that is uniquely Dhanka.

Messages about companionate marriage as the most modern form of relationship were not hard to come by, especially once girls could read the kinds of materials left scattered about the Reproductive and Child Health post, such as the following, excerpted from a brochure titled "Appropriate Age at Marriage."

> It is very important that both the woman and man are fully mature before marriage and they should be taught to understand fully this legal responsibility. In Indian culture, mothers and fathers play an important role in arranging marriages. But at the same time it is essential that two young people should be given the right to ultimately decide because they have to spend the rest of their lives together. Moreover, it is not sufficient that the families decide, but the boy and the girl have to accept each other. This is especially important now because the joint family is fast becoming extinct and the couple has to depend on each other. For these reasons, it is important that when two people make this decision they are not of tender age.[5]

Like youth in Junigau, Dhanka youth, who are at the ethnic margins of mainstream discourses of development, take such messages to heart. It was not uncommon to hear girls criticize their community for disallowing boys and girls to pursue "love," particularly those relationships that cross caste/tribe boundaries. And while it was not always allowed, girls vastly preferred arranged marriages in which both parties, the prospective bride and the groom, were allowed to see pictures of one another and talk on the telephone, as had been the case with Aparna. Hopes about marriage, narrated in the language of kismet, were not without some sense that young people had a right to a hand in their own futures.

Yet, there is an important difference between Junigau and Shiv Nagar Basti: Dhanka girls do not actually marry their boyfriends, real or imagined. Whatever their dreams may be, Dhanka girls are not running off with their lovers to be married. Though I have heard of a few cases in which girls' parents arranged a marriage to a boy of her choosing, I have yet to meet a couple married in this way. Eventually, girls inhabit a space of ambivalence that allows them to let go of other visions for what their lives might be like enough to acquiesce to their new situations without completely relinquishing those visions. One girl in the neighborhood, for instance, continued to return to the basti for months after her marriage—which everyone reported was quite happy—to try to catch a glimpse of her former lover; she was allowed to return after repeated complaints of homesickness for her mother.

It seems to me, then, that these discussions may be only partly about particular romances and their tragic endings. They also allow girls to imagine futures that may involve a given love affair, but may also refer to desires around autonomy, education, or earning power. It is telling that, in both Junigau and Shiv Nagar Basti, the terms that are used to refer to romantic love are often in English. Ahearn (2001) tracks the circulation of the term "*laif phrend*," which she links to the pervasiveness of development ideals of "success and autonomy in decision-making ability" (150). In Shiv Nagar Basti, the terms "lover," "love," and "boyfriend" were common. Particular qualities of people—being "smart" or "sweet"—were also rendered in English. While Ahearn sees this use of foreign terms as an effect of the deployment of development languages, I see these terms as allowing a space for girls to communicate and work through their own ambivalence about the community projects of which they are a part. Dhanka girls have no English-medium education and pick up English terms from popular media, especially television and movies. In this context, English terms can only partially be seen as "referring" to a particular definition; they are not completely overdetermined by connotation, but, imprecisely defined and unmoored from a systematic language ideology, they open space in language for the articulation of emotions, desires, and thoughts that are not easily rendered in the familiar referential field of Hindi. "Lover," as we have seen, does not carry meanings related to sexual intimacy, and while it clearly refers to a specific person and relationship, it also refers to thwarted dreams—that which cannot be.

In the Nepali case described by Ahearn, literacy was on the rise in the village, and development seemed to be offering opportunities for young people aside from, or in addition, to marriage. In the Dhanka case, girls can usually read and write, but very few pass through higher than eighth class; the kind of opportunities that would be implied by English-medium education, for instance, are not open to them. Further, in a context in which samuhik vivaha represents the apogee of community organizing and willingness to be developed, the best that the group has to offer its young women, love and marriage, have to be considered as a capacious field of reference or as anchoring a different grid of intelligibility. The kinds of ambivalence that girls express about their nearly inevitable decisions to abandon romantic relationships in favor of proper parentally or community-arranged marriages then needs to be seen as a kind of political subjectivity, in the sense that it is directly related to the broader project of Dhanka community building outlined above. Love is what you hope for.

It was important to maintain hope because there were always reasons to be fearful. In addition to the frequently discussed worry that once a girl was married her time for talking with friends would be taken up by housework performed for a demanding *sas* ("mother-in-law"), girls were afraid of the physical violence that can accompany marriage, even samuhik vivaha. If event organizers saw the collective wedding as guaranteed protection against dowry-related violence or spousal abuse, the girls were not convinced of its efficacy. After one of my visits to Sapna, near the Lotus Garden and the cremation ground, Mona told me in hushed tones about Sapna's sixteen-year-old daughter, Nandini, whom we met briefly in Chapter 4. According to Mona, Nandini was home with her mother because, shortly after she was married in the previous year's samuhik vivaha, she began being "tortured" (Mona used the English word) by her in-laws because her dowry was not enough. The groom's family had expected money and gifts in addition to that provided by the Samiti, despite the demands being against the rules of the samuhik vivaha. Mona was worried and wanted to know if women were "tortured" in my country. When I replied that yes, they were beaten up and abused, Mona was shocked, since we did not practice dowry and could make our own money. Why would a woman be tortured if it wasn't about dowry? But I am afraid my response offered little comfort, as Mona was clearly afraid of what might await her in her own marital home.

Girls' dreams of love, then, must be seen against this backdrop of concern about their future material and physical safety. Your lover could never abuse you because he could not demand dowry. Your husband might fall in love with you, but he might be dangerous. You could turn to the community for protection, as in samuhik vivaha, but those protections could only go so far. You could resist marriage for a little while, but it was inevitable since it constituted a parent's primary responsibility to their daughter. Girls are not simply controlled, nor do they easily resist under these conditions. Rather, they traverse back and forth between a sense of inevitability and a sense of possibility, the ambivalence both promising and perilous. Because marriage is utterly conventional, it is unavoidable. But it might contain this other quality, this romantic love, that offers to make the conventionality special, meaningful, surprising. Conventionality can be transformed if the conditions are right so that the drudgery of everyday life, the cooking and cleaning and tending to children, become part of a larger project of sustaining and enlivening a deep emotional attachment.

If Dhanka girls' mothers' labors were essential to the project of collective aspiration in the era of service, in which they were a part of Dhanka mens' efforts to evince willingness by building their dreams for uplift in concrete, today girls participate in collective aspiration through the heartfelt hope for love. Yet, there remains a sense that this is not as reliable as the concrete of an earlier time and that there may be options passing them by. To further illustrate my argument that the ambivalence that characterizes girls' attitudes to love and marriage is important for understanding Dhanka collective aspiration, I turn now to girls' discussions of education.

Education

In the kinds of modernization narratives that have characterized post-independence India, education is seen as the single, necessary ingredient for the uplift of oppressed groups. As Jeffrey, Jeffery, and Jeffery (2008) point out, there is broad accord among scholars, politicians, and development planners that education is a "tool for personal and collective development" (3). (It should be noted that, in addition to the kind of secondary and college education referred to by Jeffrey, Jeffery, and Jeffery, "education" has several meanings in the context of Shiv Nagar Basti, from the education of basti women about reproductive health to formal education in preparation for

professional work to basic literacy to enable informed voting). Any level of
social and economic disadvantage can be overcome by proper knowledge in
this view. Despite an avowed commitment to education, however, tribal girls
cannot be said to have been brought into the school paradigm. A study of
six Jaipur bastis found that only 48.38 percent of basti residents in the city
had a primary education. Of this fraction, only 5.54 percent were girls and
2.04 percent were women (Bodh Shiksha Samiti 2001). While, according to
the 2001 census, Dhanka girls had a much higher rate of literacy than many
of their tribal peers—reported at about 48 percent—most girls leave school
at a young age. Furthermore, when education is not seen as a path toward
employment, further schooling, or basic social functioning, and when it remains available to less than half of a community that is taken to be role models for other tribal groups, we must be careful about attributing transparent
meanings to terms like "literacy."

In her ethnography of young women in an OBC college, Lukose (2009)
argues compellingly that in addition to noting literacy rates and the number
of girls enrolled in schools, we must also always ask "What are the conditions under which young women gain entry into education?" and "What are
they being educated for?" (32). Indeed, in light of the relatively good rate of
Dhanka female literacy, one might be inclined to think that the community
is an exception compared to other Rajasthani tribal groups. However, very
few, if any, Dhanka young women have professional aspirations; those who
do are seen as exceptional cases. One woman who married into Shiv Nagar
Basti was a schoolteacher, a position that was said to be enabled by a particularly enlightened father-in-law who was a longtime government worker and
one of very few speakers of English in the basti. Two young Dhanka women
in a nearby neighborhood had been given scholarships to a convent school.
They were fluent speakers of English and aspired to be in the armed forces.
While their less-educated peers were obviously impressed by the girls' skills,
the dominant story about these two (out of their earshot, of course) was that
they were high and mighty.

While too much education could make someone a target of scorn, the
overall lack of schooling did not always sit well with Shiv Nagar Basti's girls.
In conversation with friends, they regularly voiced complaints about their
education and their lack of opportunity for employment. Mona, for instance,
expressed disappointment at not being able to go far enough in school to be
a service-*walli* like Priya, the auxiliary nurse midwife, or like myself, the foreign researcher who got to roam around asking questions and writing things
down. She spoke passionately of her desire to get a job in Ganesha Plaza,
a modern-style shopping complex in Jaipur that housed banks, cell-phone

service providers, retail shops for tourists, a Pizza Hut, and travel agencies. While Mona is perhaps exceptional in her maturity and ambition, we can start to see impressions of the thwarted aspirations of many Dhanka girls in her dreams of an office job with its trappings of computers, air conditioning, and credit cards.

In a 2005 conversation, I asked several girls what they would want to do for a career if they could pursue any field. Manju, one of Kanika's friends, grabbed my tape recorder and said, "I'd do what you do—I'd be a reporter." We all laughed. Who would she interview? Manju replied that unlike my stories, hers would focus on film stars. Shah Rukh Khan. Politics was too boring. The theme of girls' comments, however, was that a girl's work is already set out for her: helping her mother or going to work for her mother-in-law when she gets married. The joke about being a reporter (who does things like the anthropologist, including travel far from home) and meeting film stars was funny because of its impossibility. The young woman seemed to be saying: *Imagine me meeting someone famous, and all you can do is laugh. These two things can never fit in the same frame.*

I have already described a section of the Reproductive and Child Health publication "Appropriate Age at Marriage" that deals specifically with the issue of choice in marriage; its reiteration of an ideal of modern, companionate marriage was obvious. It is telling, then, that the same document does not embrace the "modern" view of education. I quote the document at some length to show how the question of girls' education is folded into issues of marriage and family.

> Is education important today?
>
> At present in our country, before a man has reached middle age there is a strong sense that he should develop a skill. That is why, realizing the importance of education, more people have gone to study than was the case previously. Young men have to develop their abilities in the emerging social world, so they spend their adolescence as students. This is why boys only begin to think about marriage after they have completed their education and settled into a profession. It is a good idea for him to work to establish himself. Similarly, it is necessary for a girl to complete her education and obtain a skill so that she can stand on her own two feet. Moreover, it is better if she has a career or a profession. During this time, young men and women develop their personality. They mature enough to understand what they want from their life and from their life partner.[6]

Putting aside the kinds of anguish that such a comment might create for young Dhanka men who now have little hope of securing a "profession," it is clear that girls' education does not have the same importance as boys'. It is "better" if she has a career, but more as an afterthought to the necessity of a boy's adolescence being spent as a student in training for a profession than as a real platform for intervention. In the subsequent sections of the brochure, entitled "How does young marriage affect boys?" and "How does young marriage affect girls?" respectively, no further mention is made of a girl's need for school. Young marriage is a bad idea for boys, the brochure tells us, because it interrupts their studies; for girls, its effects are physical and involve the strains of motherhood before full maturity.

As in the discourses surrounding samuhik vivaha, girls' possibilities are being defined only in relation to the horizon of an eventual, inevitable marriage. Girls' responses to this horizon were complicated and, again, ambivalent.

The complexities created in my own relationship with Mona were manifold because of her recurrent dream of being a part of the world of "service." On days when I would go with Priya on her rounds in another neighborhood or we would depart early for a function at the Reproductive and Child Health project office, Mona would be gloomy and upset as she watched us depart. She once confessed, "When you and Priya go, I have *feelings*. I *feel* when you speak in English." It took me a minute to translate her use of the English term "feel." Mona rarely, if ever, spoke in English. I was confused.

I think that Mona meant that she felt jealous or upset, perhaps angry. The lines between educated worker and recipient were being challenged in Mona's statement such that she seemed to be arguing "I could be Priya—or you— with just a bit more education." She was quite obviously correct as well, and the fact caused me no small grief each time I left. The use of the term "feeling" in English, like that of "lover" discussed above, left the emotion—and therefore its sources, remedies, intensity—ambiguous, however. Mona's "real" feelings never came through because she relied on the English word. Any real critique of her education, lack of work choices, lack of choices in marriage, or of me, was gathered up into this one term that could only "mean" imperfectly.

Not long after our conversation about Ganesha Plaza, I took Mona to the mall complex to try her first pizza at Pizza Hut. Trying to say thank you to my friend for all that she had given me—support, compassion, insight—if I was conflicted about all that is caught up in taking her to this temple to Americanization in Jaipur, I swallowed the concern because she seemed to want very badly to go on this outing together. I ordered us pizza and Cokes in English and settled into the booth. But Mona wouldn't eat. She would barely talk, and when she did, it was only to tell stories about her family, now left at home, and a time they visited a shrine in the Punjab to pray for her aunt's son.

★

My stomach sank: she didn't know.

✳

She had no idea how it would be, how uncomfortable she would feel. I had misunderstood her dream—the fantasy was better. Now we, who had constructed a fragile fiction of coevality, two friends, were staring difference in the face. One trip to Pizza Hut would change nothing. Neither of us ate much and we packed up the pizza to bring home to Kanika, who did not find it even slightly appealing. Later, when she was back in her familiar surroundings, Mona told me "They wouldn't let me in those places without you. And you spoke so much English. I don't like it. It makes me *feel*."

What She *Felt*

To say that she "felt," was, I think, Mona's way of saying she felt upset, felt emotional, felt left behind, and that she expected more from her life. She only used the phrase in relationship to skills she thought she would probably never attain, like speaking English. Though Pizza Hut was not the only time I heard her use the term, it was the most difficult. For in the end, the anthropological question of the exchange of women has always come down to the problem of the subjectivity of those exchanged. Perhaps it is easier to not know and to leave an absence at the heart of the exchange.

I have put the story of samuhik vivaha together with the story of Mona, Kanika, Aparna, and the other Dhanka girls I knew in Jaipur in order to reflect upon the story I could have told and its relationship to the other stories that, while not the stuff of traditional political analysis, make all the difference for Dhanka girls. Samuhik vivaha has undoubtedly become the centerpiece of Dhanka community organizing. Male members of the Samuhik Vivaha Samiti become prominent within the samaj; the event itself draws and demonstrates Dhanka numbers, reiterates messages about Dhanka willingness for development, and captures the attention of those few Dhanka who occupy public office and positions of authority within the state; it produces good publicity and opportunities to articulate a cohesive identity. One kind of feminist analysis might simply show the ways in which issues related to marriage and family become the ground upon which Dhanka identity claims are staged and the kinds of political effects and solidarities that are created by this traffic in marriage and exchange of women. To reiterate my earlier point, I think that these aspects of the collective weddings are undeniable. But I have tried to keep open questions about, and the possibility of, a subjectivity of the gift. I have also tried to demonstrate that we can "hear" answers to these arrangements of dowry, marriage, and family in which Dhanka girls find themselves in their discussions of love and education, answers that echo with ambivalence—sometimes hard-won, sometimes accepting, but always engaged with, rather than separate from, the broader terrain of Dhanka collective aspiration.

In Lieu of a Chapter Conclusion

Mona was not lucky in marriage. After her marriage in 2003 to a man who enjoyed taunting her and talking about other women, her domestic life was tumultuous for almost a decade. Her mother-in-law was cruel and insulting. In the early days, in the mid-2000s, Mona's family would not talk about it, except for Kanika, who scowled deeply and told me that things there were very bad. Mona was more withdrawn when we met, though we still liked to joke around. It often seems to me now that Kanika expressed many of Mona's feelings—outrage, desperation, hope—for her so that Mona could remain steady for her two young children, a girl and a boy.

When we met in 2007, we talked about what her daughter's life might be like in the future. Mona had big plans for her. *My daughter will travel the world, like you do. She will be educated. She will have breakfast in America, dinner in India. And stop to go to the toilet in Pakistan.* Everyone laughed. I was uncomfortable. But the joke is telling: Mona's dreams for her daughter were dreamed on a grand scale and in line with those of India as a nation. Her reference to Pakistan is less a statement on any particular anti-Muslim stance among Jaipuri Dhanka and more a signal of Mona's embrace of a particular kind of citizenship that is reaffirmed through the exclusion of a polarized other. If Mona and her peers were, and perhaps even continue to be, ambivalent about the community projects that happen in their name, they have imbibed a spirit of collective aspiration that explodes beyond the familiar terrain of Dhanka upward mobility through government service. Having no real models for herself or her daughter in the real space of Jaipur, Mona's fantasies extend to the globe and to rapid movement across vast distances—to what we might think of as the hyperreal world of globalization and Indian neoliberalism (see Lukose 2009; Mazzarella 2003).

Life goes on, and Mona is much happier now. She has settled into a relationship with her new family that she can tolerate and seems even to have developed some affection for her husband who, she says, is now much more willing to do as she asks. It took a great deal of effort on her part to get to this place, however—she told me that she had to fight and scrape and push (literally miming the motion of pushing down on her husband's shoulders) for years to make things different.

But I want to give the dreams of her younger years the space they deserve to grow and not to weigh them down with a retreat into the facts that made them so profoundly unlikely for Mona.

Therefore, in lieu of a conclusion, I am reminded of the young woman's words: *Maybe they go to a party and see someone. They fall in love. This lasts forever. . . . They might kiss, but most just talk. Sometimes the girl and boy are allowed to get married. Sometimes they run away together. But most just remember their lover in their heart.*

7

Of Contracts and Kaliyuga

One of the plot tricks of this ethnography is to produce, as much as describe, pieces of time I have called "eras." In Chapter 3, I wrote the story of a time, the era of service, and diagnosed all kinds of social relations as its products and conditions of possibility. In tracking the shift from one epoch to another, I have given a certain arc to my story. It is an ethnographic arrival of a sort (Pratt 1986), one that becomes legible because something that came before it has given way.

We have moved now into the present, the era of contract. Yet it is clear from the previous chapter that the dispositions and sociopolitical arrangements of this era have not supplanted those that came before it. The desires and dreams that shape Dhanka collective aspiration are still those drawn from the era of service—they have government jobs and well-fed relations and pukka homes at their heart. Young women like Mona are living in both eras in intimate ways: the confidence and willingness of their fathers, who arrange their marriages whether in samuhik vivaha or not, is not apparent in their potential spouses. Young women's ambivalence comes in part from the fact that they must believe in marriage as the best hope they have for a meaningful future, even as its material basis is eroded. Even as it becomes an unsteady foundation for a future that is increasingly, unnervingly, uncertain.

There are new problems for the ethnographer in this era. Writing about the now, this happily or frighteningly changing now, means trying to render things that seem to slip away because they are immediate—not yet history (see Hecht 2006). Perhaps my account will seem less sure of itself, less definitive. Ambivalence helped me talk about young women. I have no such narrative tool for young men. How will I conjure the sons of the era of the contract for you? Part of my concern probably arises from the simple fact that, of all of the generational cohorts I encountered in Shiv Nagar Basti, I probably spent the least time with young men between the ages of fifteen and thirty-five. I would certainly not claim that what follows in this chapter is based on the kinds of intimate connections I have described in the previous chapter; a broad sociological portrait was never my goal. Yet, we have to try to understand how young Dhanka men are grappling with the era of the contract, which entails privatization and hiring freezes that affect them especially, in a social context heavily saturated by the willingness that I have argued characterizes the dispositions of their fathers and grandfathers. Without them, the story is incomplete.

What follows, then, is perhaps a simpler offering than in other chapters. It is a set of reflections on how young men do or do not make their way in the city and in their families, with shrinking job prospects, under the regime of *thekedari*, the giving and receiving of contracts.

I have chosen to talk about thekedari, or the era of the contract, and not neoliberalism (or "liberalization," as it is known in India) because "thekedari" was the term most often used to describe a set of changes taking place in the early 2000s, when I began visiting Shiv Nagar Basti. These changes included both so-called reforms in the sectors that most affect the Dhanka as workers and consumers—water and electricity—and the increasing reliance of Dhanka laborers on private labor brokers (known as thekedars) to procure daily wage work (*mazdoori*).

In 2002, I learned about local definitions of "thekedari" from a twenty-five-year-old man and his elderly mother. They were Rajputs and recently arrived in the city from Gwalior.[1] At that point, their household consisted of four adults: Hanuman Singh, his wife, his brother, and their mother, Ramperi. They earned about Rs. 1,500 each month, with Hanuman working in a *bhel-puri* (*chaat*, or "snack") business near the old city. My research assistant, Shally Vaish, and I were asking questions about changes in the city since they arrived.

HANUMAN: It's good today. In the last two to four years the city has flourished [*acchi raunaq aa-gaye han*]. But now it's very expensive. Before the flour was Rs. 7 a kg. Now it's Rs. 8 or 9. The cost of oil and gas has also increased. The electricity bill used to run us about Rs. 800. Now it is Rs. 1,700–2,000. Even when we're running the TV and fan the same amount.

RAMPERI: [emphatically] Before the electricity was given for Rs. 15–20. Now these expensive bills come. You have to pay a bill of Rs. 2,000–2,500 for a small hut. Where do you get the money? If two people earn, it's still hard to get Rs. 4,000.

HANUMAN: If we go for *service*, nobody is going to pay you more than Rs. 1,500.

RAMPERI: It is that the electricity has gone private [*theka men*]. When things go private, poor people suffer. And the people who do the jobs [*naukri wale*]—their salary goes on increasing.

MEGAN: What is "*theka*"?

HANUMAN: It's like the way the lights have gone into private hands. "Theke-dari" means that you take a *factory* yourself, privately, and you have paid 1 crore for this. And if you have earned a profit of 10 crores, then it is yours. All the *problems* have arisen with electricity.

RAMPERI: How do we pay the electricity bill?

HANUMAN: Like if the bill is Rs. 4,000, besides that you have to pay rent. You have to pay money for food.

RAMPERI: You can get manual day labor [*kula danda*]. We earn for two days, and [then we] sit for ten days. When there is no work. What will people do? We'll see to it, otherwise the electricity will be cut. We'll remain as such [without lights].

The fact that Shiv Nagar Basti residents like Hanuman and Ramperi linked utilities reform and contract labor explicitly (an insight I will have more to say about in this chapter) gives us a glimpse into what we might think of as the story of privatization from the underneath. "The era of the contract" is the best appellation I can come up with for a story of the present that reflects these local concerns and analyses of how changes in the last fifteen years have altered daily life for Jaipur's poorest residents.

Neoliberalism, on the other hand, I understand to refer to a set of political-economic practices inaugurated around the globe since the 1970s, which include deregulation, liberalization of restrictions on foreign investment and import/export, privatization, and the withdrawal of state support from social programs. I also understand neoliberalism as a value system that holds that "the social good will be maximized by maximizing the reach and frequency of market transactions" (Harvey 2005, 3) and therefore seeks to market-ize human relations. However, taking to heart Lisa Rofel's argument that there is not "a universal set of principles from which derives, in a deterministic fashion, a singular type of neoliberal subject" (2007: 2), I see this set of practices and notion of value as powerful ideals that are rarely, if ever, enacted in practice. Neoliberalism is a useful diagnostic and descriptor for tracking global linkages or capturing resonances across a variety of geopolitical sites, but it can easily turn into a view of everything that keeps us from seeing not only local conditions and contradictions but also how people theorize those local conditions and contradictions themselves. These theorizations will take precedence here. Neoliberalism is lived as the era of the contract in Shiv Nagar Basti.

In the following section, I outline the features of the era of the contract that most affect young Dhanka men, roughly between the ages of fourteen and forty, who are employed or looking for employment. The most salient is the rise of thekedari in both state and private employment. Indeed, I discuss the ways that employment techniques designed to cut costs and limit employee benefits and rights are increasingly shared between state and non-state actors; with the rise of confusing and half-completed "public-private partnerships," the lines between the two are increasingly unclear except insofar as reservation policy only applies in government hiring. I then go on to discuss how these conditions shape the way young men see themselves in relation to older men, such as fathers and grandfathers, and in relation to one another. Again we will see how the challenges of Scheduled Tribe identity, albeit in changed and changing circumstances, create distinctions between Dhanka men, now labeled good or useless on the basis of their employment status and relationship to idealized notions of the properly employed ST. Yet, the aspirations and visions of the era of service are never entirely replaced and rumble in the wings of daily dramas. Young men must struggle in a temporality of not-yet/not-anymore that is perhaps more challenging than anything faced by their elders.

Privatization from Underneath

There are three changes that best characterize the shift from the era of service to the era of contract. The first is a statewide freeze on government hiring. Over the years, despite repeated efforts, it has been very difficult for me to obtain details about the exact parameters of this hiring freeze—for instance, a list of positions to which it applies. The lack of documentation and the policy's hearsay quality is not altogether surprising considering that the topic can be politically incendiary, with parties touting one position or the other as truly in favor of the people. What is clear is that in 2001, under a BJP-led government, the central government announced that it would cut 10 percent of government jobs, cancel vacant posts, and impose a permanent ban on new recruitment (Balagopal 2006). Many states, including Rajasthan, announced similar measures. The return of a Congress Party-led coalition in 2004 is in part attributed to pledges to end the ban and undertake "significant policy changes in favour of unemployed youth" (Balagopal 2006, 2). One year later, however, the central government's Ministry of Finance issued an "austerity measures" memorandum that not only reiterated the ban on the creation of new posts and demanded a rapid review of vacancies but also recommended privatization: "Outsourcing of routine services such as cleaning, maintenance, moving papers/dak etc., may be encouraged" (quoted in Balagopal 2006, 1).

The status of the hiring freeze remains elusive. Dhanka repeatedly stressed to me that they were not getting jobs because there was no governmental hiring. But since the government of the state has clearly hired employees since 2001, there is obviously not an all-out ban on state hiring. It seems possible, then, that the invocation of a hiring freeze is a not-infrequent way that managers within government bodies justify other kinds of hiring practices, such as temporary contracts, about which I have more to say below. I have no evidence that this is the case, but the frequency with which the hiring freeze is cited as an impediment to employment means that someone is claiming its existence, whether official or not. Recent newspaper articles promising that, contrary to popular wisdom, the public sector will hire one hundred thousand new employees and become a "growth" field, as well as the PHED's own recruitment call for 2013 with 1,294 posts, indicate both the widespread belief that there is a hiring freeze *and* that it is not universal.[2]

The second shift that young men report has taken place is increasing competition for posts and higher educational requirements. These are also hard to confirm empirically. As literacy in the state has gone up, certainly there are more candidates meeting basic requirements, thus increasing competition. As the PHED's own personnel statements, originally drafted in 1967 and 1968, are regularly updated as requirements change, they do not provide a documentary history of what might have been required for an "Assistant Driller, Boring" twenty years ago as opposed to today. Older Dhanka men regularly told me, however, that in an earlier generation all that was really required as a qualification for low-level postings was an ST certificate and a kinship link to someone already employed in the department, like a father or uncle.

The final change, and perhaps the most important for Shiv Nagar Basti residents, is the rise of thekedari, or contract labor, in both private and state employment. Dhanka men have historically been engaged in labor related to the building and maintenance of the city of Jaipur, whether as brick bakers or pipe fitters or pump mechanics. Most of these jobs have been government jobs, which remain the most coveted and revered form of employment for Dhanka men. It is for exactly this reason that they are doubly impacted by privatization: not just as consumers who must contend with higher prices for basic services, but also as potential employees who cannot find work.

Since I have been conducting research in Shiv Nagar Basti, residents have talked a great deal about the looming threat of water privatization, which would impact them directly through their connection to the PHED. If the topic has been much on the minds of all Rajasthanis, especially in Jaipur, where parts of the city were expected to run out of groundwater completely by 2009, it has even more so occupied the minds of Dhanka residents, who will suffer in very acute ways.

Dhanka fears are hardly misplaced. The privatization of this collective resource has already been threatened and is not without precedent. When I began my fieldwork in 2002, Rajasthan had just become one of the first Indian states to undertake sweeping reforms of its electricity sector. With the financial support and encouragement of the World Bank, which made reform a condition of its electricity-related loans, Rajasthan followed the "Orissa model" beginning in the year 2000, when it passed the State Reforms Act.[3] This included the constitution of a State Electricity Regulatory Commission to set market-based cost-recovery prices, the "unbundling" of the State Electricity Board,[4] and the signing of a memorandum of understanding with the central government about the state's commitment to electricity reform. The most far-reaching and controversial step was the unbundling, which meant separating electricity generation from its transmission and distribution through the creation of separate corporate entities, which were then privatized (Vadra 2012). On the ground, this has not meant the improvement of services for poor neighborhoods like Shiv Nagar Basti, but it has meant an explosion in the cost of electricity.

So while water has not yet followed suit, despite concerted efforts by multinational private corporations (see Shiva 2002), the two utilities share much in common. Water provision, particularly under the PHED, which has historically employed a large number of Dhanka men, has also been targeted by international funding agencies like the World Bank as a site of inefficiency and fiscal irresponsibility. As Trevor Birkenholtz (2010) shows in his important study of an urban infrastructure project funded by the Asian Development Bank in Jaipur, the PHED has been slotted for dissolution since 2000 when, as part of its "technical assistance program," the Asian Development Bank recommended that private-public partnerships take over water management from state bodies in the interest of eventual full-cost recovery. This is also done in the name of decentralization, since a 1994 act of the Rajasthani Constitution actually mandates the transfer of urban water supply controls away from the state and to local urban bodies.

According to Birkenholtz, this has created an untenable situation for the department, in which they seem doomed to fail: "The PHED continues to have full responsibility in water-sector planning, design and construction of delivery and treatment facilities, service provision, and operation and maintenance. But the PHED does not have autonomy from the state government in either any of their previously listed functions or in the setting of tariffs. This creates a conflict of overlapping mandates and authority, which sets the current system up for failure and opens the door to new approaches for water provision, where [public-private partnership] is framed as the only viable option" (2243).

One stopgap solution that seems to have become popular in a wide range of government departments is for the state to take on and mimic the contract-based hiring practices of private industry. Even if a younger man is able to obtain a posting within the PHED, for example, he is likely to be hired on a temporary contract. Strict regulations governing the duration of these contracts (I was told three to six months) mean that both employers and employees find creative ways to get around regularizing employment, which would include provision of benefits, job security, and other perks. One example is allowing an employee to serve out his contract, dissolving his employment, and then rehiring him under another, false, name. In 2012, I was told by one Dalit PHED employee that he had been working on a contract basis for fifteen years. Not thirty minutes later, I asked a junior engineer in the PHED about this and was told that there were no contract workers in the department at all. But his response to other questions indicated that privatization concerns are widespread among employees. Having heard that he had worked for PHED for eighteen years, I asked him if he liked his work.

JE: [Laughs] Well, there are two things. I'm in service, which is a good thing for feeding my family. And I am doing some service [for the city].
MEGAN: How do people get training? On the job?
JE: It's all on the job. But more importantly, there are no new appointees. All are old. Before there was a kind of apprentice system where a helper would follow a fitter and assist. But there was never any formal training.
MEGAN: So what will you do when all the old employees retire?

He told me the system was changing and was going to a "contract basis." By this he did not mean continuing the current practice of hiring employees on serial contracts, however, but that private companies will form to contract for all the work the employees do now—precisely in the ways envisioned by the 2005 memo from the Ministry of Finance described above. An example is the Bilsapur Dam, which is already managed by a multinational company held by Reliance Industries Limited.[5]

Thus, privatization from below blurs many of the boundaries, particularly those between state and non-state bodies, which have often shaped our analyses of neoliberalism. Even when state institutions like the PHED are not privatized per se, they adopt many of the practices that characterize the private sector, such as contract labor, and in ways that seem to disproportionately affect low-level employees. Groups like the Dhanka see themselves doubly at risk: they no longer have the jobs necessary to pay the prices of "market-led" utilities.

Fathers and Sons

Men like Ram Lal who are entering retirement from government service feel acute grief around their inability to provide good employment for their sons as their own fathers had for them. While there is little that anyone feels they can do about these changed circumstances and the waning of the era of service, stark contrasts are drawn between good, community-minded and hardworking older men and shiftless, consumeristic, and selfish youth. While older men are keenly aware of the structural changes that have taken place, they are also critical of the younger generation—particularly their *un*willingness to study and work.

In their personal narratives of work and family life in Shiv Nagar Basti, men of the era of service stress how far the Dhanka have come since the time of their fathers (*We were adivasis*), their long relationship to the city of Jaipur, their own efforts to better the collective lot of the community, and their spiritual devotion to masters who preach equality. We saw all of these themes reflected in Ram Lal's story of the building of the basti. Another view of this history can be seen in the story of Gopal Singh Mundariya. Gopal Singh finished a high-secondary education in 1972 and began a government service position in 1977. His father had also been employed by the government, but he was illiterate. Gopal Singh narrated his family's history as follows: "Our village is in Jaipur District. Dholatpura. We left that village many generations ago. The work in our village was taking care of animals. We [also] did bonded labor [*begaari*]. . . . We have been here [in Jaipur] since the time of my grandfather. Here he did physical labor [*mazdoori*]. My father was illiterate, but even still he educated us."

Gopal Singh paints his own life as a materials inspector in contrast to a history of forced and difficult physical labor, referring explicitly to bonded labor (*begaari*). This shift was enabled in part by his father's decision to educate him through a secondary graduation, to see into the future and envision a different path for his son. Gopal Singh and his father made choices and expended effort toward the proper inhabitation of a certain ethos—the cultivation of a disposition of willingness in relationship to norms of citizenship

that include civil service, literacy, and community investment. This willingness is seen as the key factor in many men's ability to obtain government
postings, build cement homes, and educate their children.

Like Ram Lal, however, Gopal Singh was upset that the efforts of two
generations seemed to be for naught. When we spoke in 2007, his own son
was employed, though actively seeking a better job. But Gopal Singh implied
that his son's situation was the exception rather than the rule. When asked
why his son was able to find steady work despite the rising unemployment
of young men, he blamed the fact that some young men simply did not have
the proper guidance. He then went on: "We are trying to build a school close
by [the basti] in five to seven years. The kids from the basti will go there. At
least they will get some knowledge. . . . *There is a generation that got left in
between*, but now a new generation is coming up (emphasis added)." The
generation that got "left in between," according to Gopal Singh, is precisely
the one that is now grappling with growing unemployment at the same time
that their inability to obtain secure jobs is seen as a moral failure by their
elders. While his own son may be okay, if underemployed, there are far more
young men who are failing to carry on the project of Dhanka collective aspiration because they lack the necessary dispositions and refuse to cultivate
them. If some blame lies with the community for not ensuring proper schooling, the ultimate responsibility is clearly seen to rest with the young men
themselves.

Indeed, there is a pervasive sense among the men of the era of service that
young men today lack the resolve and, importantly, respect for elders that
enabled their own upward mobility. I am reminded of stanzas of another of
Ravi's poems, "That era has ended":

> A mother's labor.
> The array of responsibilities
> In front of a father.
> An offspring's even slightest
> lending of a hand.
> Now that era has ended.

> The feeling of humility
> In pupils towards teachers.
> Enduring even the switch
> For the zeal for learning.
> Obeisance to the feet
> or—bowing the head.
> Now that era has ended.[6]

As noted by Ann Grodzins Gold (2009), stories of decline and *Kaliyuga* are pervasive throughout India and Rajasthan specifically. *Kali* ("black") *yuga* is the final of the four yugas, or eras, through which time cycles infinitely according to Vedic Hinduism. It is a dark age, when things are upside down, and right actions do not bring their expected rewards; as such, human life gets progressively worse until the universe is destroyed, and the cycles begin again (see Thapar 1996). Much of the evaluation of young men's lack of commitment to personal and community uplift echoes those deteriorating trends found by Gold: "less courtesy and respect within families; less neighbourliness; less sense of community; and more violence perpetuated by humans against other living beings" (2009, 367). This deterioration can be paradoxical because it is also often noted that the Dhanka are better educated than they were in the past. Paradox, however, is one of the defining characteristics of Kaliyuga: it is an upside-down time when proper actions do not produce the expected results (see Cohen 1998). It is also tempting to think of the gap between the men of the era of service and their sons as a gap between the generations, the inevitability of which is a hallmark of a modern consciousness. It is interesting that in their study of Dalit workers in Tamil Nadu, Anandhi, Jeyaranjan, and Krishnan (2002) also found older men describing the lack of respect among young men in terms of Kaliyugam. In this case, community elders were more specific than Dhanka elders about the caste-based humiliation they faced as young men, but there does seem to be a shared sense that young men in both cases do not appreciate the suffering and accomplishment of their elders.

In addition to local discourses about Kaliyuga, it is also the case that young Dhanka men have far fewer opportunities to learn to comport themselves in a manner that expresses the willingness of the era of service because there are simply fewer government jobs. Fewer young men come in contact with the rules, rituals, and pleasures of a service position.[7] They are, in fact, different than their elders. They face a work landscape in which many industries have been privatized and thus removed from the system of reservations that enabled their grandfathers and fathers to enter into government service. This may also be why few young men speak in terms of their identity as "Dhanka." Since they do not benefit particularly from their ST status, their belonging in this category matter less to them than it did to their fathers and grandfathers, who embraced ST status.

For their part, young men seem to appreciate the community-mindedness of their fathers, uncles, and grandfathers, but see their own ability to reach the economic and social status necessary to perform work for the neighborhood as being significantly limited. They recognize that while educational and job reservations may have been a path to upward mobility for their fathers and grandfathers, this path is not open to them in the same way. Much like the young men in Craig Jeffrey, Patricia, Jeffery, and Roger Jeffery's (2008) study of education, employment, and masculinity in Uttar Pradesh, young Dhanka men thus occupy an ambivalent position in relation to hegemonic notions of masculinity.

On one hand, they want the stability of their fathers' employment and oppose changes in family and gender structures, such as women going to work outside the home (unless in dire circumstances). On the other hand, they feel that competition within reserved categories for government jobs, as well as the greatly reduced number of these positions, makes this aspiration unrealistic and untenable. They are at a crossroads where they must imagine future paths while lacking access to the social capital or experiences that might help them forge such a path. It has often struck me that many of these young men are simply frustrated; they often describe what they are doing as *ghumna* ("wandering about") or *timepass* (spoken in English).

Craig Jeffrey has also written extensively about "timepass" as a way to understand what he calls the "waiting characterized by aimlessness and ennui" (2010, 4) of young Jat men in Uttar Pradesh. Like young Dhanka men, Jeffrey's interlocutors are unable to pass into full adulthood because they cannot find employment considered commensurate with their desires or educational levels. Because Jat men are "durably unable to realize their goals" (3), they pass the time by studying, cultivating "style," and engaging in political work. Timepass is thus a useful, if not ideal, set of practices that men can engage in while waiting—sometimes for generations. And herein lies an important difference from the Dhanka case I am describing: young Jat men have a vast political machinery, as well as wealthy landowners from their own caste—both rural and urban—who support them and who can become sources of status and income. Young Dhanka men do have community organizations and events, such as samuhik vivaha, but they have negligible visibility on the state or national scene and widespread poverty within the community, so that even when they might choose to engage in "Dhanka" work, its only real audience is internal—the same fathers, grandfathers, and uncles who find them lacking to begin with.

There are a handful of young men in Shiv Nagar Basti who are trying to emulate the older generation, particularly in their relentless pursuit of good government service positions. One such young man is Rakesh. Rakesh has an unusual reputation among elders, both men and women, in the basti. He is trusted as one who does not do *badmashi* ("wickedness of naughtiness") and get into fights, drink, or flirt with girls; Rakesh is regularly called on to babysit neighborhood children, with whom he is patient and kind. One reason for his popularity might be a kind of collective sympathy: Rakesh's father left his mother over ten years ago, according to neighborhood gossip, and has not returned since. Some residents have been encouraging his mother, a plump, jovial woman, to remarry. She has chosen to remain single, however, and when asked about his father, Rakesh insists that he did not leave the family but went to take a position in the Railway Department in Jodhpur.

Unlike many of his young peers, Rakesh has a steady salary from his contract work in the Railway Department, albeit without the security of a permanent posting. Like many men now entering government jobs, he is hired on the basis of three-month contracts. At the end of each contract, his employment is terminated and he is rehired under another name, a practice that points to the increasing overlap between the public and private sector in terms of employment practices.

It was not easy to procure his job. In addition to the competition he faced within the reserved Scheduled Tribe category, there was a physical fitness component, as well. Rakesh described the process as follows: "I ran 1,500 meter race and finished it in six minutes, so I got credit for that [for the posting]. I also was in boxing, but didn't get the certificate. Then I went to Bikaner and gave an interview and got selected. . . . I got credit for sports and also because I had an ST certificate.[8]" When asked how this ST certificate was obtained, Rakesh explained, "We have to produce our parents' identity card and the ration card. [But] we face difficulties because the *patwari*[9] is never there—he's always absent. And they never do work without taking a bribe. Because he's absent, we have to go to his house and give a bribe."

While the patwari's behavior is inconvenient, it is not necessarily seen as being corrupt; rather, it is expected and even inevitable. Being a gainfully employed Dhanka man does not necessarily conform to middle-class ideas about what it means to be a good employee. While Rakesh was describing his work to me, an older cousin had been sitting and listening in on the conversation. At some point, he asked me to turn off the tape recorder I was using so he could report that anyone could make an extra Rs.100 per day in a government office in the form of bribes given to peons for making sure one's paperwork rose to the top of the pile. This is an expected perk of government service, one that young men continually stressed because in many ways it could be even more reliable than government paychecks, which are notoriously late. Rather than seeing this reliance on bribery as exceptional, we need to consider the extent to which bribes are an expected and normal part of government offices, especially at the lowest levels (see Gupta 1995). Importantly, Class IV salaries, particularly when they arrive late, are not sufficient to support a family as they pay less than Rs. 6,000 per month, the lowest pay grade recorded in the Rajasthan census of government workers (Directorate of Economics and Statistics 2009).

A theme that runs across the generations, from Ram Lal's frequent invocation of his own lack of education to Rakesh's life trajectory, is that employment and the willingness it takes to find the jobs one might need to survive do not necessarily imply a particular level of schooling.[10] While Rakesh regrets the fact that a sudden and severe illness in eleventh class kept him from completing a graduation, he was very clear that education had never been important for his future—his father had told him not to worry because a father in the Railway Department office guaranteed a son a job. Though other examples have shown that this is not always the case, in Rakesh's situation, his employment was taken as a sign that education is something of a waste of time.

Even though he was only employed on a temporary, if serial, basis, Rakesh still evinced the necessary willingness to do something for himself, his family, and his community. This willingness was reaffirmed when, not long after the conversation reproduced above, Rakesh availed himself of a free railway ticket provided to ST candidates and went to Jodhpur to compete in a running race that marked the first stage in an interview for a better job in another department.

A Tale of Two Brothers

Another telling story about the era of contract can be found in the Bagri family, whom I know quite well, in the differences drawn between two brothers, Sunil and A.J. It is generally agreed upon within the family that Sunil is a good man, a hard-working son, and a credit to his parents. Because he found steady work in a garment factory, Sunil was married in 2007 and now has two children, with a third on the way in 2012. He would have liked to have found a government position like his father, who worked at a pump station for the PHED, but Sunil accepted that no position would be forthcoming with the local hiring freeze on and the expenses involved in bribing one's way into a state job. Anyway, government did not seem to be a growth industry anymore, while the textile markets in Jaipur were, and are, booming. Sunil seems set up for a nice life, though it is notable that he does not (yet?) participate in any panchayat activities or samuhik vivaha offices.

A.J., on the other hand, is seen as lazy and unfocused. On any given day, when asking his whereabouts I would be told, "Who knows? He's out roaming about. He just likes to have a good time." Marriage is not on his horizon at the moment because he does not have any kind of job that would allow his parents to find a girl suitable to their status as the extended family of two generations of government workers. Over the years I have tried to find out what A.J.'s own aspirations might have been and asked him what he would like to do for a living. His answer was immediate and excited: *I want to DJ!!* *(d-shh d-shh, pow pow, d-shh).* A.J. explained that his cousin had managed to purchase some sound equipment and sometimes took A.J. with him when he was hired out to DJ a wedding. A.J. loved this work, getting a party moving, and felt like he was good at it. But it was not steady, surely not steady enough for his family, since it was all on a booking-to-booking basis, and he was not a real employee—just given some cash for helping by his cousin. The tension between A.J. and his parents was palpable.

As in many of the cases of the young men I have been able to talk to about their work prospects and hopes for the future, the emotional and social relationship to their inability to find work is, I think, far more complicated than is seen by parents who, perhaps understandably, want the boys to embrace the values of the era of service. The last time I was in Shiv Nagar Basti in 2012, I asked Kanika if she would like to (finally) work as my official assistant, for pay. She dropped her head and laughed out a breathy retort, "Oh come on, didi, how can I roam here and there with you?" (Never mind that she roams here and there with me regularly). But she had a suggestion: "Why don't you hire A.J.?" I could see she wanted desperately for her cousin to work and, importantly, get paid. We found A.J. and I asked him if he'd like to help me interview some neighbors about their work histories, just asking basic questions like what jobs they had done in their lives and whether they'd been on a permanent or contract basis. A.J. listened with a smile that belied what I could see was rising physical discomfort. I was surprised. It seemed like easy money to me, and a fairly pleasant way to earn it. Did he hate the idea? Was he breathing oddly? He said he'd think about it and left the room quickly.

A.J. later told me through Kanika that he didn't think he could do the interviews with me. I started to suspect that his discomfort was not that the job sounded boring, but was born out of anxiety, or even fear. It is possible that A.J.'s reluctance had something to do with fears about his literacy—maybe in his own estimation he was not literate enough—but also, and in an enervated way, he seemed to doubt his ability to occupy the disposition that would allow him to travel around the neighborhood declaring himself a service worker.[11] Since I can only speculate about his internal state, I will describe his reaction only as bodily agitation.

Sunil's status within his family and, perhaps in future, his community, had almost nothing to do with the actual status of his work, and it is worth remembering that even in the aspirational model—the willing Dhanka civil servant with a wife at home in a cement house—the posts that moored the dream were rarely higher than Class IV (the lowest class of government employment). Most Dhanka men have worked as somewhat invisible office employees or low-level pump mechanics and pipe fitters, not as respected members of the administrative services. The prestige is one of relative status, with the salient comparisons being within the community and not outside.

One would also hardly call Sunil an empowered worker in any sense beyond that related to his family and community status. I met the owner of his garment factory during a brief visit to Jaipur in 2012. The owner, who I will call Mr. Aditya, had visited the United States several years earlier to take in the sights. He was keen to start importing his textiles, including high-end wedding finery, into California and wondered if I might take some samples to broker a deal.[12] I declined, telling him he needed someone much more knowledgeable about the US market for Indian clothing. During the entire conversation, Mr. Aditya and I were seated across from one another, Sunil was not invited to sit with us and stayed busy throughout the conversation, making huge stacks of plastic-packaged, embroidered kurtas or organizing hangers filled with elaborate wedding suits for men. Mr. Aditya did not refer to Sunil, the real reason for my visit, even once; Sunil's little sister, who had walked me down the road abutting a Dalit basti on which the factory was located, had not even been allowed to come inside. Flummoxed and annoyed, I made a point of telling Mr. Aditya that Sunil was a very good man, from a well-respected family in his community, and that he could not have been luckier to have him as an employee. I recounted my long friendship with his extended family and neighborhood, and extremely warm feelings about the Dhanka community in general. While I would like to think my outpourings registered and brought some kind of benefit to Sunil later on, I do not know if Mr. Aditya was even listening to me, and, even if he was, I doubt that I seemed like more than a vaguely Christian social worker in his eyes.

Mr. Aditya gifted me a silk kurta as I was leaving, despite my protestations; Sunil, with a great deal of pride, later presented me with clothing for my husband and young son that he appeared to have bought from the factory himself. Any misgivings I felt about receiving such extravagant gifts for my family were slightly assuaged by the realization that it may have been precisely his ability to *buy* garments from his own factory and present them to a family friend from the United States—one that his boss had actually met— that made the whole exchange, including my visit, meaningful for Sunil. He was and would most likely remain a disrespected manual employee in a local textile manufacturing business. But Sunil was willing to do this work (unlike

A.J., who would not or perhaps could not) because of these kinds of trade-offs: private moments of dignity that, if not understood by Mr. Aditya and outsiders, were amply understood by those gathered closely around him and loosely sensed by his foreign friend.

Many young Dhanka men are more like A.J. than Sunil. Like the Dalit/Chamar young men discussed by Jeffrey, Jeffery, and Jeffery (2008) in Bijnor District, these young men have an "image of disillusionment" and claim to be just passing time and doing the best they can. They do not espouse any great faith in the promises of education and can be bitter and defiant in the face of older men's accusations that they are not interested in study or work. Talking to such young men about their school and work histories in 2007, after several years of privatization, I was struck by the dramatic difference between their cultivated nonchalance, even apathy, in the face of increasing unemployment and insecurity, and the concern and ethos of service inhabited by the older generation.

Yet there were moments in which these same young men seemed desperate to explain things from their point of view. One such young man, Nikhil, overheard a Dhanka elder telling me that young men today had no interest in studying, implying that it was a deficit of dedication and effort that had produced the current unemployment situation. Nikhil had an entirely different explanation and jumped in with his own version of the story:

> In every family, there are difficulties. This is why studying isn't effective. At [the time I left school] I had done some studies and also done some work. I was in fourth or fifth class. I worked in an *export company* then. I had to study and also [had] a *duty* to *join*. But both jobs were going on at the same time. Then I didn't have enough time to do either fully. So my family told me to quit, to take a break, because [also] at that time [the school] took two months' fees in advance. I didn't have that kind of money then. . . . Many people choose to leave school themselves. Because there were difficulties. . . . I was really excellent at studies then. In eighth class I did very well. But at that time, because of my family's condition, I left.

In this explanation, Nikhil's choices to leave school are choices made for the community, not in opposition to it. Further, though not explicitly expressed, there is a hint of an accusation in Nikhil's account. If the chosen path of the men of the era of service were effective and open to all, he seems to say, then young men would not have to leave off their educations to help support their families. Men of the era of service are then not doing as well as they would have others believe; their promises seem like naïve faith in a system that does not, in fact, help ST men very much at all.

Nikhil's story is not unique. It is very common for families to pull children out of school when faced with an economic crisis or, as we saw in Rakesh's case, when an illness makes their continued studies difficult. The relationship between illness and men's life chances tell us a great deal about the realities of Dhanka upward mobility—illnesses can be lengthy, treatment difficult and costly, and, if one leaves school at the wrong moment, the consequences of such flights of fate can be lifelong. These patterns are not only found among the Dhanka. In their study of the city of Jaipur, S. Mohanakumar and Surjit Singh (2010; 2011) found that many families dependent on the gem-polishing and construction industries (both sectors employ Dhanka men) were forced to end children's education after the global economic meltdown of 2008. They rightly conclude that once this form of family spending is cut it can never return to pre-crisis levels. There is no going back.

Young men like A.J. tend to think that wisdom and success come not from government service and education, but from their run-ins in the bazaars of Jaipur, from older cousins and brothers, and from on-the-job experience. It is not uncommon for boys from Shiv Nagar Basti to get into physical conflict with other young men in the bazaars; alcohol may fuel these altercations. These spaces can thus be dangerous or exhilarating, depending on the personality and prowess of the particular young man. There is a cultivated "cool" that comes with recounting these stories to sisters, neighbors, and visiting anthropologists upon their return. When asked about their day's activities, a boy fresh from a fight might simply say, "I was wandering around today." This attitude is, of course, performed for the boys' own community; for, as noted by Amita Baviskar in her account of other adivasi men in urban spaces, "young men partake of a bazaaria modernity that is cool, but that rarely translates into higher social status beyond more egalitarian treatment in everyday encounters" (2007, 280). Experience in the bazaars makes a young Dhanka man cool with his friends and female relatives who are forbidden to visit the markets on their own—not with the world at large.

Life under Thekedari

Gopal Singh, whom we met earlier in this chapter, has educated all of his children—four daughters and a son—and helped them seek employment. In general, he thinks those Dhanka who cannot read and write work very hard. Yet, he also aligns himself with a group of five to seven families in the basti who have chosen to "progress" beyond the conditions of the uneducated. Despite seeing a strong work ethic in his fellow Dhanka, he commented, "You know, our samaj is not immune to the influence of the greater society. Our *janjati* is not going to get out of its present mindset that this is our way of life: eat and drink, get married, have kids. This is what our life is. Some families are progressing and bettering their lives. But some have vices." Those who were working to better their families, he went on to say, were also dedicating time and effort to build a special Dhanka school for the area, as well as starting a cottage industry cooperative for women. Gopal Singh thus distances himself from those who simply focus on the daily worries of food and family, and yet he also identifies with them. His shifting use of "their" and "our" points to conflicted practices for drawing sharp distinctions within his own samaj, even if he also acknowledges, indeed reinforces, these distinctions. He is part of a cadre of Dhanka men who we might think of as the successfully upwardly mobile.

Men who must take work on a temporary, contract basis and become dependent on thekedars recognize that they are seen to be missing something "as men," as hinted at by Gopal Singh's distinctions between "us" and "them." Chandrashekar, the husband of my friend Richa, often talked of his struggles as a temporary employee in the PHED. While he was happy to be earning some money, he felt that he was never taken seriously either in his office or at home because he only worked on a contract basis. Other day laborers were even more adamant: thekedari meant that they were at the mercy of contractors, private labor suppliers, who had no loyalty to their workers unless they happened to be Dhanka themselves. The presence of thekedars in Shiv Nagar Basti was a matter of some debate, with some young men claiming that there were many men in the area who served as middlemen for workers, while others claimed that the contractors all came from outside and that this was one of the main factors in the instability of Dhanka employment—the *lack* of a firm, tribally based system for contracting labor.

In other words, thekedars were not criticized as exploiters (though occasionally there were criticisms of the contract system as a whole). Dhanka men wanted contractors loyal to their community.[13] Similarly, men who were struggling to find a government service position tended not to criticize their more successful peers, at least not openly. In contrast to the view espoused by critics of the Indian reservation system that SCs and STs resent their communities' "creamy layer" of elites, these men of service are valued and seen as assets. Geert de Neve finds a similar situation in south India where "the upward mobility of neighbors and friends is taken as an indication of the direction in which this local community of Vanniyars, as a whole, is moving and of the opportunities ahead for those eager to improve their lot. It gives hope to those who are still struggling as workers. . . . Most workers do not scorn more successful neighbors" (2004, 89).

While men such as Gopal Singh may attribute the difference between service and thekedari men to personal drive and commitment or simple preference—and while in some cases this may be true—men who cannot find full-time government employment are not wrong when they argue that the labor market is becoming more difficult. Between 1997 and 1998 and 2001 and 2002, the total number of state employees in Rajasthan decreased from 481,000 to 445,000 (Directorate of Economics and Statistics 2009). Of the half a million state workers who were employed in 2009, 27.19 percent belonged to Scheduled Castes and Scheduled Tribes. But it is interesting to note that of these 127,493 workers, only 9,565 were "gazetted," meaning that they were employed in Classes A and B or given the authority to verify identity and other official documents. Since most Dhanka households in Shiv Nagar Basti earn quite a bit less than Rs. 6,000 per month (the lowest income bracket recorded in official statistics) they are also in the most vulnerable positions when layoffs and hiring freezes occur. Indeed, these were precisely the kinds of positions that the Ministry of Finance recommended outsourcing in 2005. Outside government service, in the industries where Dhanka men are likely to seek work, the situation is equally grave. Mohanakumar and Singh found that a significant proportion of labor households in the gem-polishing and construction industries were pushed down into the lowest income strata, making less than Rs. 3,000 per month (2010, 11). As the median income for Dhanka households I interviewed in 2002 was Rs. 3,125 per month, they can hardly be seen to have been doing well by these standards, even before privatization really took off in Rajasthan.

It is also not necessarily the case that government employment today provides what it was able to provide for the Dhanka in the past. Rakesh's story above hints at government hiring practices that reproduce some of the essential features of the labor system known locally as or "thekedari." While thekedari is technically a system of subcontracting and labor located in the private sphere, in practice, government and private employment involve many of the same structures and practices. Both require bribes to secure a position, both are run through ties of kinship and caste/tribe, and both employ contracts in order to maximize profit, in the name of "efficiency." Rakesh described the most common system for getting around the problem of temporary contract work—both for the employers who do not have to waste time training new employees and for workers desperate to keep their jobs from month to month—that involves official mis-documentation and subterfuge.

There are important differences, however. Of these, perhaps the most important is that while the security of government service is increasingly difficult to obtain, there are institutional measures in place—free rail tickets, physical competitions, and so on—to guarantee that groups like the Dhanka have a chance at that security. Reservations, despite the intense controversy over their categories and future, have worked for the Dhanka. Shiv Nagar Basti is offered up as the physical instantiation of the promise of affirmative action for tribals, and one of the modes of willingness is taking up the mantle of this promise. One does not have infinite choice—the Dhanka have relationships with specific departments like the PHED *because of* a history of caste oppression in the management of waste—but there are legal safeguards that can still be invoked should the occasion arise.

In the world of the private contract, things still run along kin and caste/tribe lines, but there are no such safeguards. I was often told that just because a thekedar showed up to gather workers one day, there was no guarantee that he would show up again. Dhanka dreams of collective aspiration are most visibly embodied in forms—houses, buildings, well-run sewers—that require saving and investment over time. They require the ability to plan and make arrangements for the future. Quite literally, Shiv Nagar Basti and its pukka houses becomes a space of aspiration that reinforces both the sense of community identity and the notion that things can get better—that doing what it takes can bring rewards.

The increasing instability of Jaipur's labor market and the threat of the privatization of the utilities in which Dhanka men have worked for generations make the model of masculinity developed during the era of service untenable for most young and middle-aged men today because they cannot count on a particular income from year to year—or even month to month. The Dhanka are stranded in a zone between the era of service, in which constitutional promises of uplift and empowerment provided the horizon of collective aspiration, and the era of the contract, in which communities are supposed to embrace "self-help" and leave behind the non-modern reliance on caste-based identity and legal affirmative action in the form of reservations. The young men who are "left behind" are precisely the young men who are currently being married and attempting to set up homes and families but without the stability of government work that allowed older generations of Dhanka men to build their hopes in concrete and without the (caste-based) connections to get ahead in a privatized economy. The investment in the community that is the heart of Dhanka collective aspiration has become something of a trap, then, in which the insularity of the tribal form threatens to limit, if not end, the ability to strive for the future. And yet this trap may yet be the Dhankas' best hope. It is, after all, Kaliyuga, in which things are upside down.

8

Conclusion: On Collective Aspiration

In many ways, the Dhanka story is a success story.[1] A modern idea, the idea that differential access to state resources could produce positive changes, gave Shiv Nagar Basti and other Dhanka enclaves in Jaipur working water taps and cement homes. Reservations are a platform that has enabled material changes and generated aspirational practices. They achieved, in other words, precisely what they were intended to achieve, at least for a time. It is worth remembering that the Indian Constitution in which they are ensconced was written by, and reflects the political philosophy of, not an upper-caste elite, but a Dalit leader, B. R. Ambedkar. Ambedkar fought a taxing public battle with Gandhi and incurred the wrath of other leaders across the political spectrum in the 1930s to demand separate electorates for historically oppressed groups. He held firmly to the idea that a religiously inflected majoritarian democracy holds particular kinds of perils for minoritized, oppressed communities that must be *highlighted and grappled with*, rather than wishfully written out of a nation-state's founding moment in a performative "we the people" (see Spivak 1990). Neither Gandhi's self-reflexive and penitent Hindu, nor Nehru's unmarked modern subject, become the singular founding figure of the individual at Indian independence.

Ambedkar's Dalit citizen, the subaltern citizen, the one *marked* by history and deserving of compensatory discrimination, is a figure that dominates the political imagination of groups like the Dhanka.[2] Ambedkar insisted that the state is not the neutral arbiter of an ethnically divided nation; instead, even at the moment of constitution, marked groups are only ever hailed as citizens in their embodied specificity (feminist political theory has also often emphasized this point [Brown 1995; Pateman 1989; Sunder Rajan 2003]). Thus, any history of struggles around recognition and redress is always a study of multiple axes of meaningful social difference. What Dhanka success looks like has been different for women and men; it is different across generational cohorts. This has been an ethnography of the political imaginaries of marked citizens, and thus has had several different tales to tell. There are many more.

✶

The Dhanka story has lessons for us not only about the particularities of the Indian political landscape but also about the role of collective aspiration in our contemporary world. Within the academic Left in the United States, it often feels like modern ideals such as race- or gender-based affirmative action were given up with little compunction in the face of legal and electoral challenges. Because inequality did not go away, these dreams and accompanying practices seemed facile, as tending toward a divisive and disciplining "identity politics." But groups like the Dhanka did not choose the terms under which they would be marked by the state, which only recognized them at all through the category "ST." (Remember their flickering on the edges of colonial records and their continual struggles to hide and stay out of the way: *We were adivasis.*) Their attachment to this category is not one political choice among many, cynically undertaken for its effectiveness, but an attachment that goes to the heart of how they understand their situation and its potential improvement as part of a political landscape in which they are rendered insignificant.

What if those of us who play roles as commentators on and observers of such processes gave up on modern ideas like affirmative action just when we actually need them most? What if we have become so concerned about the coercions of the imperative to be an aspirational citizen that we have neglected aspiration altogether? What if we have forgotten about all the ways in which our current configurations in, for instance, higher education in the United States are products of kinds of collective aspiration similar to those evinced by the Dhanka ST in Jaipur? Surely it must matter that one of my own mentors told me, upon reading this manuscript, that she herself would never have been a professor without US affirmative action policy in the 1970s.

While I have been in conversation with Berlant's (2011, 3) idea of cruel optimism at various moments throughout this book, it bears reiterating one important difference between the contexts of our descriptions: the world she describes, in which "the fantasies that are fraying" are things like "upward mobility, job security, political and social equality, and lively, durable intimacy" is not the world inhabited by many people outside the bourgeois middle classes of the west today. Of course, Berlant never claims that it is. Her account should give us pause precisely because she seems to have described the lens through which many of us in academic social sciences and humanities see the world around us: a genre-less world of the impasse. If we turn our attention to on-the-ground political life in South Asia, we see a very different landscape of fantasy and hope and disappointment. Genre abounds. New worlds are regularly declared born. More than anything, there is struggle. The ongoing, hard work of cultivating the capacity to aspire (Appadurai 2004) in the messiness of political imaginaries that are never innocent, and yet have a promise about democratic participation and material equality at their heart.

For the remaining pages of this conclusion, I propose to take the reader on a brief visit to two more sites of struggle that are connected to the preceding ethnography. Both contain, I want to suggest, a telling suggestion about where global imaginaries for collective aspiration might get a new lease on life. Yet each struggle plays out precisely through attachments to political-legal categories that constrain as much as they enable. This is part of their generativity. Through this exercise, I am suggesting that we use the tools of ethnography and the global scope of anthropological research to reorient the center of political theory toward those places where the struggles over collective aspiration are most obvious. India, today, is one of those places.

I. The Gujjar Agitations

One of the important contexts for this book, which I have yet to discuss in detail, is a series of violent clashes between a middling caste of agriculturalists, the Gujjars, and the Rajasthani police in the summer of 2007 and again in 2008.[3] Led by a retired army colonel, Kirori Singh Bainsla, the Gujjar Arakshan Sangharsh Samiti demanded the inclusion of the Gujjars in Rajasthan's Scheduled Tribe category. Though Gujjars had been declared an "other backward class" (OBC) in 1993, they felt that they had not sufficiently benefited from reserved seats in educational institutions, government employment, and legislatures. Their argument was in many ways simple: like the Minas, Rajasthan's largest Scheduled Tribe, the Gujjars had been labeled a criminal, or "notified," tribe by the British colonial government. The Minas were made a Scheduled Tribe in 1955, however, and the Gujjars were not. Having a majority within the ST category (54 percent) had allowed Minas to corner the benefits of reservations, which were not forthcoming to Gujjars, who had to share the OBC category with groups such as the numerically and politically powerful Jats. Thus, the Gujjar Arakshan Sangharsh Samiti argued that Gujjars should be declared a Scheduled Tribe.

The Gujjars' demand was nothing new—the case for their inclusion in the ST category was first put forth in the 1960s[4]—but in 2007, members of the

Samiti blocked four national highways, and their efforts resulted in a violent clampdown by police. Reports vary somewhat, but at the end of May twenty-five or twenty-six people were killed during clashes between Gujjars and others in eastern Rajasthan; many of these were Gujjar protesters.[5]

In the subsequent hours and days, the protests spread to Delhi, Uttar Pradesh, Haryana, Uttarkhand, and Madhya Pradesh. They came to an end only on June 4, when the chief minister of Rajasthan and member of the BJP, Vasundhara Raje, agreed to appoint a three-person high-powered committee to look into the Gujjars' claims. The committee was to be headed by a retired high court judge, Jas Raj Chopra, and was tasked with submitting a report on the matter in three months (the actual report did not appear until December).[6]

Little changed on either the state's or the Gujjars' side for the next year. On May 23, 2008, a new round of public demonstrations began. As in 2007, the agitations were met with violence. The planned protest resulted in the deaths of seventeen people in Bayana village in Bharatpur. In response, protestors blocked NH-11, an important traffic route between Jaipur and Delhi. The following day, twenty protesters were killed in Dausa. In both locations, protesters gathered the bodies of the dead and refused to cremate them until their demands were met. Throughout early June talks between Gujjar leaders and the Raje government repeatedly broke down; Bainsla was charged with sedition in addition to murder and conspiracy, and the situation appeared at a standstill.

Then, unexpectedly, on June 18, Bainsla called off the agitation after a meeting with Raje. In what seemed to many a complete about-face, he accepted terms that had previously been unacceptable: the Gujjars promised to stop their protests and, in exchange, a special category would be made for them—along with the Banjara, Gadia Lohar, and Raika communities[7]—and a separate 5 percent reservation awarded, on top of the 49 percent already guaranteed to SCs, STs, and OBCs, whose reservations remained untouched.[8]

*

National and international media attention was trained on Jaipur in May 2007 and 2008. For many Indian English news commentators, the explosion of the Gujjar agitations confirmed stereotypes about Rajasthan and its backward, caste-ist politics. Headlines such as that of *India Today* on June 11—"Caste in Conflict: Caste Cauldron between Gujjars and Meenas"— were common. US outlets decried the ironies of communities arguing that they should be recognized as "more backward" than their previous designation in order to achieve upward mobility.[9] Local debate seemed focused on whether Gujjar leaders who drove SUVs and had mobile phones could really represent their community or whether they were a "creamy layer" of opportunists who needed to be skimmed off so that benefits could reach the real, deserving needy.[10] The Chopra Report itself discussed a wide gulf between those urban Gujjars leading the ST battle and the poor and impoverished Gujjars in rural areas for whom they purportedly spoke. To be fair, Bainsla and others were always clear that neither they nor their immediate families would benefit from the ST designation directly. But the question of the creamy layer loomed large and ST inclusion was almost entirely seen as a strategic *choice* undertaken by a leadership eager to exploit any weakness in the reservation system.

In all of the public debate on the Gujjar agitations, the tone has been decidedly cynical. They have become something of a symbol of how far gone the reservation system is, when groups are fighting and dying over tiny percentages of quotas in the face of much bigger problems like drought, rural poverty, and even starvation deaths.[11] Surely these problems should occupy center stage, but the logic that reservations are antithetical to real pro-poor politics misses an important point: quota politics are as much about inclusion as they are about getting ahead, whether this is inclusion on the list of STs, as witnessed in the violent clashes between the Gujjars and the police, or, as we have seen in the case of the Dhanka, inclusion in the ongoing project of building the capital city and participating in the project of Indian modernity through government employment.

While it is undoubtedly the case that regimes of belonging and inclusion always necessitate and depend on exclusions (van Schendel 2011), it seems worthwhile to think a great deal more about why inclusion is read as divisive and dismissed as backward caste-ism in the "new" India so often extolled in glossy metro spreads in Delhi and special reportage in *The New York Times*. There is a special hypocrisy at work when groups like the Dhanka watch the highest level civil servants (Class I and Class II) who are their supervisors and bosses give birth to a globalized generation who neither believe in nor are willing to countenance the continuation of exactly the same institutional formations that enabled their own security. The social science literature is bearing out the insight that much of the project of state privatization is being carried out by the very actors who benefited from state support and protection. For example, in the case of India, Smitha Radhakrishnan's in-depth study of global IT workers shows that the majority of them are the children of civil servants; in other words, "most of those who make up what has been dubbed India's 'new' middle class had parents who were a part of the 'old' one" (2011, 42).

The Dhanka do not believe that difference can dissolve into equality—in assimilation or the end of caste, for instance—yet they demand that the dream of inclusion remain available. "We were adivasis" is not a prelude to an imagination of similitude—*We were adivasis and we would like to be otherwise, like you*—but a demand to be both different and included, to leave the future undetermined in a not-yet, a hopeful *what if*, precisely because what is on offer from today's elites is found lacking (see Pandey 2009). They do not want land, or statehood, or sovereignty, though these have been important goals for adivasis elsewhere. They do not want more loans or a job in a call center. They want a concrete house and a government posting. The politics of inclusion as manifest in the Gujjar agitations is about the continued importance of making demands in ways that are neither militantly separatist nor entrepreneurial, but aspirational. The difference matters.

Appadurai's recent reflections on the capacity to aspire remind us that concrete desires can speak to much broader demands. As he describes it, "aspirations to the good life," which are often articulated as specific desires for particular kinds of consumer goods or employment, are directly tied to some of the most basic local beliefs one can hold (2004, 68). These include those related to "life and death, the nature of worldly possessions, the significance of material assets over social relations, the relative illusion of social permanence for a society, the value of peace or warfare" (68). While he is unclear about the mechanism whereby these broader values get submerged below a choice between one pair of shoes and another, which is their outward manifestation and frequently depoliticized by economists seeking to understand them as "choices," he seems to be implying that at the same time that subaltern voices are strengthened, those who would serve as their allies also learn to *listen* differently (66). It has often seemed to me that what is *heard* in contemporary debates about affirmative action is simple, individual interest; but what is being articulated is a much more complicated set of statements about constitutional guarantees and the necessity of community and the impossibilities of life in the era of the contract.

In this sense, I am even willing to go beyond Appadurai to say that we need not consider aspiration to be a content-less capacity. One of his motivating questions—"whether cultural recognition can be extended so as to enhance redistribution" (63)—has had a social incarnation since 1950: reservation policy. It seems to me that starting a global conversation about recognition and redistribution here, with the history of Indian affirmative action, could engender a very different set of analytics, not to mention politics, with which to consider the claims of aspirational groups, one that starts with concrete histories and does not end with the dismissal that affirmative action policy has not done what it ought and should therefore be abandoned.

II. A Ruling from the Ministry of Tribal Affairs

On March 5, 2014, I received the following e-mail from Kalu Ram Kayath, a former commissioner and dedicated provocateur in Dhanka causes:

> my dear magan
>
> very good news Ministriy of trible affi New Delhi withdrawn letter dates 13.07.2010. for ST DHANKA, RAJASTHAN

He had attached the document itself as a .pdf file, with its official filing number, copious signatures, and emblazoned letterhead. Of course, Kalu Ram's telegram-like note did not need any explanation. The implications of the new memo were clear: the Ministry of Tribal Affairs had ruled on the Dhankas' side. The 2010 memo that forbid officials to give ST certificates to Dhanka not hailing from Abu Road had been rescinded. From now on they were going to get the official certificates to which they were entitled and which would get them government jobs. They had won.

The victory was a huge relief after the anxiety around this issue during my last trip to Jaipur in December of 2012. As soon as my fall class ended, I brought the working draft of this manuscript—a thick, spiral-bound document—to Shiv Nagar Basti as proof that I had, indeed, been working on a book all this time. That it was almost, but not quite, done. *But Meghna-bai, how long does it take to publish a book in your country? Give it to me and I'll get it done next week!* various friends told me. *We need you to publish this now!*

In general, people agreed that the title, *We Were Adivasis*, was pretty good. Many nodded their heads and said, "Yes, that's right. We *were* adivasis." Maybe there was even more confidence in this assertion; it seemed to matter more than ever before. The Dhanka were still not getting their ST certificates then, and they blamed another Scheduled Tribe, the Mina, for their illegal exclusion. They said the Mina didn't want any competition in the ST category and were working on squeezing them out. My last conversations before leaving were all about how I might help publicize Dhanka struggles against the 2010 memo from the Ministry of Tribal Affairs. I planned to write an article about it but wondered if any of the normal channels—the media or the courts or the bureaucracy itself—would be effective (see Moodie 2013b). There was rising anxiety, even desperation, around the issue.

And then they won.

The Ministry of Tribal Affairs' decision to rescind the 2010 memo has to be attributed, in large part, to the efforts of Kalu Ram himself and his strategic use of a new tool in peoples' struggles across India: the Right to Information. In the last fifteen years, India has seen the emergence and growth of a broad-based coalition known as the National Campaign for the Right to Information that demands greater governmental transparency and accountability. The national social movement around access to information grew out of a number of more local struggles against development (Baviskar 2010). In Rajasthan, a group called the Mazdoor Kisan Shakti Sangathan (Workers' and Farmers' Power Union), or MKSS, began organizing rural farmers to demand information about vital drought relief works and development projects in their area. Through events known as *jan sunvais* ("public hearings"), in which actual conditions were compared against public records (for instance, had a particular road actually been repaired and in the manner recorded in government documents?) they were able to bring to light discrepancies and impel immediate action on the part of apathetic or corrupt local officials. According to Amita Baviskar, these efforts "punctured" the hegemonic power of the state and enabled a moment in which the poor were actually able to speak truth to power (136). The demands garnered such broad-based support that in 2000 Rajasthan became one of the first states to pass a Right to Information Act. A national Right to Information Act followed in 2005.

On the basis of the 2005 decision, all government departments and public sector organizations have been ordered to put in place processes and officials to handle public requests for information; new Public Information Officers, for instance, are being trained in many departments. It is to such officers that Kalu Ram has submitted frequent petitions on behalf of the Dhanka seeking not only to repeal the 2010 memo but also to publicly name and shame particular officials whom he and other Dhanka elders feel are personally responsible for their current plight.

For example, on February 8, 2011, Kalu Ram used the Right to Information (RTI) to ask for an explanation as to why a particular official of the National Commission of Scheduled Tribes in Jaipur (incidentally, the same official who authored the infamous 2010 memo that barred Dhanka from ST certificates), was able to use government funds to purchase a laptop computer. Unsatisfied with the response he received in March, and after a series of bureaucratic runarounds, Kalu Ram filed several appeals until he ended up pleading his case at a hearing of the Central Information Committee in Delhi. The committee ruled that the original question—whether the official in the Jaipur office actually had the authority to use public funds to buy a laptop—had never been answered satisfactorily. It demanded a copy of the letter justifying the laptop purchase (see Moodie 2013b for more details). A bureaucrat's mundane transaction, purchasing a computer with public funds, which might otherwise have gone unremarked, now not only is questioned but also must be made part of the public record.

Kalu Ram's ability to navigate the terrain of a new RTI process cannot be disconnected from his personal history as a civil servant. As other observers have pointed out, RTI activism is entirely premised on the existence of a vast documentary record for many state projects, which means that groups and individuals who lack either basic or bureaucratic literacy may have trouble demanding implementation of the laws (Baviskar 2010; Webb 2012). His ability to raise questions in the appropriate language and pursue claims when they repeatedly take him as far as Delhi is grounded in the Dhanka history of reservations in multiple ways. Reservations provided Kalu Ram not only with a job in which he encountered and used the language of the state on a daily basis (while learning its rituals and rankings). That same reservation also provided him a secure retirement (a state pension), which now affords him the means for full-time activism and travel. Kalu Ram's victories are unintended outcomes of reservation policy.

While I would not want to dismiss concerns about the way that RTI quests can require new brokerage relations with government officials (Webb 2012), it is also the case that, as Baviskar argues, the inclusive organizational strategy of the National Campaign for the Right to Information has also meant including the state, such that much RTI activism tries to work with, rather than against, the state. In this sense, it is quite different from other social movements. As Baviskar puts it, "The emphasis on *hamari sarkar* (our government), asserting ownership, is a key element of democratizing the state and reducing the distance between state and citizen" (2010, 143). The campaign has always had supporters within the government, and many of the most visible figures in local movements, including several of the founders, have backgrounds in government service.

It may be that such struggles are precisely where we encounter the creativity of subaltern citizenship—a creativity that emerges *because of*, not in spite of, proximity to those state institutions the theorization of which usually produces subalterneity as an exclusion, or outside. They should garner our attention and support because they defy teleological accounts of political modernization and speak to the messy conditions of the political everyday. The subaltern civil servant is the "fragment," to use Gyanendra Pandey's term, the "interruption," that demands a new set of questions about democratic participation (dare we say civility?) (2009). There are new possibilities emerging that do not doom us to a search for the social movement that is truly and finally an alternative (or a revolution); rather, the kind of activism that has emerged around RTI produces a heady blend of constitutional promises and grassroots strategies that may reinvigorate the possibilities of accountable democracy.

Throughout my account, I have stressed the ingenuousness of Dhanka efforts to conduct themselves as exactly the kinds of aspirational citizens the constitutional regime of recognition asks them to be. I have tried to show that, rather than seeing the promises contained within the tribal role of reservation policy as simple ruses of power, we must attend to the ways that subaltern communities continue to use the available resources—state languages of development; local, gendered codes of comportment including willingness and respectability; long histories of doing what it takes to get out of the way and get by—to demand that the nation-state make good on its twinned commitments to universal, democratic participation and social uplift for the poor and oppressed. In an era of cynicism, it is important to document hope.

*

And yet.

*

If there is one central lesson of feminist theorizations of citizenship, it is that it is always inflected by locally relevant categories of difference. When I wrote the above paragraph, I incarnated an equal-opportunity subaltern civil servant—"he or she"—knowing full well that today this figure is very unlikely to be a woman. The extent to which community striving depends on a particular gender configuration, particularly through marriage, should, I hope, give us all pause. Throughout the previous chapters, I hope to have shown the ways in which Dhanka intimate life and Dhanka political life are inextricably intertwined in the promises of collective aspiration. I have argued that it is in marriage—as a community institution, a site of sociality, and a horizon of imagination—that we can most clearly see Dhanka negotiations of the politic-legal category "Scheduled Tribe" and the way that these negotiations require the cultivation of different dispositions by Dhanka women and men.

In describing the specifically gendered sociality that emerges in the spaces of the home and the neighborhood I have *also* tried to point to possibilities that things could be otherwise, to other dreams, and have tried to avoid taking for granted that particular kinds of attachments and dispositions have necessary outcomes. I do not see Dhanka futures as irrevocably patriarchal—there are no timeless traditions here but only (always) emerging worlds. I have learned to see domesticity as possibility, for instance, and to take seriously the lessons we might learn from young women who negotiate an ambivalent relationship to community-building projects that shape their lives but from which they are largely excluded. We will have to stay focused on multiple valences of practices like "keeping house" to notice and support the emergence of worlds more in line with Dhanka girls' heretofore thwarted imaginations for their own futures. We may have to give up some of our own most dearly held dreams. This is, if ever there was one, a time to put critical feminist ethnography at the heart of political practice.

A Short Glossary

adivasi—The literal translation of this term is close to "earliest inhabitant" or "those who originally dwelled [in a place]." The term seems to have been used first to refer to the "Adivasi
Mahasabha" of Chhotanagpur in 1938 and was popularized in the 1940s by A. V. Thakkar,
a social worker and advocate for tribal peoples (who was also a highly visible member of
the Indian National Congress (Hardiman 1987, 13n34). It is used now as a general term to
refer to India's tribal populations, particularly by those who are invested in transnational
discourses of indigeneity.

jati—Often translated as "caste," this term refers to groupings and subgroupings of individuals who recognize themselves as belonging to a community or lineage. "Jati" is regionally
specific and not generalizable across the subcontinent, unlike "varna," which refers to one
of the four groups described by Vedic texts as Brahmin, Kshatriya, Vaishya, and Shudra.

janjati—Usually translated into English as "tribe," as in the *Oxford Hindi-English Dictionary*.
"Janjati" refers to a jati or caste in which the prefix "jan" ("folk" or "group") indexes an
origin prior to jati. One translation therefore might be "primitive caste." Dhanka commonly
use this term interchangeably with "adivasi" to refer to themselves in historical materials.

Scheduled Caste (SC)—The official, legal term used to refer to caste groups included in the Indian Constitution's list, or "schedule," of former Untouchables who are eligible for reserved
seats in government service, legislatures, and educational bodies; special protections under
criminal law; and supplementary development-related funds.

Scheduled Tribe (ST)—The official, legal term used to refer to communities included in the
Indian Constitution's list, or "schedule," of tribal peoples who are eligible for reserved seats
in government service, legislatures, and educational bodies; special protections under criminal law; and supplementary development-related funds. Eligibility is based on five very
general criteria, laid down by the Chanda and Lokur Committees in the 1960s: presence of
primitive traits, distinctive culture, geographical isolation, shyness of contact with outsiders, and backwardness.

Note: Scheduled Caste and Scheduled Tribes are often referred to together, as "SC/ST."

Notes

Chapter One

1. *Basti* is usually translated as "slum," though it may refer to a wide range of dwelling spaces, from stick-and-tarp squatters' camps to what in American English might be termed "bad neighborhoods" with permanent structures. Shiv Nagar Basti is of the latter type.

2. According to the Jaipur Municipal Corporation, Jaipur is now ranked eleventh in population among India's megacities (Government of Rajasthan 2006, http://jnnurm.nic.in/wp-content/uploads/2010/12/CDP-Jaipur1.pdf).

3. My work in Dhanka basti began in 2002 while I was conducting dissertation research on state-sponsored programs for women's empowerment in Rajasthan. I visited the neighborhood with a friend's NGO that was, at that time, running a reproductive health post in Ram Lal's house, under the auspices of a joint World Bank-Government of Rajasthan initiative called the Reproductive and Child Health (RCH) Kacchi Basti program. The NGO workers were not aware that the majority of the inhabitants of the neighborhood were members of the Dhanka tribe until I conducted a very informal social study for them. While the NGO's relationship with the basti eventually deteriorated and ended, my own personal relationships with Ram Lal and his family, as well as other Dhanka residents, grew over time. I therefore spent a great deal of the period of my dissertation research (the academic year 2002–2003) in Dhanka basti and have returned for several visits in the intervening years. Thus, this book is based on fifteen months of ethnographic research conducted between 2002 and 2012. My relationship with the city of Jaipur predates this project, beginning with undergraduate study in 1996.

4. While I discuss *sati* and *satimatas* in Chapter 4, here it bears noting that while English speakers tend to use the term "sati" to refer to an act—following British colonial usage—the term "sati" actually refers to "a good woman," which is something one is transformed into even before death. In the Rajput ideology that dominates contemporary discussions of widow immolation in Rajasthan, "becoming a sati" is a process of transformation that involves making a vow—a *vrat*—to carry out an act of self-destruction (see Harlan 1992). Most feminist commentators have rightly insisted that we mark a difference between "sati as a discourse" (Mani 1986) and the "primary violence" (Sangari and Vaid 1996, 240) of the immolation of women on the funeral pyres of their husbands. I therefore use "sati" for the discourse and "immolation" for the violent act.

5. These official histories tend to begin with the abolition of sati in 1829 in Bengal (Uberoi 1996).

6. There are studies that talk about gender and social reform among adivasi groups somewhat indirectly, such as Hardiman 1987 and Baviskar 2008. A feminist reading of Bhil rebellions and social reform movements that attends explicitly to questions of gender and sexuality is a truly worthwhile project that has yet to be undertaken. For a discussion of social reform outside the direct colonial ambit, see Bhagavan 2001. It is also important to keep in mind Anjali Arondekar's (2012) insight that while social reform debates may provide a political framework, they do not determine the meaning of all reform efforts—particularly those that are community-based—in all places and at all times (250).

7. This is less the case when we are able to track changing caste practices over several generations. I think of G. Arunima's discussion of changes in matrilineal kinship among the Nayar in Malabar (1996), Prem Chowdhry's study of the Jats (1994), and, in a different vein, Maria Mies's study of the lace makers of Narsapur (1982) as good examples wherein non-elite marriage practices are given in-depth consideration alongside an analysis of British-inflected notions of respectability and nationalist aspirations to good Indian womanhood.

8. The subject line of this letter reads, "Clarification on the Synonymous/Phonetic Similarity name of Dhanak, Dhanuk, Dhankia as Scheduled Castes; and Dhanka, Tadvi, Tetaria, Valvi as Scheduled Tribes in the State of Rajasthan." I stumbled upon the source while searching for another reference to the Dhanka. (Accessed on February 15, 2011, http://ncst.nic.in/writeread data/linkimages/MTA_Clarification_for%20Dhanka_in_Rajasthan3405967512.pdf.)

9. Some groups historically labeled "tribes," such as the Meo, are Muslim; Muslims as a group are not eligible for reservations.

10. Unnithan-Kumar incisively challenges this popular view and shows that tribal women are not "more free" than other Hindu and Muslim women but are similarly positioned with regard to the inheritance of resources such as land.

11. As I discuss in Chapter 2, the current criteria for tribal recognition were laid down by the Chanda and Lokur Committees in the 1960s and are as follows: (1) presence of primitive traits, (2) distinctive culture, (3) geographical isolation, (4) shyness of contact with outsiders, and (5) backwardness. The profound ambiguity of these categories is the source of a great deal of political turmoil around tribal definition in Rajasthan today.

12. Though my use of the term "disposition" is intended more as something of an evocation, or a citation nearby, rather than a direct reference, readers may note its relationship to the work of French sociologist Pierre Bourdieu. There is some ambiguity in Bourdieu's own use of "dispositions" and their relationship to another well-known term, "habitus." Sometimes they seem interchangeable, as when he comments that "the word *disposition* seems particularly suited to express what is covered by the habitus (defined as a system of dispositions)" (1977, 214n1). And it may not even be particularly useful to worry about the distinction. It does seem to me, though, that "disposition" refers specifically to the work of cultivation that it takes to orient oneself in a particular way, referring to "the immense preliminary labour that is needed to bring about a durable transformation of bodies and to produce ... permanent dispositions" (2001, 38). Dispositions are also about recognition—how one is able to see who is a part of the group—and that recognition (and therefore exclusion) is the necessary condition for the emergence of groups at all. (It is not a coincidence, I think, that this term emerges most importantly in Bourdieu's work on masculine domination and discussions of a sense of honor). Dispositions are structures, but not deterministic. They are a "predisposition, tendency, propensity, or inclination" (1977, 214n1, italics removed).

13. In this way, the statement is not dissimilar to the statement "In the past, we were a bit 'Chamar,'" about which Manuela Ciotti has written (2006). She stresses that Manupur Chamars in Uttar Pradesh are keen to narrate their backwardness into the past and embrace a modernist, progressive narrative of history in which their present is considerably better by virtue of education. (Education, not incidentally, guaranteed by reservations for Scheduled Castes). Unlike Dhanka in Jaipur, Manupur Chamars do not, for instance, find the cultural model of the cycle of *yugas* (each of the four eras through which time repeatedly moves, according to some Hindus) particularly convincing, preferring to find the causes for misfortune in upper-caste oppression—particularly the historic refusal to educate Untouchables. It is telling that the group with whom Ciotti worked do not try to legitimate their claims for rights and equality by locating themselves within Hindu tradition; for instance, they do not try to locate themselves in the epics such as the Mahabharata. It is tempting to say that proving their antiquity is less important to Chamars because they do not have the burden of proving indigeneity. The story is more complicated, however, because they do embrace Ambedkar's retelling of the ancient history of caste in which Dalits and adivasis, now called Adi Hindus, are part of the original population of South Asia who were driven south, dispossessed, and conquered by invading Aryans (207–209). The comparison could perhaps be fruitfully developed, but is beyond my scope here.

14. There are important differences between the Australian case described by Povinelli, which has placed a high premium on the promise of the "authentic," and the Indian case, of course, where contests over the original inhabitation of the subcontinent are a terrain of historical debate and Hindu nationalist assertion (Baviskar 2007).

15. Stuart Corbridge (1988) writes, "The main propositions of this ideology [of tribal economy and society] . . . are (1) that the concept of a tribe is given and unproblematical; (2) that the tribals of South Bihar are the original inhabitants of Jharkhkand, where they still predominate; and (3) that tribal politics and tribal policies are effective because individual tribes are themselves undifferentiated, united and geographically concentrated" (1).

16. This term comes from Gahlot and Dhar (1989).

17. Ann Grodzins Gold (2009) notes similar narratives in rural Rajasthan (see also Gold and Gujjar 2002).

18. See Williams 1973.

19. Dumont (1980) comments: "For modern common sense, hierarchy is a ladder of command in which the lower rungs are encompassed in the higher ones in regular succession" (65).

20. Srinivas notes that the view of caste as a single ladder of ranked groups was an important part of British colonial imaginings of India. Struggles around where a group should be located point to the paucity of this model but, for Srinivas, do not call it into question.

21. The focus on Brahmins to the exclusion of other upper castes has been one of the most often-cited critiques of Sanskritization theory. It led to the proposition of several other terms such as "Rajputization" (Sinha 1962). To be fair, Srinivas tried to account for this variation, which he saw as regional, in later iterations of the theory. For instance, in *Caste in Modern India*, he noted that "though, over a long period of time, Brahminical rites and customs spread among the lower castes, in the short run the locally dominant caste was imitated by the rest. And the locally dominant caste was frequently not Brahmin" (Sinha 1962, 44).

22. The Bhil comparison is especially relevant because many believe that the Dhanka are an offshoot of the Bhil tribe. I discuss this possible historical link in Chapter 2.

23. "Liberalization" in India is a term most often used to refer to a set of changes post 1991. It is frequently used interchangeably with "neoliberal," which in the Indian context I take to generally refer to a shift from India's more protectionist-style socialism to policies intended to

"open" Indian markets. As many commentators have noted, it also coincides with the rise of Hindu nationalism as part of a middle-class common sense (see Mazzarella 2003, Oza 2006); to smooth over the potential contradiction, neoliberalism in India stresses that India will join the global market in its own way.

24. Besides simply being a moment of classism and condescension, such a commentary belies the extent to which, as Leela Fernandes and Patrick Heller (2006) argue, "Sociocultural inequalities and identities . . . are an integral part of the process of middle class formation" (497).

25. I leave aside here frequent complaints in everyday talk and in the media by upper castes that they are experiencing downward mobility—a state of affairs they often attribute to affirmative action and the rise of lower-caste movements.

26. The desire to "give back" has been noted as one of the most notable characteristics of beneficiaries of affirmative-action programs in the United States. Bowen and Bok (2000) note that African-American graduates of elite schools are significantly more likely to be involved in community organizations than other African-Americans or white Americans.

27. More "classic" formulations along this line are Leacock 1972; Mies 1982; and Meillassoux 1981. Recent authors in this vein would include Boris and Parreñas 2010; Tadiar 2004; and Vora forthcoming.

28. It is clear in Mahmood's account that women participating in the piety movement are making and remaking its parameters as much as they are "participating" in them. But it does seem to me that the codification and ritual involved provides a kind of structure, even an aspirational one, *organized around gender*, that is not to be found in many contexts.

29. This argument is different than, though not unrelated to, arguments about, for instance, the politics of gay marriage in the United States. Michael Warner's (1999) critique of state regulation of intimacy and pleasure, as well as the exclusions created by marriage, are broadly applicable in many contexts. However, his tendency to define "majoritarian" and "queer" predominantly, if not entirely, in relation to the intimacy of sexuality (whether this is his intention or not—and I do not think it is) means that his analysis cannot capture the nuance that a more intersectional analysis might require. So, for groups for whom "kinship and exogamy" have not "receded" (139)—arguably there are such groups in Warner's own context—we might encounter a wholly different politics of marriage.

30. Shah Bano had been abandoned by her husband of forty years in the late 1970s. She took him to court under the ostensibly secular Code of Criminal Procedure (CCP) of 1973 to demand that he pay maintenance. The courts all agreed, and in 1985 the Supreme Court of India ordered Shah Bano's ex-husband to pay her maintenance. The decision was seen as a victory by feminists, who attempted to translate the energy behind the case into a step toward the drafting of a Uniform Civil Code that would give Indian women the right to avail themselves of non-religious law. Some Muslim groups, however, vocally decried the decision as an erosion of their right to be judged under Islamic law and the imposition of Hindu law under the guise of secularism. Shah Bano herself was persuaded by influential clerics to repudiate the decision in her favor, and in 1986 the Muslim Women (Protection of Rights in Divorce) Act was passed. This law made it impossible to seek maintenance under the CCP and further specified the *mehr* and *iddat*, two customary forms of payment to Muslim women upon divorce, to which Muslim women are entitled (see Engineer 1984; Menon 2000).

31. I take my approach here to be in conversation with much recent work on "the education of desire" in colonial and postcolonial settings. Ann Stoler's (2002) work, for instance, has focused on the management and enactment of intimate domains—domesticity, sexuality, affection—in order to examine "how power shaped the production of sentiments and vice

versa" (12). Similar approaches have been taken in recent ethnographies of the co-constitutive links between intimate life and what we might call global economic logics (see Wilson 2004; Faier 2009).

32. In my reading of Spivak, ethical singularity is a possible goal and occasionally a fragilely achieved moment, but not a condition for intimacy. It is its quickened state.

33. Veena Das's (2007) description of ethically accountable fieldwork is also apt here: "When I reach bedrock I do not break through the resistance of the other, but in this gesture of waiting I allow the knowledge of the other to mark me" (17).

34. Feminist scholarship cautions us against the fetishization of voice—either as a presence or an absence (Arondekar 2009; Visweswaran 1994). Indeed, as Gloria Raheja and Ann Gold (1994) have argued about women's verbal worlds in north India, we need not read silence as acquiescence. "Submission and silence may be conscious strategies of self-representation deployed when it is expedient to do so, before particular audiences and in particular contexts" (11). Ethnography, unlike history, does allow us to get some sense of these shifting contexts, not with the intent of giving voice to another, but to look at "the discontinuity, the interpenetration of the hegemonic and the subversive, and their varied deployments, from moment to moment in everyday life" (16).

Chapter Two

1. The letter was actually forwarded by the minister for tribal affairs in Delhi to the chief secretary of the government of Rajasthan but originally written by the National Commission for Scheduled Tribes (NCST).

2. A taluka is an administrative unit, often comprised of a town or several villages.

3. The exact text reads: "Since Abu Road taluka of Banaskantha districts of Bombay State was transferred to Sirohi district of Rajasthan, as a consequence, 'Dhanka' including Tadvi, Tetaria and Valvi was listed at S. No. 5 under 3 in Abu Road taluka of Sirohi District under the State of Rajasthan having area restricting meaning that Dhanka, Tadvi, Tetaria Valvi [sic] tribal groups of Abu Road Taluka were only eligible for S.T. certificate."

4. Dhanka insist that this claim was tendered by members of the Mina community. I have come to be skeptical about many such claims as they may just as easily reflect an anti-Mina sentiment that I have noted has been on the rise in Rajasthan since I began my fieldwork there. Certainly, the Gujjar agitations of 2007–2008 did a great deal to pit the Dhankas and the Minas against one another, and my preference is not to add fuel to this fire as it seems counterproductive for both communities. It is true, however, that the individual who authored the letter is from the Mina community.

5. I discuss the NCST letter and its implications more thoroughly elsewhere (see Moodie 2013b).

6. Gahot and Dhar make the comment in their *Castes and Tribes of Rajasthan* that "there are 12 tribes found in the state during 1981 Census. Of these, six are rather insignificant" (1989, 208). I find the statement extremely telling about the invisibility of the Dhanka, even within tribal studies of Rajasthan.

7. Crispin Bates makes a similar point: "both the concept [of tribe] and its object have always been a political construct. Rather than ask 'who were the adivasis' therefore, it might be better to ask 'who wants to define them', since the definition of original or anterior inhabitants is usually a preliminary to the establishment of claims to political or economic power or (alternatively) reflects the power of an existing elite, exerting its cultural hegemony" (1995a, 17).

8. I use "role" here rather than the more commonly used term "slot" to emphasize the scripted yet performative—and hence, unpredictable—aspects of enacting Scheduled Tribe identity. It also seems to me that there has been something of a simplification of Michel-Rolph Trouillot's (1991) notion of the "savage slot," which is cited as inspiration for later uses. In my reading, Trouillot is demonstrating the role of the Janus-faced savage (both noble and frighteningly other) in an early modern worldview that is the historical condition of possibility for the emergence of nineteenth-century anthropology, including colonial anthropology. His interest is not particularly in the institutional (state or colonial-corporate) structures that define the savage—in fact, he wants to think about the pre-histories that make the emergence of these structures possible—but more in a pervasive imaginative project that involves Europe reflecting on itself; indeed, he calls it the West becoming the West. Thus, while both Tania Li (2000) and Bengt Karlsson (2003) illuminate important issues surrounding the politics of claiming tribal or indigenous identity in divergent national or transnational arenas, these "slots" are of an altogether different kind.

9. There seems to be a growing, global interest in the question of India's genetic diversity; genetic studies are also used to map historical migrations. (See, for example, Thanseem et al. 2006; on the emergence of genetic information as biocapital, see Sunder Rajan 2006).

10. A quick list of Bhil participation in anticolonial revolts makes this clear. Bhils led violent agitations against the British in 1856 and in 1912 (under the Bhagat leader Govind Giri). They were participants in Gandhian actions including the Salt March and the Quit India movement and in 1940 convened a meeting that declared their intent to overthrow British rule (Lobo 2002).

11. The Dhanka relationship to the state is closer to that described by Kriti Kapila for the Gaddis in Uttaranchal: "Gaddis' everyday relationship to the state to an extent is 'extractive', in that they have a strong sense of what can and should be derived from the state as an entitlement. But their sense of political identity historically comes less from confrontation with the state than from a process of negotiation, compromise, and strategy . . . They see themselves as abiding by the state agenda in order to derive benefits and to influence and shape the agenda as much as possible at the local and regional level" (2008, 128).

12. Indeed, a good deal of work has to be done to make "adivasi" equivalent to the international language of "indigenous peoples."

13. On this legal issue, see Galanter 1984, Chapter 11.

14. Galanter argues that the latter has been a somewhat more contentious category. Beginning in the early twentieth century, the question of who belonged in the "depressed classes" that were to be the target of legal and philanthropic efforts drew strong disagreement (1984, 122). Galanter is perhaps correct in the sense that fewer court cases have been tried, historically, around ST status and that STs have, until recently, had fewer public debates over inclusion and exclusion. If we think of the struggles for statehood (Jharkhand and Chattisgargh) and separatist movements in the northeast (the Nagas, for instance) as in some ways constituting reactions to the inadequacies of reservation policy in addressing the struggles of tribal groups, however, the history can be cast somewhat differently.

15. The bulk of the work of the Lokur Committee, which was conducted over a two-month period, was in compiling specific lists for inclusion and exclusion in the schedules. Their recommendations were not heeded (see Galanter 1984, 137–138).

16. K. S. Singh, well-known author of *The People of India* series argues, rather, that the beginning of special tribal regulation began with a tribal uprising in the Arakan Hills in the 1820s (McMillan 2005, 112).

17. This was itself a paternalistic and erroneous view, as many tribals participated in violent resistance against British rule throughout the nineteenth century and because some who had contact with the Congress rejected it because of its base in exploitative caste structures (see Hardiman 1987; Bates 1995a)

18. Elwin's oft-cited comment that tribals should be placed in a national park—which critics liken to a "zoo"—was made in the closing pages of his 1939 ethnography of the Baiga. He later regretted the comment (Guha 1999, 156).

19. Bhil Minas are a separate tribe, descended from both groups, and recognized in a separate category.

20. It is important to keep in mind that the Dhanka were not officially part of Rajasthan's Scheduled Tribe roster until 1976, after the Removal of Area Restrictions (Amendment) Act. Census data, therefore, jumps from 1931 to 1981.

21. I leave aside here the thorny issue of whether "Dhanak" and "Dhanka" are or were the same community.

22. In the work of Michel Foucault, "strategy" is most often used to talk about the power that crystallizes in the state apparatus (see Foucault 1978, 92–93). But it applies equally to those forms of resistance that emerge in any given epoch. His assertion "there is no power that is exercised without a series of aims and objectives. But this does not mean that it results from the choice or individual subject" (95) could apply to state power and resistance alike. It is thus useful for thinking about how current Dhanka efforts to make claims on the state both rely on and exceed its power, even as they are articulated almost entirely within its own terms.

23. Jaipur would probably not be included on many historians' mapping of Bhil country. This may be precisely because groups like the Dhanka are generally left out of studies of Bhils in western India. It remains to be seen what such a remapping might do to our sense of this region and seems a highly worthwhile line of research.

24. At the time of the publication of *Tribal Life in Gujarat: An Analytical Study of the Cultural Changes with Special Reference to the Dhanka Tribe*, P. G. Shah was the president of the Gujarat Research Society, which he also helped found in 1936. He was also a past-president of the Anthropological Society of Bombay. Shah studied the Dhanka to fill out the ethnological picture of Gujarat as it was seen as the only tribe not yet studied by anthropologists. Shah was obviously greatly influenced by the work of Margaret Mead, and his ethnography considers culture "traits, habits, and practices" that are relatively stable as well as a force that can change "personality structure" (6). The fieldwork on which the book is based was conducted by graduate students, overseen and visited by Shah, over a period of three years (7). The Gujarat Research Society also pursued extensive anthropometric studies (Datta-Majumder 1947, 161), so it is perhaps not surprising that the final three chapters of *Tribal Life in Gujarat* are entitled "Anthropometry of the Gujarat Tribes," "Serological Study of Gujarat Tribes," and "Psychological Evaluation of the Dhanka Tribe."

25. Pavagadh is a small mountain forty-six kilometers from Vadodara in present-day Gujarat. It was an important site near Champaner in the fifteenth century. It has been claimed that Champaner was the seat of a Bhil dynasty and that the Bhils held what is now the city of Ahmedabad until the eleventh century (*Gazetteer of the Bombay Presidency* 1901, 9: part 1).

26. Chauhan Rajputs were also in power in parts of present-day Rajasthan, including Udaipur.

27. Another name for Durga or Parvarti; the latter is a consort of Shiva.

28. The Archaeological Survey of India says that Mahmud Begada defeated Patai Rawal, the last Rajput holdout in the region, after a twenty-month siege from 1483 to 1484. After

his victory, Mahmud Begada renamed Champaner "Muhammadabad" (Sivananda and Bhagava 2009, 13).

29. Shah goes on to report that while it was originally believed that each of these groups were basically endogamous local variations of a larger community (no mention is actually made of "Valvi" or its history), it was later found that Tetarias identify themselves as Bhils and not as Dhanka; in fact, a Dhanka would not take food from a Tetaria. Some Tadvi Bhils, he explains, have also embraced Islam while Tadvi Dhanka have been Hinduized by Vishwanath Maharaj so that one finds "both Hindu and Muslim groups" among the Tadvi (23).

30. While some accounts of Bhil history, such as that recorded in K. D. Erskine's (1908) *Gazetteer of Udaipur State,* seem to accept the possibility that Bhils are the Nishadas referred to in the epic, other accounts are skeptical. The author of the Khandesh volume of the *Gazetteer of the Bombay Presidency* (1880, 12:80n1), comments in a footnote, for instance, that "there is no more reason for identifying the Nishadas with the Bhils than with many other of the rude hill races." It is unclear whether this note was written by James M. Campbell, editor of the gazetteer series, or Mr. W. Ramsay, C.S., whom Campbell identifies as having written drafts of many of the sections within the volume.

31. As further proof of Dhankas' low status, Nath reports that, "In Pipergota, a Bhil is having a Dhanaki concubine for a number of years. But he does not live with her. He accepts no food from her. So his purity is unaffected and he remains a member of the Bhil society" (1960: 62).

32. The author's reference here is to a version of Enthoven's (1920) *Tribes of Bombay* republished in 1983. I have been unable to locate this version of the book, but according to a 1975 edition, the author's statement here is not entirely accurate. The Tadvi are described as half-Muslim and half-Bhil (156), but they are labeled a "mixed" tribe; that is, a tribe in which Bhils have mixed with members of another community. The Dhanka, however, are classed among the "Aborigines, Wild Tribes, and Wandering Castes" (Enthoven 1902, 92) and as a "hill and forest tribe" (Enthoven 1975, 156). In fact, Enthoven is among those who see "Bhil" as an externally attributed category used to refer to many separate groups. He comments: "The name Bhil is often given to half-wild tribes such as Chodhras, Dhankas, Dhodias, Katkaris, Konknas, and Varlis" (1975, 151).

33. Many thanks to Nishita Trisal who figured out how to digitize the 1879 gazetteer and found this reference while working as my research assistant.

34. From the *Census of the Native States of Rajputana 1881*: "Owing to a very pronounced repugnance to being enumerated, a repugnance which in some instances led to a disturbance of the peace, no accurate Census could be taken of the Bhil population in the States of Oodeypore, Partabgrah, Dungarpur and Banswara, and the authorities had to be contented with counting houses and allowing an average of four persons to each house" (6).

35. *Gazetteer of the Bombay Presidency* 1880, 12:83.

36. Ibid., 6:34.

Chapter Three

1. Interestingly, Ravi's categories only vaguely correspond to those recognized in the ethnographic record and discussed in Chapter 2.

2. I am extremely grateful to the talented Hindi scholar Sneha Desai for her thoughtful translation of Ravi's poetry. Her work was enabled by a Faculty Research Grant from the Committee on Research at UC Santa Cruz.

3. Its opening stanza: "Become a beautiful bride today/our darling daughter/So beautifully adorned today, our darling daughter."

4. For this reason, some readers may note a relationship between my use of the term "willingness" and Tania Li's (2007) discussion of "the will to improve" in the ethnography of that title. While this was not necessarily an intentional citation, I am certainly convinced by Li's vivid ethnographic account of a "stubborn will" that persists among actors she refers to as "trustees" to do something to better Indonesian people and landscapes. Following Foucault, she shows that these trustees do not work through domination or coercion, but through interventions intended to persuade people to do "as they ought" (Li 2007, 5; this a phrase she borrows from David Scott (1995, 202–203). The case I am describing here is similar in the sense that it is likewise related to a form of (post)colonial governmentality—namely, the administration of tribes—that requires certain social enactments. However, Li's focus remains on an official and authorizing will—even as it is hardly singular and often thwarted. I am framing the question of will in the other direction: willingness is a Dhanka project, not a state project of governmentality, even as it emerges in a discursive and practical space profoundly shaped by governmental logics. Because of their subaltern sociopolitical status, Dhanka are hardly trustees in the sense used by Li, even if that might be one of their goals. Their willingness is therefore both acquiescent and resistant in a way that makes critiques such as Li's more difficult: willingness begins from a different place, one that is Dhanka, and that is constitutional, as much as it is governmental.

5. He also reports that they had begun collective marriages for the sake of the modernization of the group, which I discuss in the next chapter.

6. On the other hand, one hegemonic masculinity project that has been explored is the martial, aggressive, high-caste Hindu masculinity promoted by the Sangh Parivar (Hansen 1996). Interestingly, there are genealogical resonances with what Lloyd and Susanne Rudolph have called the "Rajput ethic," by which they mean "valor without regard to consequences" (1984, 41), which may have to do with colonial constructions of effeminacy among the colonized populace (Sinha 1995). It is important to note, however, that the ideal Hindu leader is an unmarried, celibate brahmachari, one who is in control of his sexual potency and uses it for the protection of the nation, because, as Paola Bacchetta argues, "the operative sexuality binary here is not so much hetero versus homo; rather it is asexuality versus both heterosexuality and homosexuality" (1999, 148).

7. On the building of Jaipur, see Sachdev and Tillotson 2002.

8. In fact there was a rivalry between the Arya Samaj and the Radhasoami satsang because so many samaj-ers converted to Radhasoami (Juergensmeyer 1991, 47).

9. Mayer's insights are interesting to think about here, because it is true that in this case Dhanka men who do social work—which is almost all Dhanka men of the era of service—are supposed to expect nothing in return for themselves and the notion is supported by Radhasoami tenets. I am grateful to Alpa Shah for pointing me to this reference.

10. P. G. Shah mentions the influence of Vishwanath Maharaj in his 1964 ethnography. It is interesting to note that Shah rejects the interpretation of the Dhanka embrace of the guru as an instance of Sanskritization, Hinduization, or Westernization, preferring to see their devotion as part of a trend toward "modern" reformers like Dayanand Saraswati and the Arya Samaj. He links this trend (in something of a contradiction) to "influence of contact with European or American ways of living" (Shah 1964, 70).

11. This was not the first time I was surprised by Dhanka knowledge of Jaipur and its environs via previous work assignments. In 2007, I arranged for a group of Dhanka friends (who sorely needed the money) to fix a broken pipe at the home of a dear friend with whom I've stayed since my undergraduate days, in the upscale C-Scheme area of Jaipur. Upon arrival, the Dhanka leader of the team, Mohan Lal, said "Oh! This is the doctor's house." My friend's late

husband had, indeed, been a pediatrician. Mohan Lal recounted the story of digging the tube well at the doctor's house about a decade earlier. Clearly water works are also a mnemonic for mapping the social landscape of Jaipur's elites by subalterns.

12. See "Indian Print Artisans at Work" by Amy Yee, *The New York Times*, May 26, 2011.

13. During my visit to the basti in 2007, a banner was hung at the front of the temple construction depicting religious figures and announcing an upcoming Bharatiya Janta Party (BJP) event. When I asked elder Dhanka men about the sign—"Are you now supporting the BJP? I can't believe it!"—they said that they were not, that the BJP gets up to a lot of mischief, but that they thought the picture was pretty. It's unclear to me whether this explanation was simply for my benefit or not, since my shock surely conveyed disapproval.

Chapter Four

1. I draw some inspiration here from an ongoing conversation in Caribbean studies about the relationship between respectability and reputation. In a 1969 article, Peter Wilson attempts to go beyond the paradigm of the domestic in the study of Caribbean society to think about informal groupings and internal differentiations (70). As part of his analysis, he exposes a double standard of sexual morality for men and women, in which men are supposed to be virile and behave in ways that subvert dominant laws, while women are supposed to be modest and embody an ideal of "respectability." Respectability is especially conferred upon women by marriage— that is, through "a degree of approximation to standards of the external, legal society" (78). For Wilson, men's social system of reputation is more empowering than women's respectability as the former enables groupings of individuals beyond the household and thus increases potential resistance to colonialism. Women's embrace of the church, on the other hand, puts them morally in line with the colonizing force. Over two decades later, in an analysis of Wilson's argument, Jean Besson finds fault with precisely this distinction, arguing that it obscures understandings of Afro-Caribbean women and works as an apology for gender inequality. Afro-Caribbean women are not "passive imitators of colonial culture" (Besson 1993, 18–19) but also resist colonialism, compete among themselves for status, and engage in nonconformist religious activities. Thus we cannot assume a priori the complex of ideas and practices that will constitute respectability. It is better seen as a historical, ethnographic question than a given framing structure.

The importance of the colonial context for the debate on reputation and respectability cannot be overlooked, and the similarities between Wilson's framework and discussions of the formation of an upper-caste, domestic "Indian womanhood" in the late nineteenth century bear noting. However, Partha Chatterjee's (1993) oft-cited description of the way in which late nineteenth-century nationalists in Bengal "resolved" the woman question is almost the inverse of Wilson's view of similar dynamics in the Caribbean. For Chatterjee the woman's world of the home becomes the site of the "authentic," rather than the oppositional groupings of men along lines of reputation; but, as in Wilson's analysis, women are folded into the picture in a rather uncomplicated way.

Chatterjee has been critiqued on a number of counts, the most common being his historical framing, which ends in the 1880s and thus neglects the very prominent presence of women in the twentieth-century nationalist movement (John 2000; Rege 2006). But one of his basic insights, that the nationalist movement was premised on the deep separation of a feminine realm of the domestic from the public, corrupted world in which Indian men encountered colonial power, has been important for understanding the imbrication of figurations of gender with the construction of the Indian nation-state. What has been less emphasized in Chatterjee's analysis is that only certain women were able to even aspire to this respectable status, which entailed proper comportment, limited education, and restricted contact with the world outside the home (Rege 2006, 28). As Uma Chakravarti argues, it was a high-caste Hindu woman who became the nationalist symbol of Indian womanhood, with the Vedic *dasi* and, by extension, all low-caste and tribal women, left beyond the pale (1989).

2. Though not the source of the title for this chapter, I am reminded here of Spivak's assertion that the force of feminist struggle comes from "the actual players contemplating the possibility that to organize against home-working is not to stop being a good woman, a responsible woman, a real woman (therefore with husband and home), a woman; and only then walk with us in a two-way response structure toward a presupposition that is more than a task merely of thinking on both sides: that there are more than one way of being a good woman" (1999, 391). The intervention, then, is as much for feminists as for their interlocutors, an incitement to figure out how to "join those within the cultural inscription who join to lift the stricture" (391) and, I would ad, in ways feminists do not always recognize.

3. As Kalpana Ram notes in her study of a marginalized fishing community in South India "The task of ethnographic writing in this case is bound up with the ultimately political challenge of shedding assumptions derived from the majority culture" (1991, xi).

4. One of the most infamous rape cases in the history of feminist organizing in India, the "Mathura case," also involved a young adivasi woman whose sexual life was put on public trial, though the specificity of her adivasi-ness tends to be glossed over in historical accounts (see Gangoli 2007). The prevalence of sexual violence perpetrated against SC/ST women was a topic that occupied many commentators around what has become known as the "Delhi rape case" in 2012 (see, for example, Geetha 2013 and Teltumbde 2013).

5. In British representations, the colonized was always wild, regardless of whether castes or tribes, while the colonizer represented civilization. But differences between castes and tribes were drawn based on an understanding of different "*forms* of wildness, each with its distinctive politics of gender and time" (Skaria 1997, 727; emphasis added). Notably, while castes were feminized in European constructions (see also Sinha 1995), tribes and certain martial castes were notably masculinized. Masculinity included particular traits that were valued by the British and thought to make tribal groups in some ways closer to the colonial power; these included "honesty, loyalty, independence, lack of religious dogmatism, and sense of humor" (733).

6. Skaria argues:

> These two attitudes—*adivasi* society as highly male, and *adivasi* women as highly sexual and erotic figures—were in all likelihood common to late nineteenth- and early twentieth-century Indian middle-class attitudes towards tribes. Both were different from colonial ascriptions . . . Colonial officials often cast savage women not as wildly sexual beings but as responsible and stabilizing figures in the family; middle-class writers, in contrast, reserved these qualities for middle-class women, denied the sexuality of upper- or middle-caste women, and displaced that ascription of sexuality onto the "tribal woman." . . . The emphasis on the sexuality of the *adivasi* women continues today (1997, 741).

Though it deserves greater study, a similar pattern seems to hold for Rajasthan.

7. In 2006, BBC reporter K. S. Shaini tracked down Kosi Elwin in Madhya Pradesh and found her living in "penury," with "little money and no land." Elwin divorced her in 1949 and rarely spoke or wrote of her later in his life.

8. Srinivas (1962, 1966) further argues that this particular kind of mobility was given greater importance by the advent of the British census, which attempted to fix both identity and rank of castes. Srinivas does not treat Sanskritization as a kind of universal, timeless process. He is quite clear about its crescendo in the early twentieth century around the census.

9. This pity may also be because of the connection between renting and migration. In 2002–2003, a young Bihari couple moved into one of the basti's more *kaccha* ("unfinished, impermanent") houses and paid rent; their Dhanka neighbors, especially women, expressed a great deal of sympathy for the couple. This is all the more interesting because many Dhanka residents attributed declining conditions in the city to the in-migration of so-called Biharis and other Bengali-speakers (see Moodie, 2010).

10. To some extent, children confound these rules, often playing in mixed-gender groups. By around age ten, however, this is much less common and gender mixing happens mostly in the context of care (i.e., one child babysitting another).

11. In a small and rather unscientific survey of married Dhanka female respondents, which I conducted in late 2002, well over half reported that they did not work outside the home. While this was not a rigorous statistical study, it does point to a local preference for housewifery when it is possible.

12. I have been told by non-Rajput friends that Rajput women—particularly those of "royal" or noble lineages—are especially good at managing their marital relations and keeping men content in marriage.

13. The introduction to the Commission of Sati (Prevention) Act reads "An act to provide for the more effective prevention of sati and its glorification and for matters connected therewith or incidental thereto."

14. One reason the song may be more important than the film itself is that the soundtrack features a young Asha Bhosle on vocals and is one of her earliest successful albums.

15. Sapna technically owned her home, having paid the previous resident Rs. 31,000 for it, but as the graveyard is public property, everyone there is technically a squatter.

Chapter Five

1. Pipal is the local name for *ficus religiosa*.

2. On the double meaning of tree imagery for young women, Ann Grodzins Gold points both to their rootedness in place and to their "vulnerability to the winds and whims of fate and men" (2002, 286).

3. Trees are strong but "the girl-tree identity holds implications of openness to damage" (Ramanujan quoted in Gold 2002, 286).

4. When the pipli ki shaadi took place, the "mandir" was still a simple shrine to the god Shiva; construction of the temple described in a previous chapter had not yet begun.

5. Rochana Majumdar makes this point well when she says, "Whether we look at travel literature or early anthropology, marital practices in foreign lands have long tantalized outsider observers with their apparent promise to unlock the secret of an "oriental" culture" (2009, 6).

6. On the Hindu Code Bill (see Som 1994; Rao 2009; Ambedkar 2013); for a summary of the Shah Bano case, see Introduction, 21n22.

7. Sangari and Vaid note that this is a deliberate historical turn, as the Jaipur-Amber region was not a frequent site of sati or apparently ideologically invested in its practice, unlike in Jodhpur and Udaipur. Jaipur was in fact the first state of the Rajputana region to outlaw the

immolation of widows (1996, 245). As an aside, the Dhanka recognize the historical region of Jaipur-Amber as Dhundar, not Shekhawat.

8. Kumkum Sangari and Sudesh Vaid convincingly argue that while on one hand Rajputs try to illustrate the special, "martial" status of their community via widow immolation, on the other hand they have needed to broaden ideological support for the practice. Since the 1950s, Rajputs in Rajasthan have been able to widen social support for widow immolation beyond the Rajput community by marshalling a sense of the sati as the symbol of a general Rajasthani womanhood that crosses class and caste lines (1996, 263). This womanhood is based on the ideal of the *pativrata* ("one devoted to the husband/lord") who is defined by her existence and behavior *in marriage*. As Sangari and Vaid put it: "all women of Rajasthan are upheld as exemplary: unmarried girls are virtuous, wives are faithful, never seek divorce, and widows do not remarry" (264). While the Rajputs (notably with the support of Brahmin and Bania communities) have sought to make the pativrata the ideal for all Rajasthani women, they have also, of course, implicitly defined this ideal in contrast to "other" unnamed women, including working women, non-Hindu women, Westernized women, remarried and divorced women, and widows who seek new marriages (290). For communities like the Dhanka, there are conflicting responses to the idea of the pativrata.

9. Other reformers held similar views. Jyotirao Phule, for instance, started a home for women and the children they bore from intercaste relationships (see Geetha 2007, 96–105).

10. Ambedkar continued, "To leave inequality between class and class, between sex and sex which is the soul of Hindu society untouched and to go on passing legislation relating to economic problems is to make a farce out of our Constitution and to build a palace on a dung heap. This is the significance I attach . . . to the Hindu Code Bill" (quoted in Pandey 2013, 68–69).

11. A Banjara by birth, Govind Giri led Bhils to revolt against the ruler of Dungarpur State, from which he was exiled. His attempt to establish a Bhil Raj was thwarted by the British Army, who attacked his holdings on Mangarh Hill and sentenced him to prison (Vashishtha 1997).

12. There does seem to be good evidence for such shifts in many other sites across India (see Arunima 1996, Chowdhry 1994; Oldenburg 2002).

13. *Ram Lila*—plays that reenact stories from the Ramayana—are performed every fall. The Adarsh Nagar Daessera Maidan, where the samuhik vivaha was held, is an especially large and popular site for *Ram Lila*.

14. The organization's English title would be something like The Dhanka People's Collective Marriage Committee.

15. These are the ages reported by Dhanka men and women I know. As is apparent in this and other chapters, girls are sometimes below the legal age. I mention it here because these are clearly invoked as ideals.

16. See Chapter 2 for a discussion of these numbers and the Dhanka ST category. The Dhanka claim that they themselves have seventy to eighty thousand members in Rajasthan, which makes the joint figure with Tadvi, Tetaria, and Valvis less credible. For the purposes of this book, I have assumed that Dhanka leaders are correct about their numbers, though I do acknowledge that they have a political stake in making it seem as large as possible.

17. This is according to Björkman and Chaturvedi 2001. It should be kept in mind that this is an estimate because no census had recorded caste information since 1931, until the 2011 census.

18. Bashiruddin Ahmed articulates the classic view of the relationship between caste and electoral behavior succinctly: "Caste provides an extensive basis for organization of democratic politics. The need to organize and articulate support in an open polity inevitably turns those

engaged in political competition toward organizations and solidary groups in which the masses are found . . . caste identities and solidarities become the primary channels through which electoral and political support is mobilized within the political system" (1970, 980). While Ahmed's analysis remains helpful and streamlined, his assertion that caste becomes less important in urban areas or as the result of internal differentiation is not as convincing as it perhaps was in 1970.

19. This is probably not entirely accurate as Dhanka from all over the state and Gujarat also attended, but the claim does help stress Dhanka numbers in the Jaipur region.

20. Translation by Maru Chowdhury and author.

21. Translation by Maru Chowdhury and author.

Chapter Six

1. "Smart" in this case means handsome or well turned-out, not intelligent; it was by far the most commonly used adjective for describing an appealing boy.

2. Here, I am influenced by Berlant's diagnosis of the activity of the *critic* who is likely to have (often unreflexive) stakes in identifying and diagnosing the politics, or lack thereof, of any kind of cultural disposition.

3. I think here also of Ramamurthy's use of the term "perplexity" to describe the contradictory positioning of Dalit women as consumers in Andhra Pradesh. The term allows her to disrupt a notion of the "centered subject," in which the women she worked with might have a singular position in relation to global commodity chains, and to capture the "joys and aches of the global everyday, often simultaneously" (2003, 525). The intervention here also seems to be about pointing to wonderment and consternation.

4. Such characterizations fly in the face of what is usually presumed about tribal girls, even within the tribes themselves, that they mature sexually and are eager for sex at a very young age. I knew of no cases of unplanned pregnancy out of wedlock among girls in Shiv Nagar Basti, and abortions, such as were discussed, were all by married women seeking to space births rather than hiding illicit affairs. This is not to say that physical encounters never happen but, rather than being somehow "freer," girls in the neighborhood are subject to the same strict social code as other Hindu and Muslim girls in the area.

5. Translated by the author and Shally Vaish.

6. Translated by the author and Shally Vaish.

Chapter Seven

1. As I described in Chapter 2, many groups in Rajasthan claim a Rajput ancestry. What is more interesting than Hanuman Singh's *jati* is that his family was, especially at that time, one of the very few non-Dhanka residents in this part of the neighborhood. Their outsidership and lack of a long relationship with the city and the PHED may have enabled them to see and comment on certain aspects of privatization in a different way than their Dhanka neighbors.

2. See "No Hiring Freeze: 100,000 Public Sector Jobs Are up for Grabs," *Hindustan Times*, September 11, 2013. For PHED recruitment figures for 2013, see "Rajasthan PHED Recruitment 2013," http://onlineapplicationform.in/rajasthan-phed-recruitment.html. It is telling that the majority of the PHED openings are for "helpers," those low-ranking positions most likely to be held by SC/STs.

3. The World Bank's enthusiasm can be explained by their attention to the link between electricity and prosperity and to the fiscal drain represented by what one World Bank researcher

(Lal 2006, 2) terms "large-scale theft" by consumers and corruption among politicians who oversee the sector.

4. State Electricity Boards, or SEBs, were created by the 1948 Electricity Supply Act, which effectively nationalized the utility, while keeping control basically in the hands of individual states (Kumar and Chatterjee 2012).

5. Reliance Industries Limited is an Indian conglomerate with interests/holdings in oil, petrochemicals, retail, and telecommunications.

6. Translation by Sneha Desai.

7. On the cultivation of civility, see Bear 2007.

8. Some government positions require candidates to demonstrate a certain level of physical fitness; there are also "sports" reservations for outstanding athletes. I assume that Rakesh is here referring to the first form of physical testing and not a specific competition to "win" a sports seat.

9. *Patwari* is a term used to refer to clerks and record keepers of many kinds. The term technically refers to a "registrar."

10. This is quite a different attitude toward education than may be present in other aspiring communities. Craig Jeffrey reports, for instance, that among Jats, education has been seen as the key to upward mobility over the last several decades (2010).

11. While this is not the term I use to describe myself in Shiv Nagar Basti, the overlap between my own methods and the work of government officials and NGOs certainly puts my work in the category of service work broadly conceived.

12. The extraordinary embroidery, which cost up to Rs. 50,000 for a fancy wedding suit, was done exclusively by men referred to as "Bengalis." These men were located and contracted by Bengali thekedars.

13. Bikramaditya Kumar Choudhary reports a similar finding that waste pickers in Delhi do not think thekedars are exploitative but are seen as guardians of the community who provide housing and other resources (2003, 5241).

Chapter Eight

1. There are not many such "success stories" recorded in the anthropological literature. For another, however, see Parry 1999.

2. In his introduction to the edited volume *Subaltern Citizens and Their Histories*, Gyanendra Pandey argues that the notion of the subaltern citizen is useful not simply because it points to ways that "citizen" is often qualified or called into question by "subaltern" as a descriptor. Rather, the more radical claim is that "it is 'citizen' that qualifies subalterneity, not 'subaltern' that qualifies (or describes) the status of citizenship" (2010, 4). This shift records citizenship as a historical fact (since many states around the world now recognize at least formal equality), rather than only an aspirational yet-to-be, and asks about how people *live* within specific historical-political circumstances. The question of what subaltern citizens seek when they engage in political struggles then becomes paramount, as I have argued throughout earlier chapters.

3. I have written about the Gujjar agitations and some of their unexpected consequences for the Dhanka elsewhere (Moodie 2013a; 2013b).

4. At a Gujjar Mahasabha convention at Dholpur in 1965, the community argued both for a Gujjar regiment in the army and ST status. See T. K. Rajalakshmi's article, "Stir and Standoff," in *Frontline* 25, no. 13 (July 4, 2008).

5. *People's Union for Civil Liberties (PUCL) Bulletin* 27, no. 8 (August 2007).

6. The appointment of the commission was widely seen as a move of deflection on the part of Raje, who had promised to help Gujjars with their claim in her 2003 election *yatra*; Justice Chopra himself was given no choice in participating in the research and writing the report (Justice Jas Raj Chopra, pers. comm.). The report did not, in fact, resolve anything. It did not support the Gujjars' claim, but it also made a recommendation that they be given extensive funds for further development, especially in rural areas that the committee found to be abysmally lacking in basic services.

7. "Rajasthan to Move Bill on Quota for Economically Backward," *Indiaenews.com*, June 19, 2008.

8. Many of Bainsla's own followers were disappointed and concerned by the outcome. There were charges that the colonel had whittled away the bargaining committee and some members had not signed the agreement. They pointed out that Raje's solution was, in fact, no solution, as a Supreme Court ruling has long held that no state can have more than 50 percent reservations. This reservation, which took Rajasthan over the 50 percent mark, would open the state to judicial scrutiny. To make things even more complicated, several days after announcing the separate quota for Gujjars and others, Rajasthan became the first state to announce a reservation for economically backward (forward) castes, to include Rajputs, Brahmins, and other high castes. Thus, the state had gone to a 68 percent quota system and was even more likely to be subject to judicial examination that would invalidate all new reservations.

9. In an article titled "Indian Shepherds Stoop to Conquer Caste System," Amelia Gentlemen begins her coverage in *The New York Times* on June 3, 2007: "A fight for the right to be downwardly mobile exploded this week in north India, as a powerful community of Indian shepherds asserted that the best way to rise up in modern society was to take a step down in the regimented class hierarchy here. Tension over the still-rigid caste classifications, which underpin the Indian social system, spilled over into riots across Rajasthan State, with at least 23 people killed."

10. See, for example, an article by Sobhana K, "Lavish in protest," *The Indian Express*, June 13, 2008, http://www.indianexpress.com/news/lavish-in-protest/322017.

11. Throughout my original fieldwork in 2002–2003, the issue of starvation deaths among adivasi groups in Rajasthan loomed large. Reports started emerging during the winter months that a number of children from the Saharia tribe had died in southern districts due to hunger in September. See, for example, Neelabh Mishra, "Hunger Deaths in Baran," *Frontline* 19, no. 24 (2002). Such cases had already prompted the People's Union for Civil Liberties to enter a writ in the Supreme Court (see *People's Union for Civil Liberties [PUCL] Bulletin*, November 2001, accessed May 16, 2014, http://www.pucl.org/reports/Rajasthan/2001/starvation-writ.htm).

Bibliography

Abu-Lughod, Lila. (1993) 2008. *Writing Women's Worlds: Bedouin Stories.* Berkeley: University of California Press.

Agnes, Flavia, Chandra Sudhir, and Monmayee Basu. 2004. *Women and Law in India.* New Delhi: Oxford University Press.

Ahearn, Laura M. 2001. *Invitations to Love: Literacy, Love Letters, and Social Change in Nepal.* Ann Arbor: University of Michigan Press.

Ahmed, Bashiruddin. 1970. "Caste and Electoral Politics." *Asian Survey* 10 (11): 979–92.

Ambedkar, B. R., and Sharmila Rege. 2013. *Against the Madness of Manu: B. R. Ambedkar's Writings on Brahmanical Patriarchy.* New Delhi: Navayana Publishers.

Anandhi, S., J. Jeyaranjan, and Rajan Krishnan. 2002. "Work, Caste, and Competing Masculinities: Notes from a Tamil Village." *Economic and Political Weekly* 37 (43): 4397–4406.

Appadurai, Arjun. 2004. "The Capacity to Aspire: Culture and the Terms of Recognition." In *Culture and Public Action*, edited by Vijayendra Rao and Michael Walton, 59–84. Stanford, CA: Stanford University Press.

Arondekar, Anjali. 2009. *For the Record: On Sexuality and the Colonial Archive in India.* Durham, NC: Duke University Press.

———. 2012. "Subject to Sex: A Small History of the Gomantak Maratha Samaj." In *South Asian Feminisms*, edited by Ania Loomba and Ritty A. Lukose, 244–66. Durham, NC: Duke University Press.

Arunima, G. 1996. "Multiple Meanings: Changing Conceptions of Matrilineal Kinship in Nineteenth- and Twentieth-Century Malabar." *The Indian Economic and Social History Review* 33 (3): 283–307.

Babb, Lawrence A. 1986. *Redemptive Encounters: Three Modern Styles in the Hindu Tradition.* Berkeley: University of California Press.

Bacchetta, Paola. 1999. "When the (Hindu) Nation Exiles Its Queers." *Social Text* 17 (4): 141.

Balagopal, K. N. 2006. "Withdraw the Clandestine Move to Freeze Employment." *People's Democracy: Weekly Organ of the Communist Party in India (Marxist)* 30 (3) (January 15): 1–3. http://pd.cpim.org/2--6/-1152006_balagopal.htm.

Banerjee, Prathama. 2006. *Politics of Time: "Primitives" and History-Writing in a Colonial Society.* New Delhi: Oxford University Press.

Bannerman, A. D. 1902. *Census of India, 1901.* Vol. 25, *Rajputana.* Lucknow: Newal Kishore Press.

Basu, Srimati. 2005. "Introduction." In *Dowry and Inheritance,* edited by Srimati Basu. London: Palgrave Macmillan.

Bates, Crispin. 1995a. "Race, Caste and Tribe in Central India: The Early Origins of Indian Anthropometry."In *The Concept of Race in South Asia,* edited by P. Robb, 219–259. Delhi: Oxford University Press.

———. 1995b. "Lost Innocents and the Loss of Innocence: Interpreting Adivasi Movements in South Asia." In *Indigenous Peoples of Asia,* edited by R. H. Barnes, Andrew Gray, and Benedict Kingsbury, 103–19. Association for Asian Studies, Inc. Monograph and Occasional Paper Series 48.

Baviskar, Amita. (1995) 2008. *In the Belly of the River: Tribal Conflicts over Development in the Narmada Valley.* 3rd ed. New Delhi: Oxford University Press.

———. 2007. "Indian Indigeneities: Adivasi Engagements with Hindu Nationalism in India." In *Indigenous Experience Today,* edited by Marisol de la Cadena and Orin Starn, 275–304. Oxford: Berg.

———. 2010. "Winning the Right to Information in India: Is Knowledge Power?" In *Citizen Action and National Policy Reform: Making Change Happen,* edited by John Gaventa and Rosemary McGee, 130–152. London and New York: Zed Books.

Bear, Laura. 2007. *Lines of the Nation: Indian Railway Workers, Bureaucracy, and the Intimate Historical Self.* New York: Columbia University Press.

Berlant, Lauren Gail. 2008. *The Female Complaint: The Unfinished Business of Sentimentality in American Culture.* Durham, NC: Duke University Press.

———. 2011. *Cruel Optimism.* Durham, NC: Duke University Press.

Besson, Jean. 1993. "Reputation and Respectability Reconsidered: A New Perspective on Afro-Caribbean Peasant Women." In *Women and Change in the Caribbean,* edited by Janet H. Momsen, 15–37. Bloomington: Indiana University Press.

Béteille, Andre. 1974. "Tribe and Peasantry." In *Six Essays in Comparative Sociology,* 58–74. Delhi: Oxford University Press.

Bhagavan, Manu. 2001. "Demystifying the 'Ideal Progressive': Resistance through Mimicked Modernity in Princely Baroda, 1900–1913." *Modern Asian Studies* 35 (2): 385–409.

Bhambhri, C. P. 2005. "Reservations and Casteism." *Economic and Political Weekly,* February 26, 806–808.

Bhatt, Amy, Madhavi Murty, and Priti Ramamurthy. 2010. "Hegemonic Developments: The New Indian Middle Class, Gendered Subalterns, and Diasporic Returnees in the Event of Neoliberalism." *Signs: Journal of Women in Culture & Society* 36 (1): 127–52.

Birkenholtz, Trevor. 2010. "'Full-Cost Recovery': Producing Differentiated Water Collection Practices and Responses to Centralized Water Networks in Jaipur, India." *Environment & Planning A.* 42 (9): 2238–53.

Björkman, James Warner, and Het Ram Chaturvedi. 2001. "Panchayati Raj in Rajasthan: The Penalties of Success." In *The Idea of Rajasthan: Explorations in Regional Identity,* edited by Karine Schomer, Deryck O. Lodrick, and Lloyd I. Rudolph, 117–60. New Delhi: Manohar.

Bodh Shiksha Samiti. 2001. *Bridging the Gaps: The Situational Context and Educational Efforts for Deprived Children in Jaipur City.* Jaipur: Bhalotia Printers.

Boris, Eileen, and Rhacel Salazar Parreñas. 2010. *Intimate Labors: Cultures, Technologies, and the Politics of Care.* Stanford, CA: Stanford University Press.

Borooah, Vani K., Amaresh Dubey, and Sriya Iyer. 2007. "The Effectiveness of Jobs Reservation: Caste, Religion and Economic Status in India." *Development and Change* 38(3): 423–45.

Bourdieu, Pierre. 1977. *Outline of a Theory of Practice.* Cambridge: Cambridge University Press.

———. 1984. *Distinction: A Social Critique of the Judgment of Taste.* Cambridge, MA: Harvard University Press.

———. 2001. *Masculine Domination.* Cambridge: Polity Press.

Bowen, William G., Derek Curtis Bok, and James Lawrence Shulman. 2000. *The Shape of the River: Long-Term Consequences of Considering Race in College and University Admissions.* Princeton, NJ: Princeton University Press.

Brown, Wendy. 1995. *States of Injury: Power and Freedom in Late Modernity.* Princeton, NJ: Princeton University Press.

Brueck, Laura. 2012. "At the Intersection of Gender and Caste: Rescripting Rape in Dalit Feminist Narratives." In *South Asian Feminisms*, edited by Ania Loomba and Ritty A. Lukose, 224–43. Durham, NC: Duke University Press.

Butler, Judith. 1993. *Bodies That Matter: On the Discursive Limits of "Sex."* New York: Routledge.

———. 2006. *Gender Trouble: Feminism and the Subversion of Identity.* New York: Routledge.

Census of the Native States of Rajputana 1881: Review of the Census Operations and Tables Shewing the Population & C., Enumerated in the Native States of Rajputana. 1882. Bombay.

Chakravarti, Uma. 1989. "Whatever Happened to the Vedic Dasi? Orientalism, Nationalism, and a Script for the Past." In *Recasting Women: Essays in Indian Colonial History*, edited by KumKum Sangari and Sudesh Vaid, 27–87. New Delhi: Kali for Women.

———. 2006. *Gendering Caste: Through a Feminist Lens.* Calcutta: Stree.

Chatterjee, Partha. 1993. *The Nation and Its Fragments: Colonial and Postcolonial Histories.* Princeton, NJ: Princeton University Press.

———. 2004. *The Politics of the Governed: Reflections on Popular Politics in Most of the World.* New York: Columbia University Press.

Chaudhury, Pradipta. 2004. "The 'Creamy Layer': Political Economy of Reservations." *Economic and Political Weekly*, May 15, 1989–1991.

Chin, Aimee, and Nishith Prakash. 2009. "The Redistributive Effects of Political Reservation for Minorities: Evidence from India." Discussion Paper No. 4391, Institute for the Study of Labor (IZA), Bonn, Germany, http://econpapers.repec.org/paper/izaizadps/dp4391.htm.

Chopra, Radhika, Caroline Osella, and Filippo Osella, eds. 2004. *South Asian Masculinities: Context of Change, Sites of Continuity.* New Delhi: Women Unlimited.

Choudhary, Bikramaditya Kumar. 2003. "Waste and Waste-Pickers." *Economic and Political Weekly* 38 (50): 5240–42.

Chowdhry, Prem. 1994. *The Veiled Women: Shifting Gender Equations in Rural Haryana, 1880–1990.* Delhi: Oxford University Press.

———. 2007. *Contentious Marriages, Eloping Couples: Gender, Caste, and Patriarchy in Northern India.* New Delhi: Oxford University Press.

———. 2009. "'First Our Jobs Then Our Girls': The Dominant Caste Perceptions on the 'Rising' Dalits." *Modern Asian Studies* 43 (2): 437–79.

Ciotti, Manuela. 2006. "'In the Past We Were a Bit "Chamar"': Education as a Self- and Community-Engineering Process in Northern India." *Journal of the Royal Anthropological Institute* 12 (4): 899–916.

Cohen, Lawrence. 1998. *No Aging in India: Alzheimer's, the Bad Family, and Other Modern Things.* Berkeley: University of California Press.

Collins, Patricia Hill. 1999. "Moving Beyond Gender: Intersectionality and Scientific Knowledge." In *Revisioning Gender,* edited by Myra Marx Ferree, Judith Lorber, and Beth B. Hess, 261–84. Thousand Oaks, CA: Sage Publications.

Connell, R. W. 2005. *Masculinities.* 2nd ed. Berkeley: University of California Press.

Corbridge, Stuart. 1988. "The Ideology of Tribal Economy and Society: Politics in the Jharkhand, 1950–1980." *Modern Asian Studies* 22 (1): 1–42.

———. 2000. "Competing Inequalities: The Scheduled Tribes and the Reservations System in India's Jharkhand." *Journal of Asian Studies* 59 (1): 62.

Crenshaw, Kimberle. 1991. "Mapping the Margins: Intersectionality, Identity Politics, and Violence against Women of Color." *Stanford Law Review* 43 (6): 1241–99.

Das, Veena. 2007. *Life and Words: Violence and the Descent into the Ordinary.* Berkeley: University of California Press.

Datta-Majumder, N. 1947. "Anthropology During the War." *American Anthropologist* 49 (1): 159–64.

Deliège, Robert. 1985. *The Bhils of Western India: Some Empirical and Theoretical Issues in Anthropology in India.* New Delhi: National.

De Neve, Geert. 2004. "The Workplace and the Neighborhood: Locating Masculinities in the South Indian Textile Industry." In *South Asian Masculinities: Context of Change, Sites of Continuity,* edited by R. Chopra, C. Osella, and F. Osella, 60–95. New Delhi: Kali for Women.

Derné, Steve. 1994. "Hindu Men Talk About Controlling Women: Cultural Ideas as a Tool of the Powerful." *Sociological Perspectives* 37 (2): 203–27.

———. 2008. *Globalization on the Ground: Media and the Transformation of Culture, Class, and Gender in India.* Delhi: Sage Publications.

Devika, J. 2005. "The Aesthetic Woman: Re-Forming Female Bodies and Minds in Early Twentieth-Century Keralam." *Modern Asian Studies* 39 (2): 461–87.

Devy, G. N. 2006. *A Nomad Called Thief: Reflections on Adivasi Silence.* New Delhi: Orient Longman.

Directorate of Economics and Statistics, Rajasthan. 2009. *A Report on Census of State Government Employees: Rajasthan.* Jaipur.

Dirks, Nicholas B. 2001. *Castes of Mind: Colonialism and the Making of Modern India.* Princeton, NJ: Princeton University Press.

Dumont, Louis. 1980. *Homo Hierarchicus: The Caste System and Its Implications.* Chicago: University of Chicago Press.

Engineer, Asghar Ali. 1987. *The Shah Bano Controversy.* Bombay: Orient Longman.

Enthoven, Reginald Edward. 1902. *Census of Bombay.* Vol. 9, *Part I: Report.* Bombay: Government Central Press.

———. (1920) 1975. *The Tribes and Castes of Bombay.* Vol. 1. Delhi: Cosmo Publications.

Erskine, K. D. 1883. *Gazetteer of Udaipur State.* Ajmer: Scottish Mission Industries Co.

———. 1908. *A Gazetteer of the Udaipur State with a Chapter on the Bhils and Some Statistical Tables.* Ajmer: Scottish Mission Industries Co.

Faier, Lieba. 2009. *Intimate Encounters: Filipina Women and the Remaking of Rural Japan.* Berkeley: University of California Press.

Fernandes, Leela. 2006. *India's New Middle Class: Democratic Politics in an Era of Economic Reform.* Minneapolis: University of Minnesota Press.

Fernandes, Leela, and Patrick Heller. 2006. "Hegemonic Aspirations." *Critical Asian Studies* 38 (4): 495–522.

Foucault, Michel. 1978. *The History of Sexuality: Volume 1.* New York: Vintage Books.

Gahlot, Sukhvir Singh, and Banshi Dhar. 1989. *Castes and Tribes of Rajasthan.* Jodhpur: Jain Brothers.

Galanter, Marc. 1984. *Competing Equalities: Law and the Backward Classes in India.* Berkeley: University of California Press.

———. 2002. "The Long Half-Life of Reservations." In *India's Living Constitution: Ideas, Practices, Controversies,* edited by Z. Hasan, E. Sridharan, and R. Sudarshan, 306–18. London: Anthem Press.

Gangoli, Geetanjali. 2007. *Indian Feminisms: Law, Patriarchies, and Violence in India.* Aldershot, VT: Ashgate.

Gazetteer of the Bombay Presidency. Vol. 6, *Rewa Kantha, Narukot, Cambay, and Surat States.* 1880. Bombay: Government Central Press.

———. Vol. 12, *Khandesh.* 1880. Bombay: Government Central Press.

———. Vol. 9, *Gujarat Population: Hindus.* 1901. Bombay: Government Central Press.

Geetha, V. 2007. *Patriarchy.* Kolkata: Stree.

———. 2013. "On Impunity." *Economic and Political Weekly* 48 (2): 15–17.

Gellner, David N. 1991. "Hinduism, Tribalism, and the Position of Women: The Problem of Newar Identity." *Man* 26 (1): 105–25.

George, Annie. 2006. "Reinventing Honorable Masculinity: Discourses from a Working-Class Indian Community." *Men and Masculinities* 9 (1): 35–52.

Ghosh, Kaushik. 2006. "Between Global Flows and Local Dams: Indigenousness, Locality, and the Transnational Sphere in Jharkland, India." *Cultural Anthropology* 21 (4): 501–34.

Ghurye, G. S. 1980. *The Scheduled Tribes of India.* New Brunswick, NJ: Transaction Books.

Gold, Ann Grodzins. 2002. "Children and Trees in North India." *Worldviews: Global Religions, Culture, and Ecology* 6 (3): 276–99.

———. 2009. "Tasteless Profits and Vexed Moralities: Assessments of the Present in Rural Rajasthan." *Journal of the Royal Anthropological Institute* 15 (2): 365–85.

Gold, Ann Grodzins, and Bhoju Ram Gujar. 2002. *In the Time of Trees and Sorrows: Nature, Power, and Memory in Rajasthan.* Durham, NC: Duke University Press.

Goyle, Anuradha, Harsha Saraf, Preeti Jain, Neetu Shekhawat, and Swati Vyas. 2004. "A Profile of Roadside Squatter Settlements and Their Families in Jaipur City." *Journal of Social Science* 9 (2): 13–18.

Guha, Ramachandra. 1999. *Savaging the Civilized: Verrier Elwin, His Tribals, and India.* Chicago: University of Chicago Press.

Guha, Sumit. 1998. "Lower Strata, Older Races, and Aboriginal Peoples: Racial Anthropology and Mythical History Past and Present." *The Journal of Asian Studies* 57 (2): 423–41.

Gupta, Akhil. 1995. "Blurred Boundaries: The Discourse of Corruption, the Culture of Politics, and the Imagined State." *American Ethnologist* 22 (2): 375.

Gupta, Charu. 2010. "Feminine, Criminal, or Manly?: Imaging Dalit Masculinities in Colonial North India." *Indian Economic Social History Review* 47: 309.

Hansen, Thomas Blom. 1996. "Recuperating Masculinity: Hindu Nationalism, Violence, and the Exorcism of the Muslim 'Other.'" *Critique of Anthropology* 16 (2): 137.

———. 1999. *The Saffron Wave: Democracy and Hindu Nationalism in Modern India.* Princeton, NJ: Princeton University Press.

Hardiman, David. 1987. *The Coming of the Devi: Adivasi Assertion in Western India.* Delhi: Oxford University Press.

Harlan, Lindsey. 1992. *Religion and Rajput Women: The Ethic of Protection in Contemporary Narratives*. Berkeley: University of California Press.

Harvey, David. 2005. *A Brief History of Neoliberalism*. Oxford: Oxford University Press.

Hecht, Tobias. 2006. *After Life: An Ethnographic Novel*. Durham, NC: Duke University Press.

Jaffrelot, Christophe. 2003. *India's Silent Revolution: The Rise of the Low Castes in North Indian Politics*. Delhi: Permanent Black.

———. 2006. "The Impact of Affirmative Action in India: More Political Than Socioeconomic." *India Review* 5 (2): 173–89.

Jeffrey, Craig. 2010. *Timepass: Youth, Class, and the Politics of Waiting in India*. Stanford, CA: Stanford University Press.

Jeffrey, Craig, Patricia Jeffery, and Roger Jeffery. 2008. *Degrees Without Freedom? Education, Masculinities, and Unemployment in North India*. Stanford, CA: Stanford University Press.

Jenkins, Laura Dudley. 2003. *Identity and Identification in India: Defining the Disadvantaged*. London: Routledge.

Jenkins, Rob. 2004. "In Varying States of Decay: Anti-corruption Politics in Maharasthra and Rajasthan." In *Regional Reflections: Comparing Politics Across India's States*. Rob Jenkins, ed. Oxford: Oxford University Press. 219–252.

John, Mary E. 2000. "Alternate Modernities? Reservations and Women's Movement in 20th Century India." *Economic and Political Weekly*, October 28, WS22–WS29.

Joshi, Vidyuta. 1987. *Submerging Villages: Problems and Prospects*. Delhi: Ajanta Publications.

Juergensmeyer, Mark. 1991. *Radhasoami Reality: The Logic of a Modern Faith*. Princeton, NJ: Princeton University Press.

Kapila, Kriti. 2004. "Conjugating Marriage: State Legislation and Gaddi Kinship." *Contributions to Indian Sociology* 38: 379–409.

———. 2008. "The Measure of a Tribe: The Cultural Politics of Constitutional Reclassification in North India." *Journal of the Royal Anthropological Institute* 14: 117–34.

Karlsson, Bengt G. 2003. "Anthropology and the 'Indigenous Slot': Claims to and Debates about Indigenous Peoples' Status in India." *Critique of Anthropology* 23 (4): 403–23.

Kumar, Alok, and S. K. Chatterjee. 2012. *Electricity Sector in India: Policy and Regulation*. New Delhi: Oxford University Press.

Kumar, Vivek. 2005. "Understanding the Politics of Reservation: A Perspective from Below." *Economic and Political Weekly*, February 26, 803–806.

Lal, Sumir. 2006. *Can Good Economics Ever Be Good Politics? Case Study of the Power Sector in India*. World Bank Working Paper No. 83. Washington, DC: The World Bank.

Lane, David Christopher. 1992. *The Radhasoami Tradition: a Critical History of Guru Successorship*. New York: Garland Pub.

Leacock, Eleanor. 1972. Introduction to *The Origin of the Family, Private Property, and the State*, by Frederick Engels. New York: International Publishers.

Li, Tania Murray. 2000. "Articulating Indigenous Identity in Indonesia: Resource Politics and the Tribal Slot." *Comparative Studies in Society & History* 42 (1): 149.

———. 2007. *The Will to Improve: Governmentality, Development, and the Practice of Politics*. Durham, NC: Duke University Press.

Liechty, Mark. 2003. *Suitably Modern: Making Middle-Class Culture in a New Consumer Society*. Princeton, NJ: Princeton University Press.

Lobo, Lancy. 2002. "We Belong to Bharat, Not Hindustan." *Communalism Combat*, February, http://www.sabrang.com/cc/archive/2002/feb02/forum.htm.

Lukose, Ritty A. 2009. *Liberalization's Children: Gender, Youth, and Consumer Citizenship in Globalizing India*. Durham, NC: Duke University Press.

Lynch, Owen M. 1969. *The Politics of Untouchability: Social Mobility and Social Change in a City of India*. New York: Columbia University Press.

Maharatna, Arup. 2005. *Demographic Perspectives on India's Tribes*. New Delhi: Oxford University Press.

Mahmood, Saba. 2005. *Politics of Piety: The Islamic Revival and the Feminist Subject*. Princeton, NJ: Princeton University Press.

Major, Andrea. 2006. "Self-Determined Sacrifices? Victimhood and Volition in British Constructions of Sati in the Rajput States, 1830–60." *History & Anthropology* 17 (4): 313–25.

Majumdar, Rochona. 2009. *Marriage and Modernity: Family Values in Colonial Bengal*. Durham, NC: Duke University Press.

Maloo, Kamala. 1987. *The History of Famines in Rajputana, 1858–1900 A.D.* Udaipur: Himanshu Publications.

Mani, Lata. 1986. "The Production of an Official Discourse on Sati in Early Nineteenth-Century Bengal." *Economic and Political Weekly* 21 (17): WS32–WS40.

———. 1998. *Contentious Traditions: The Debate on Sati in Colonial India*. New Delhi: Oxford University Press.

Mankekar, Purnima. 1999. *Screening Culture, Viewing Politics: An Ethnography of Television, Womanhood, and Nation in Postcolonial India*. Durham, NC: Duke University Press.

Mathur, Agam Prasad. 1974. *Radhasoami Faith: A Historical Study*. Delhi: Vikas Pub. House Pvt. Ltd.

Mayer, Adrian C. 1981. "Public Service and Individual Merit in a Town of Central India." In *Culture and Morality: Essays in Honour of Christoph Von Furer-Haimendorf*. Delhi: Oxford University Press.

Mazzarella, William. 2003. *Shoveling Smoke: Advertising and Globalization in Contemporary India*. Durham, NC: Duke University Press.

Mbembe, Achille, and Sarah Nuttall. 2004. "Writing the World from an African Metropolis." *Public Culture* 16 (3): 347–371.

McMillan, Alistair. 2005. *Standing at the Margins: Representation and Electoral Reservation in India*. New Delhi: Oxford University Press.

Meillassoux, Claude. 1981. *Maidens, Meal, and Money: Capitalism and the Domestic Community*. Cambridge: Cambridge University Press.

Menon, Nivedita. 2000. "State, Community, and the Debate on the Uniform Civil Code in India." In *Beyond Rights Talk and Culture Talk: Comparative Essays on the Politics of Rights and Culture*, edited by Mahmood Mamdani, 75–95. New York: St. Martin's Press.

Michelutti, Lucia. 2008. *The Vernacularisation of Democracy: Politics, Caste, and Religion in India*. New Delhi: Routledge.

Middleton, C. Townsend. 2011. "Across the Interface of State Ethnography: Rethinking Ethnology and Its Subjects in Multicultural India." *American Ethnologist* 38 (2): 249–66.

Mies, Maria. 1982. *The Lace Makers of Narsapur: Indian Housewives Produce for the World Market*. London: Zed Press.

Miyazaki, Hirokazu. 2004. *The Method of Hope: Anthropology, Philosophy, and Fijian Knowledge*. Stanford, CA: Stanford University Press.

Mody, Perveez. 2002. "Love and the Law: Love-Marriage in Delhi." *Modern Asian Studies* 36 (1): 223.

Mohanakumar, S., and Surjit Singh. 2010. *Impact of Economic Crisis on Workers in the Unorganized Sector in Rajasthan.* IDSJ Working Paper-155. Institute of Development Studies, Jaipur.

———. 2011. "Impact of the Economic Crisis on Workers in the Unorganized Sector in Rajasthan." *Economic and Political Weekly* 46 (22): 66–71.

Mohanty, Chandra Talpade. 2003. *Feminism without Borders: Decolonizing Theory, Practicing Solidarity.* Durham, NC: Duke University Press.

Moodie, Megan. 2010. "'Why Can't You Say You Are from Bangladesh?': Demographic Anxiety and Hindu Nationalist Common Sense in the Aftermath of the 2008 Jaipur Bombings." *Identities* 17 (5): 531–59.

———. 2012. "Religion and the Subaltern Civil Servant." Paper presented at "The Sacred and the City" Workshop on Urban South Asia, Stanford University, Stanford, CA, October 4–5.

———. 2013a. "Upward Mobility in a Forgotten Tribe: Notes on the 'Creamy Layer' Problem." *Focaal* 65: 23–32.

———. 2013b. "Bureaucratic Literacy and the Politics of Complaint: Untold Story from Rajasthan." *Economic and Political Weekly* 48 (45&46): 71–75.

Narayan, Uma. 1997. *Dislocating Cultures: Identities, Traditions, and Third-World Feminism.* New York: Routledge.

Nath, Y. V. S. 1960. *Bhils of Ratanmal: An Analysis of the Social Structure of a Western Indian Community.* Baroda: Maharaja Sayajirao University of Baroda.

Oldenburg, Veena Talwar. 2002. *Dowry Murder: The Imperial Origins of a Cultural Crime.* Oxford: Oxford University Press.

Osborne, Evan. 2001. "Culture, Development, and Government: Reservations in India." *Economic Development and Cultural Change* 49 (3): 659–685.

Oza, Rupal. 2006. *The Making of Neoliberal India: Nationalism, Gender, and the Paradoxes of Globalization.* New York: Routledge.

Pandey, Gyanendra. 2009. "Can There Be a Subaltern Middle Class? Notes on African-American and Dalit History." *Public Culture* 21 (2): 321–342.

———. 2010. "Introduction: The Subaltern as Subaltern Citizen." In *Subaltern Citizens and Their Histories: Investigations from India and the USA,* edited by Gyanendra Pandey, 1–12. London: Routledge.

———. 2013. *A History of Prejudice: Race, Caste, and Difference in India and the United States.* Cambridge: Cambridge University Press.

Parry, Jonathan. 1999. "Two Cheers for Reservation: The Satnamis and the Steel Plant." In *Institutions & Inequalities: Essays in Honour of Andre Béteille,* edited by Ramachandra Guha and Jonathan P. Parry, 128–69. New Delhi: Oxford University Press.

Patel, Arjun. 1999. "Becoming Hindu: *Adivasis* in South Gujarat." In *Untouchable: Dalits in Modern India,* edited by S. M. Michael, 103–30. Boulder, CO: Lynne Rienner Publishers, Inc.

Pateman, Carole. 1989. *The Disorder of Women: Democracy, Feminism, and Political Theory.* Stanford, CA: Stanford University Press.

Povinelli, Elizabeth A. 2002. *The Cunning of Recognition: Indigenous Alterities and the Making of Australian Multiculturalism.* Durham: Duke University Press.

Prasad, Archana. 2003. *Against Ecological Romanticism: Verrier Elwin and the Making of an Anti-Modern Tribal Identity.* New Delhi: Three Essays Collective.

Prasad, Vijay. 2001. *Untouchable Freedom: A Social History of a Dalit Community.* Delhi: Oxford University Press.

Pratt, Mary Louise. 1986. "Fieldwork in Common Places." In *Writing Culture: The Poetics and Politics of Ethnography*, edited by James Clifford and George E. Marcus, 27–50. Berkeley: University of California Press.

Pyburn, K. Anne. 2004. *Ungendering Civilization*. New York: Routledge.

Radhakrishnan, Smitha. 2011. *Appropriately Indian: Gender and Culture in a New Transnational Class*. Durham, NC: Duke University Press.

Raheja, Gloria Goodwin, and Ann Grodzins Gold. 1994. *Listen to the Heron's Words: Reimagining Gender and Kinship in North India*. Berkeley: University of California Press.

Rajputana Agency. 1879. *The Rajputana Gazetteer*. Calcutta: Office of the Supt. of Govt.

Ram, Kalpana. 1991. *Mukkuvar Women: Gender, Hegemony, and Capitalist Transformation in a South Indian Fishing Community*. London: Zed Books.

Ramamurthy, Priti. 2003. "Material Consumers, Fabricating Subjects: Perplexity, Global Connectivity Discourses, and Transnational Feminist Research." *Cultural Anthropology* 18 (4): 524–50.

Rao, Anupama. 2009. *The Caste Question: Dalits and the Politics of Modern India*. Berkeley: University of California Press.

Ray, Raka. 2000. "Masculinity, Femininity, and Servitude: Domestic Workers in Calcutta in the Late Twentieth Century." *Feminist Studies* 26 (3): 691–718.

Ray, Raka, and Seemin Qayum. 2009. *Cultures of Servitude: Modernity, Domesticity, and Class in India*. Stanford, CA.: Stanford University Press.

Reddy, Chandan. 2008. "Time for Rights? Loving, Gay Marriage, and the Limits of Legal Justice." *Fordham Law Review* 76 (6): 2849.

Rege, Sharmila. 2006. *Writing Caste, Writing Gender: Reading Dalit Women's Testimonios*. New Delhi: Zubaan.

Rofel, Lisa. 2007. *Desiring China: Experiments in Neoliberalism, Sexuality, and Public Culture*. Durham, NC: Duke University Press.

Rose, Nikolas. 1999. *Powers of Freedom: Reframing Political Thought*. Cambridge: Cambridge University Press.

Rudolph, Susanne Hoeber, and Lloyd I. Rudolph. 1984. *Essays on Rajputana: Reflections on History, Culture, and Administration*. New Delhi: Concept.

Sachdev, Vibhuti, and G. H. R Tillotson. 2002. *Building Jaipur: The Making of an Indian City*. New Delhi: Oxford University Press.

Sangari, KumKum, and Sudesh Vaideds. . 1989. *Recasting Women: Essays in Indian Colonial History*. New Brunswick, NJ: Rutgers University Press.

Sangari, KumKum and Sudesh Vaid. 1996. "Institutions, Beliefs, Ideologies: Widow Immolation in Contemporary Rajasthan." In *Embodied Violence: Communalising Women's Sexuality in South Asia*, edited by Kumari Jayawardena and Malathi DeAlwis, 240–96. London: Zed Books.

Sarkar, Sumit, and Sarkar, Tanika. 2008. *Women and Social Reform in Modern India: A Reader*. Bloomington: Indiana University Press.

Sarkar, Tanika. 1993. "Rhetoric Against Age of Consent: Resisting Colonial Reason and Death of a Child-Wife." *Economic and Political Weekly*, 28 (36): 1869–78.

———. 2000. "A Prehistory of Rights: The Age of Consent Debate in Colonial Bengal." *Feminist Studies* 26 (3): 601.

Satyanarayana, K., and Susie Tharu. 2013. *The Exercise of Freedom: An Introduction to Dalit Writing*. New Delhi: Navayana Publishing.

Schaller, Joseph. 1995. "Sanskritization, Caste Uplift, and Social Dissidence in the Sant Ravidas Panth." In *Bhakti Religion in North India: Community, Identity, and Political Action*, edited by D. N. Lorenzen, 105–16. Albany, NY: SUNY Press.

Scott, David. 1995. "Colonial Governmentality." *Social Text* 43, 191–220.

Scott, Jefferson Elsworth. 1904. *In Famine Land: Observations and Experiences in India During the Great Drought of 1899–1900*. New York & London: Harper & Bros.

Shah, Alpa. 2007. "'Keeping the State Away': Democracy, Politics, and the State in India's Jharkhand." *Journal of the Royal Anthropological Institute* 13 (1): 129–45.

———. 2010. *In the Shadows of the State: Indigenous Politics, Environmentalism, and Insurgency in Jharkhand, India*. Durham: Duke University Press.

Shah, P. G. 1964. *Tribal Life in Gujarat: An Analytical Study of the Cultural Changes with Special Reference to the Dhanka Tribe*. Bombay: Gujarat Research Society.

Shiva, Vandana. 2002. *Water Wars: Privatization, Pollution, and Profit*. Cambridge, MA: South End Press.

Singh, K. S., B. K. Lavania, D .K. Samanta, S. K. Mandal, and N. N. Vyas.. 1998. *People of India: Rajasthan*. Mumbai: Popular Prakashan.

Singh, Maharaj Charan. 1983. *Spiritual Heritage: A Transcription from Tape-Recorded Talks of Maharaj Charan Singh*. Dera Baba Jaimal Singh, Punjab, India: Radha Soami Satsang Beas.

Sinha, Mrinalini. 1995. *Colonial Masculinity: The "Manly Englishman" and the 'Effeminate Bengali' in the Late Nineteenth Century*. Manchester: Manchester University Press.

Sinha, Surajit Chandra. 1962. "State Formation and Rajput Myth in Tribal Central India." *Man in India*. 42 (1): 35–80.

Sivananda, Vi, and Atul Bhargava. 2009. *Champaner Pavagadh*. New Delhi: Director General, Archaeological Survey of India.

Skaria, Ajay. 1997. "Shades of Wildness: Tribe, Caste, and Gender in Western India." *Journal of Asian Studies* 56 (3): 726.

Smarika. 2003. Dhanak Welfare Association, Jaipur.

Solanki, Munshi Ram. 2003. "Our Society: An Introduction." In *Smarika*. Dhanak Welfare Association, Jaipur.

Som, Reba. "Jawaharlal Nehru and the Hindu Code: A Victory of Symbol over Substance?" *Modern Asian Studies* 28 (1): 165.

Spivak, Gayatri Chakravorty. 1985. "Can the Subaltern Speak? Speculations on Widow Sacrifice." *Wedge* 7/8: 120–130.

———. 1990. "Constitutions and Culture Studies." *Yale Journal of Law & the Humanities* 2 (1): 133–47.

———. 1999. *A Critique of Postcolonial Reason: Toward a History of the Vanishing Present*. Cambridge, MA: Harvard University Press.

Sreenivas, Mytheli. 2008. *Wives, Widows, and Concubines: The Conjugal Family Ideal in Colonial India*. Bloomington: Indiana University Press.

Srinivas, M. N. 1962. *Caste in Modern India and Other Essays*. Lucknow: Asia Publishing House.

———. 1966. *Social Change in Modern India*. Berkeley: University of California Press.

Stoler, Ann Laura. 2002. *Carnal Knowledge and Imperial Power: Race and the Intimate in Colonial Rule*. Berkeley: University of California Press.

Strathern, Marilyn. 1988. *The Gender of the Gift: Problems with Women and Problems with Society in Melanesia*. Berkeley: University of California Press.

Sunder Rajan, Kaushik. 2006. *Biocapital: The Constitution of Postgenomic Life*. Durham, NC: Duke University Press.

Sunder Rajan, Rajeswari. 2003. *The Scandal of the State: Women, Law, and Citizenship in Post-colonial India*. Durham, NC: Duke University Press.

Tadiar, Neferti Xina M. 2004. *Fantasy-Production: Sexual Economies and Other Philippine Consequences for the New World Order*. Hong Kong: Hong Kong University Press.

Teltumbde, Anand. 2013. "Delhi Gang Rape Case: Some Uncomfortable Questions." *Economic and Political Weekly* 48 (6): 10–11.

Thanseem, Ismail, Kumarasamy Thangaraj, Gyaneshwer Chaubey, Vijay Kumar Singh, Lakkakula V. K. S. Bhaskar, B. Mohan Reddy, Alla G. Reddy, and Lalji Singh. 2006. "Genetic Affinities among the Lower Castes and Tribal Groups of India: Inference from Y Chromosome and Mitochondrial DNA." *BMC Genetics* 7: 42–11.

Thapar, Romila. 1996. *Time as a Metaphor of History: Early India*. Delhi: Oxford University Press.

Trouillot, Michel-Rolph. 1991. "Anthropology and the Savage Slot: The Poetics and Politics of Otherness." In *Recapturing Anthropology: Working in the Present*, 17–44. Santa Fe, NM: SAR Press.

Tsing, Anna. 2007. "Indigenous Voice." In *Indigenous Experience Today*, 33–68. Oxford: Berg Publishers.

Uberoi, Patricia. 1996. *Social Reform, Sexuality, and the State*. New Delhi: Sage Publications.

Unnithan-Kumar, Maya. 1997. *Identity, Gender, and Poverty: New Perspectives on Caste and Tribe in Rajasthan*. Providence, RI: Berghahn Books.

———. 2000. "The State, Rajput Identity, and Women's Agency in 19th and 20th Century Rajasthan." *Indian Journal of Gender Studies* 7 (1): 49–70.

Upadhyaya, K. D. 1964. "Indian Botanical Folklore." *Asian Folklore Studies* 23 (2): 15–34.

Vadra, Ratna. 2012. "State Level Initiatives of Power Sector Reforms in India." *The Journal of Institute of Public Enterprise* 35 (3&4): 81–95.

Vaidyanathan, A. 2002. "The Pursuit of Social Justice." In *India's Living Constitution: Ideas, Practices, Controversies*, edited by Zoya Hasan, E. Sridharan, and R. Sudarshan, 284–305. London: Anthem Press.

van Schendel, Willem. 2011. "The Dangers of Belonging: Tribes, Indigenous Peoples, and Homelands in South Asia." In *The Politics of Belonging in India: Becoming Adivasi*, edited by Daniel J. Rycroft and Sangeeta Dasgupta, 19–43. New York: Routledge.

Vashishtha, Vijay Kumar. 1997. *Bhagat Movement: A Study of Cultural Transformation of the Bhils of Southern Rajasthan*. Jaipur: Shruti Publications.

Visweswaran, Kamala. 1994. *Fictions of Feminist Ethnography*. Minneapolis and London: University of Minnesota Press.

Vizenor, Gerald Robert. 2008. *Survivance: Narratives of Native Presence*. Lincoln: University of Nebraska Press.

Vora, Kalindi. Forthcoming. *Life Support: Race, Gender, and New Socialities in the Vital Energy Economy*. University of Minnesota Press.

Warner, Michael. 1999. "Normal and Normaller." *GLQ: A Journal of Lesbian & Gay Studies* 5 (2): 119.

Webb, Martin. 2012. "Activating Citizens, Remaking Brokerage: Transparency Activism, Ethical Scenes, and the Urban Poor in Delhi." *PoLAR: Political & Legal Anthropology Review* 35 (2): 206–22.

Williams, Raymond. 1973. *The Country and the City*. New York: Oxford University Press.

Wilson, Ara. 2004. *The Intimate Economies of Bangkok: Tomboys, Tycoons, and Avon Ladies in the Global City*. Berkeley: University of California Press.

Wilson, Peter J. 1969. "Reputation and Respectability: A Suggestion for Caribbean Ethnology."
    Man 4 (1): 70–84.

Wilson, William J. 1990. *The Truly Disadvantaged: The Inner City, the Underclass, and Public
    Policy.* Chicago: University of Chicago Press.

———. 2009. *More Than Just Race : Being Black and Poor in the Inner City.* New York: Norton
    & Company.

Yang, Anand A. 1989. "Whose Sati? Widow Burning in Early Nineteenth-Century India." *Journal
    of Women's History* 1 (2): 8–33.

Yashaschandra, Sitansu. 1995. "Towards Hind Svaraj: An Interpretation of the Rise of Prose in
    Nineteenth-Century Gujarati Literature." *Social Scientist* 23 (10/12): 41–55.

Index